PLATONIC NOISE

o o o o o o o o o o o o o o o

J. Peter Euben

PRINCETON UNIVERSITY PRESS · PRINCETON AND OXFORD

Copyright © 2003 by Princeton University Press
Published by Princeton University Press, 41 William Street,
Princeton, New Jersey 08540
In the United Kingdom: Princeton University Press, 3 Market Place
Woodstock, Oxfordshire OX20 1SY

Library of Congress Cataloging-in-Publication Data
Euben, J. Peter.
Platonic noise / J. Peter Euben.
p. cm.
Includes bibliographical references and index.
ISBN 0-691-11399-8 (hc : alk. paper) — ISBN 0-691-11400-5 (pbk. : alk. paper)
1. Greek literature—History and criticism. 2. Politics and literature—United
States—History—20th century. 3. American fiction—20th century—History and
criticism. 4. Literature, Comparative—Greek and American. 5. Literature,
Comparative—American and Greek. 6. Political science—Greece—Athens. 7. American
fiction—Greek influences. 8. Arendt, Hannah. Human condition. 9. Politics and
literature—Greece. I. Title.

PA3071 .E93 2003
880.9'001—dc21   2002030722

British Library Cataloging-in-Publication Data is available
This book has been composed in Sabon and Carlson Open Face
Printed on acid-free paper. ∞

www.pupress.princeton.edu
Printed in the United States of America

1 3 5 7 9 10 8 6 4 2

To the memory of my sister Laura Emily Pett,

whose death so greatly diminished the generosity,

warmth, and humor in the world.

Child of an old blind man, Antigone,
to what regions, or to what men's city
have we come? Who on this day shall receive Oedipus
the wanderer with scanty gifts? . . .
But come my child, if you see any seat
either near ground unconsecrated or near the
precincts of the gods, stop me and let me sit there,
so that we may find out where we are; for we have come
as strangers, and must learn from the citizens. . . .

—SOPHOCLES, *Oedipus at Colonus*, 1–4, 8–12 (Lloyd-Jones translation)

Griefs, at the moment when they change into ideas, lose their power to injure our heart.

—MARCEL PROUST

Contents

Acknowledgments

Since I am someone who learns more from conversation than from books, my friends and interlocutors are my coauthors, however much they may wish to deny such complicity. Most of the blame can be given to Don Moon and George Shulman, who have both read most of what I have written, and tried their best to make it clearer and deeper. Wendy Brown, William Connolly, Jason Frank, Patrick Deneen, Michael Janover, Tracy Strong, Ann and Warren Lane, Dana Villa, Melissa Orlie, Gary Shiffman, and Roxanne Euben have read one or more chapters. Their insights, learning, and generous intelligence have alerted me to crucial absences, discursive liberties, and overstatement. Then there are those friends and colleagues with whom I continue to have general conversations about political theory and politics: Sheldon Wolin, Kirstie McClure, Arlene Saxonhouse, Terence Ball, Tracy Strong, George Kateb, Stephen Salkever, John Wallach, Josiah Ober, John Schaar, and Hanna Pitkin.

Since all but one of these chapters began as lectures or talks, I owe much to the people who invited me and to the people who responded with suggestions and questions. These include Andy Sabl, Robert Meister, Ronnie Lipschutz, Susan Bickford, and my new colleagues at Duke, Rom Coles, Kim Curtis, and Elizabeth Kiss. Over the years Nan Keohane has taken time from her hectic schedule to talk with me about various issues discussed in this book.

A conversation with George Kateb about my need to confront the role of loss and death in Platonic political theory brought me up short and to the themes of this book, especially those of its final chapter. That intellectual challenge became something more with the unexpected death of my sister Laura, to whom this book is dedicated, though I suspect only chapter 4 would have given her pleasure. Penultimately, I want to thank the anonymous reviewers of Princeton University Press and Ian Malcolm for his encouragement and suggestions.

Finally, it would be ungrateful not to give thanks to Zoe Sodja, Cheryl Van De Veer, and especially Betsy Wootten, who typed the manuscript for this technologically challenged academic. Their patience with my lousy typing, barely legible handwriting, and various pastings and wandering arrows is a testament to their intelligence, fortitude, and friendship.

Though all the chapters, save the introductory chapter 1, have been published elsewhere, none has simply been reprinted. In the case of chapters 5 and 6, the changes have been limited to a few revisions, additions, and cross-references. In the case of chapter 2, the last third of the essay has been rewritten; the same is true of chapter 3, which was originally limited to Arendt's Hellenism. Chapter 4 has been less extensively revised, but here, too, I have added several pages, rewritten others, and, as elsewhere, referred to previous and subsequent chapters to make this more of a book than a collection of essays. Chapter 7 appeared in a substantially shorter version in *Political Theory*.

I would like to thank the University of Minnesota Press for permission to reprint chapter 4, which originally appeared in *Public Space and Democracy*, edited by Marcel Hénaff and Tracy B. Strong (2001), and chapter 5, which first appeared in *Vocations of Political Theory*, edited by Jason A. Frank and John Tambornino (2000); Cambridge University Press for permission to reprint chapter 3, originally entitled "Arendt's Hellenism," which appeared in *The Cambridge Companion to Hannah Arendt*, edited by Dana Villa (2000); and *Polis* for permission to reprint "On the Uses and Disadvantages of Hellenic Studies for Political and Theoretical Life" as part of chapter 2. The essay appeared in vol. 15, nos. 1 and 2 (1998): 45–76.

PLATONIC NOISE

∘ ∘ ∘ ∘ ∘ ∘ ∘ ∘ ∘ ∘ ∘ ∘ ∘ ∘ ∘

I

Introduction

Philip Roth's *The Human Stain*[1] is a novel about a light-skinned "black" man named Coleman Silk who opts to pass as a "white" Jew. Coleman eventually becomes a professor of classics and reforming dean at a small New England liberal arts college. But he is undone by a charge of racism when he wonders out loud whether the two missing students in his class are "spooks" and they turn out to be African American women. Since his chosen path to success has meant renouncing his family, symbolically if not literally killing his mother, and rejecting his heritage, one might think he got what he deserved, even if the charge of racism was absurd. In that case, the novel would be a morality play in which a callous, self-serving, and selfish man received an appropriate punishment. One would be wrong.

To dismiss Coleman as merely self-interested is a comforting simplification for the same reason that regarding Dostoevsky's Grand Inquisitor as a self-aggrandizing, hypocritical power seeker rather than someone driven by love of humanity and created by our desperate need for authority and meaning is one. In both cases it lets us off the moral hook. It is true that Coleman reaps the benefits of the privileges whiteness brings. It is also true that he is traumatized by the racism he experiences before deciding to reject his past for a self-defined future. And it is true that passing seems to provide an adrenaline rush he cannot do without. Indeed, because Coleman tells no one (including his Jewish wife) his secret, his life is a constant performance on a stage as large as his existence. He seems to thrive on taking risks and challenging chance (such as having children), then reveling in his seeming triumph (all of them miraculously turn out white). But these risks are taken in the name of the American dream of freedom. It is this more than the privilege of whiteness, the experience of racism, or the pleasure of performance that drives him. Why should he be unable to live the American dream simply because he happens to be "black"? Why should he be precluded from "accepting the democratic invitation to throw our origins overboard if to do so contributes to the pursuit of happiness" (334)? He is the child of chance, not a victim of fate. He leaves the baggage of the past behind him where it belongs.

There is another figure in literature who believed that he was the child of chance, that he had escaped his fate and past and was self-made, Sophocles' Oedipus. So it is not surprising that the epigraph for the novel comes from *Oedipus Tyrannos*.

> OEDIPUS: What is the rite of purification? How shall it be done?
> CREON: By banishing a man or expiation of blood by blood.

It is the genius of Roth's novel that it first juxtaposes the myth of American self-fashioning with Greek tragedy and then juxtaposes them with the Monica Lewinsky affair and the impeachment of President Clinton. Thus Coleman becomes a character in a Greek tragedy he teaches. The narrator imagines himself and Coleman watching the latter's life as if it were a play on the southern hillside of the Athenian Acropolis in the theater sacred to Dionysus "where before the eyes of the thousand spectators, the dramatic unities were once rigorously observed and the great cathartic cycle was enacted annually" (314).

The Human Stain is a protest and polemic against purity: the epistemology of it, the culture of it, and the political consequences of it. We assume that our categories capture the world in a way that enables us to be masters of our fate. But given Oedipus, the title of Roth's first chapter, "Everyone Knows," drips with irony and foreboding. As it turns out, none of us know very much about themselves, others, or the human condition itself. We do not know why what happens happens the way it does, what it is that underlies the anarchic train of events, or the uncertainties, mishaps, disunity, and shocking irregularities that define human affairs. Nobody *knows*, and any claim to such knowledge constitutes a banalizing of experience. "Intention? Motive? Consequence? Meaning? All that we don't know is astonishing. Even more astonishing is what passes for knowing" (208–9).

Later, after Coleman has been accused of racism and resigns in fury at the charge, after his wife has died as a result, after he has taken up with a younger, deeply scarred woman, after they have been run off the road by her Vietnam vet husband, the narrator returns to the theme. "For all that the world is full of people who go around believing they've got you or your neighbor figured out, there really is no bottom to what is not known. The truth about us is endless. As are the lies" (315). Out of ignorance we turn people into abstractions, projecting our moralism onto them in a way that makes us feel safe and knowing. The narrator calls this fantasy of purity terrorism, an ecstasy of sanctimonious self-righteousness and virtue-mongering at once infantilizing and inhuman. To hell with propriety and appropriateness, with making people comfortable with the demands by the high-minded for core values, civic responsibility, WASP dignity, women's rights, black pride, and Jewish ethical self-importance, and with the desire to bring things to closure. "The human desire for a beginning, a middle, and an end . . . is realized nowhere so thoroughly as in the plays Coleman taught. . . . But outside classical tragedy of the fifth century B.C.E. the expectation of complete, let alone of a just and perfect, consummation is a foolish illusion for an adult to hold" (314–15).[2] The novel's final image in its concluding chapter, "The Purifying Ritual," drives the point home. It is a scene out of Currier and Ives. "Only rarely," the novel concludes, "at the end of our century, does life offer up a vision as pure and as peaceful as this one: a solitary man on a bucket, fishing through eighteen inches of ice in a lake that's continually turning over its water atop an arcadian mountain in America" (361). Except that this solitary man, Les Farley, is a killer. He was taught to be a killer in Vietnam and brought his lesson home by killing Coleman Silk and his lover, Les's ex-wife, whom he had beaten regularly.

One thing all the characters in the book think they know is that Fate is a primitive notion that makes no sense in a land of self-made men and women. We can reinvent ourselves, choose a lifestyle, be all we can be, even if that means discarding our past as excess baggage. Coleman Silk believes this. Though he must ritually murder his mother, the rewards for him are worth it. He refuses to be a victim of racial tyranny whereby a man's color is his fate. Why allow one's prospects to be unjustly limited by so arbitrary a designation as race, allow one's future, his future, to be in someone else's hands? "All he's ever wanted from earliest childhood was to be free; not black, *not even white* . . ." (my emphasis).[3] He thinks of himself as "the greatest of the great pioneers for this 'I' against the despotism of the 'we' " (120, 108).

Like Oedipus, Coleman thought he had it made, that he had beaten the system, though he was conscious of his double life in a way Oedipus was not. As we saw, he challenged chance and won. But he had beaten the odds only to be "blindsided by the uncontrollability of something else entirely" (335), the charge of racism. He had decided to forge a distinct historical destiny only to be ensnared by a history he had not counted on. And it could not be otherwise insofar as one's fate is constituted by one's past deeds and words, which forge an identity and character over time and through action. It is the mother whom he has callously discarded in his reinvention who makes the point. "There is no escape," she tells her son who is trying to make one. "Your attempts to escape will only lead you back to where you began" (140). Like Oedipus's, Coleman's fate is accidentally formed and inescapable. His mother again: "You're white as snow and think like a slave" (139).[4]

Every one of us is stained: cruel, error-prone, perverse, enjoying the crudest pleasures. The stain is our sexuality and excrement, the trail we leave behind and the imprint we make, our unique smile and look, the thumbprint that distinguishes us from others. It is also our dirty hands, our deeds and words that mark our presence in time and space.[5] All animals, including men and women, are driven by preconscious instincts and elemental passions. But humans are the only ones who can make themselves other than who they are. The human world is always out of joint because we are becoming someone other than we were a moment ago, though the trajectories of such changes are both distinctive and allusive. Finally, and most fundamentally, the human stain is our "horrible, elemental imperfections" (242).

Instead of lamenting our sins and imperfections, Roth celebrates them in both the structure and the "argument" of the novel. "Closure! They [a professor is talking about students] fix on the conventionalized narrative with its beginning, middle and end—every experience, no matter how ambiguous . . . or mysterious, must lend itself to this normalizing, conventionalizing anchorman cliché" (147).[6] Substantively, Roth refuses to chastise, invite confessions, or endorse self-abnegation, all of which accrue significance only in a murderous Manichaean discourse of purity. Roth's gods are Greek. They are the gods of life, impure and lustful, corrupt rather than innocent, created in the image of man. And men are flawed. That is their condition and a precondition of their nobility. Coleman, like Clinton, moved through the world with mixed motives, imprecise aims, half-blind to the forces that shaped him.

Any revulsion, contempt, or attempt to cleanse the stain is "a joke," like trying to wash the grain out of a piece of redwood. Or it is an act of self-loathing. In the end, "human stain" is a redundancy, and Bill Clinton is accused of being human. His vilification came less from his deeds than from our need for a scapegoat.

> It was strange to think, while seated there with all his [Coleman's] colleagues, that people so well educated and professionally civil should have fallen so willingly for the venerable dream of a situation in which one man can embody evil. Yet there is this need, and it is undying and it is profound. (306–7)

There is a sincerity that is worse than falseness and an innocence that is "worse than corruption" (147). The longing for it—for an Edenic utopia before or without sin, the erotic desire for childlike purity and asexual sexuality, for noble actors with clean hands—embodies a hatred for the world and for the activity of politics, which, Aristotle suggests, defines our distinctively human status.

Here is Richard Posner's condemnation of Clinton. It is an example of what infuriates Roth.

[Clinton] committed repeated and varied felonious obstructions of justice over a period of almost a year, which he garnished with gaudy public and private lies, vicious slanders, tactical blunders, gross errors of judgment, hypocritical displays of contrition, affronts to conventional morality and parental authority, and desecration of a revered national symbol. Literally the office of the President. And all this occurred against a background of persistent and troubling questions concerning the ethical tone of the Clinton Administration and Clinton's personal and political ethics.[7]

The Human Stain is, appropriately enough, a "flawed" novel. There are stilted scenes, stock characters that embody Roth's own vision of political correctness, and a clichéd reading of the 1960s. But the novel does capture a sense of Greek tragedy. "In the tragic perspective," Jean-Pierre Vernant writes,

acting, being an agent, has a double character. On the one hand, it consists in taking counsel with oneself, weighing the for and against and doing the best we can to foresee the order of means and ends. On the other hand, it is to make a bet on the unknown and the incomprehensible and to take a risk on a terrain that remains impenetrable to you. It involves entering the play of supernatural forces . . . where one does not know whether they are preparing for success or disaster.[8]

Like the tragedians, Roth seems to deny that the relations of human beings to society and to each other, if properly understood and properly enacted, can realize a harmonious identity without profound loss.

More important, Roth brings an ancient text into conversation about contemporary politics and culture in a way I try to do in the following chapters. But conversation is too "nice" a word, for Roth engages the Greeks with the passion and struggle Nietzsche might have admired.

II

In "Cities of Reason,"[9] Oswyn Murray tells the story of how national traditions influenced the interpretation of animal behavior. Animals studied by Americans rush about frantically with incredible energy and at last achieve their desired goal by chance. Animals observed by the Germans sit still and think and finally arrive at a solution out of their inner consciousness. Murray's conclusion is not the obvious one that the character of the observer affects the interpretation of results, but that the character of the experiment itself was "predetermined" by the mental attitudes of the experimenter. His point is that a similar national response to the phenomenon defines the study of the polis. "To the Germans the polis can only be described in a handbook of constitutional law; the French polis is a form of holy Communion; the American polis combines the practices of a Mafia convention with the principles of justice and freedom.[10]

In some respects, the Greek historian or political theorist has a thornier problem than the behavioral psychologist, since she or he has to "establish the limits of the factual." For example, are political myths evidence of rationality or irrationality? How are such myths related to rhetoric, on the one hand, and to logical argument on the other? Or is the distinction between the two overstated? When and with what consequences is an invidious contrast established between members of cultures who are deemed prisoners of their myths, and more rational societies that possess their culture rather than being possessed by it? How have such distinctions constructed views of agency and contrasts between those capable of autonomous thought and action, and those who, lacking reflective consciousness,[11] are fated to live as they do? The answers to such questions concerning the field of evidence determine to a large extent the result of any inquiry into the polis's rationality.

No matter what substantive answers one gives to such questions, the form those answers take is likely to beg the question. That is because our very forms of inquiry presume rationality. At least that is so insofar as "we as observers are in the business of making models, of understanding through systemization." In the interests of system and systemization we accept or reject evidence because it conforms to other evidence. But above all, "[W]e do not believe in the untidiness of reality."[12] Even worse, we use our models to *create* evidence; we extrapolate from what we take to be a fact by rational arguments to further "facts." Thus there is a complex relationship between model and argument from analogy; the concept of a warrior or democratic society allows transference of individual phenomena from one historical society to another across time and space.

Murray draws two conclusions from this situation. The first is that there are a number of senses in which the more complete, the more coherent a picture of any aspect of the polis is, the more false it is likely to be, or at least the more certain it is that the construct is that of a single observer. Here, the coherence of any society is a coherence that belongs to the observer rather than the society. The second is that if conflicting approaches result in conflicting interpretations, then we must "resign" ourselves to interpretive pluralism. But if, by some chance, conflicting approaches result in congruent conclusions, we are "on the way to establishing that the phenomena exist independently of the observers."[13]

Murray's warnings—present in the jokes about British apes with their stiff upper lips, ruthlessly enterprising American apes, hierarchical and communitarian Japanese apes, and promiscuous French apes[14]—become a screed in the case of Jorge Luis Borges, who once complained of "those

parasitic books which situate Christ on a boulevard, Hamlet on La Cana-
biere or Don Quixote on Wall Street." Like all men of taste, the narrator
of "Pierre Menard" goes on, "Menard abhorred these useless carnivals,
fit only—as he would say—to produce plebian pleasures of anachronism
or (what is worse) to enthrall us with the elementary idea that all epochs
are the same *or* are different" (my emphasis).[15]

If Roth provides a "model" for the chapters that follow, Murray provides a warning about and Borges a chastisement of them. For the former,
my claim for the generative possibilities of juxtaposing ancient and modern is likely to produce Athenian Americans, and any light I might possibly throw on texts, issues, and theories will leave the surrounding contexts
in darkness. In part, this seems to me an inescapable fact of understanding. In this I agree with Rorty and Gadamer: there are virtually no limits
to our ability to redescribe any society or text and thereby recontextualize
it. I am not sure I would call metaphysicians "control freaks," as Rorty
does, but I do think it is a mistake to believe that we can "now in the
present construct a filing system which will have an appropriate pigeon
hole for anything that might possibly turn up in the future."[16] Given this
"fact," a number of strategies are possible, all of which are employed in
the following chapters. The first is simply to do the serious intellectual
work as well as one can. Another is to accept the warning and incorporate
it in the structure of argument by creating a dynamic that makes textual
strategies and purposes as visible as possible. A third is to do what I do
in chapter 4—create an exaggerated, even playful, comparison that intro-
duces an element of irony and self-parody into that dynamic. Finally, and
paradoxically, one must make the personal, political, and epistemological
stakes in any particular juxtaposition explicit.

As for Borges, the easiest thing to say is that he wants to eliminate
political theory, or, rather, to reinstate the chasm between it and literature.
But his real object is a case against the instrumentalization of learning,
the desire to make art and knowledge useful, relevant, easily accessible,
presentistic, and practical. And he has a case. Let me make it for him.

Presentism is a proclivity to analyze contemporary culture and politics
using only contemporary texts, theories, and methods. The problem is
that these texts, theories, and methods often mirror the society they are
studying. While we can learn much from looking into a mirror, if we look
in it too much and for too long, our activity becomes a kind of narcissism.
Thus we need distant mirrors that are premodern texts, unpopular theories, peculiar locutions, and political or cultural non sequiturs to better
map the outlines of the contemporary.

Presentism is also a belief or assumption that what is new is best, most
self-reflexive, least subject to false consciousness. Too many believe that
we here and now are the culmination of history; that what came before

was aiming to be what we are, and that our sophistication dwarfs that of our more gullible, less modern or postmodern predecessors. Depressingly, this view is often held by those who regard themselves as repudiating narratives of progress.

The demand that courses, issues, or books be relevant to me or us presumes that education is and should be defined by what I am or we are now, rather than by what we might become. It ignores how much of education is serendipitous, and how often we learn most from texts and ideas that were initially alien and alienating. When students insist that *The Republic* is boring—something I also thought the first time I read it—I ask them whose problem that is. I ask this not to belittle their intelligence but to insist on their responsibilities as readers.

Let me be clear that I am not opposed to relevance. What I find dangerous (even in my own work) is having relevance determine the agenda and purpose of thinking in ways that allow the present to play tyrant to the future. Though it sounds paradoxical, I am for relevance of result and in the long run, not of intention or in the beginning. Surely Borges believes this too, since his position presupposes it.

The demand that our work be practical usually means that it should be useful. The problem is that those who judge what is useful are those who hold cultural, political, economic, and academic power. The call for practicality can be theoretically radical, but it is more often a counsel of docility and adaptation to professional norms.

More than this, if it is true that the conditions of our lives are never transparent to us, then the demand for practicality, like the demand for relevance, is a recommendation of ignorance. Oedipus (in *Oedipus Tyrannos*) is a very practical man. As such, he translated everything he encountered into a problem that he could solve. But he was, as Jonathan Lear suggests, so impatient for an answer that he never fully grasped the problem.[17] And it was, as we know, one hell of a problem.

My responses to Murray and Borges, such as they are, are practical and theoretical. The practical one is this: Do the juxtapositions "work" in the sense of opening up paths that are worth following? Or do they lead to dead ends? My theoretical defense relies on Nietzsche's essay "On the Uses and Disadvantages of History for Life," though, given my disagreements with Nietzsche and his enormous popularity, it is a somewhat peculiar choice.

Yet Nietzsche's essay (which is the subject of chapter 2) helps us negotiate between idealizing "the Greeks," suffocating them with academic paraphernalia, and making them *too* useful. To mimic, worship, or otherwise idealize the Greeks is to become their acolytes rather than their students. Ultimately, such idealization is a form of disengagement, of making them decorative rather than allowing them to invigorate our political, cultural, or intellectual lives. It is true that Nietzsche talks about the need for us to unlearn the present and give ourselves a second nature rooted in some other time. But the "us" refers to his contemporaries who live in the present, not somewhere else. (I will make the same argument about Hannah Arendt's Hellenism in chapter 3.) And to the extent that we regard the past as so much purer and grander than our present, we are tempted to turn away in disgust from our own corrupt time, leaving all as it is.

Nietzsche insists that the "usefulness" of classical texts lies in sustaining their capacity to surprise and provoke. More generally, he insists that knowledge must exist for life, which means resisting both preemptory critiques and inundating ourselves with mountains of commentary that leave them and us supine. It also means that the search for knowledge must be driven by passion and need, by a hunger to understand, a sense of absence, and a profound engagement with the fact of mortality.

This requires, if it does not entail, sustaining a tension between proximity and distance in regard to one's own time and an earlier Greek time. Yet in many respects the Greeks are a "primitive culture" that has more in common with the "backward" cultures of our own day than with advanced industrial societies, as a study of Greek religious rituals and social practices attests. It is Nietzsche's insight that it is just this "primitivism" that makes the Greeks untimely, that enables them to work on our time and provide hope for a future time. For such "primitivism," in fact, connects with powerful drives for life, with instincts that are not so much lost as reinvested or redeployed in ways that are self-annihilating.

Each of the following chapters begins with a Greek text, author, or epoch, or has one as its primary referent. Each takes that referent—be it a Sophoclean play or passage from one, a Platonic dialogue (such as *The Republic* or *Phaedo*), Aristotle, or the Stoics—and juxtaposes it with a contemporary text or thinker to explore a substantive issue. But only the following chapter on Nietzsche's essay on history elaborates the "methodological" challenges to this practice raised by Murray and Borges. I chose Nietzsche because my political and theoretical commitments are so different from his, and because I admire his heroic efforts to make the Greeks untimely in a timely manner. In this way, he is both an inspiration and a rebuke to what I am doing. He appears as a critical voice reminding me (or the reader when I default) of how hard it is to use the Greeks without abusing them. I suppose one could think of him as a skeptical interlocutor, something like an unsilenced Thrasymachus who helps set the terms of the subsequent dialogue despite Socrates' efforts to shame him.

Chapter 3 reads Greek tragedy (or rather, a tragedy) through the eyes of Hannah Arendt and explores Arendt's Hellenism through the lens of tragedy. The tragedy I chose is *Oedipus at Colonus* because the "Wisdom of Silenus" she quotes from the play in the final paragraph of *On Revolu-*

tion prefaces her most dramatic claim for the redemptive power of politics, itself perhaps her most provocative challenge to contemporary ways of thinking about political life. I also want to save Arendt from (her) Hellenism and save the Greeks from Arendt. Since she is and has been the most cited theorist in my work (though I have only recently begun directly to confront her work), this salvage operation is a kind of self-reckoning.

Chapter 4, which has a somewhat wider circle of interest and concern, provides something like comic relief amid the themes of loss and mortality that find expression in this book. It asks a somewhat absurd question about whether television comedies can play a role in contemporary America analogous to the role Aristophanic comedy played in democratic Athens. The answer is clearly "no," but the exploration of the question raises a series of substantive questions about popular and elite culture, humor and politics, unmediated communication and mass media, and ancient and modern democracy.

Chapter 5 is a story about what might be called the social ontology of political theory. Less pompously put, it is an exploration of why people theorize, and an argument that they are driven to by an acute sense of loss which has personal, political, and epistemological dimensions. It is loss that animates political theory as an enterprise and forms its problematic, but also threatens political and theoretical agency by tempting thinkers into nostalgia or certainty. This sense of loss existing at the heart of triumph is articulated by the "choral ode to man" in *Antigone*. Though the ode receives direct attention only in chapters 5 and 7, the sensibility it expresses informs the entire book.

Like chapter 4, chapter 6 begins with a question: is there an illuminating analogy to be drawn between the experience of political dislocation and theoretical struggle to understand it that accompanied the eclipse of the polis and our experience of globalization, as process and ideology, and our attempts to understand *it*? I begin with a brief sketch of the polis, drawing on Aristotle, then shift to an equally brief sketch of the Hellenistic period and the Stoics; then to the revival of interest in them (especially in the work of Martha Nussbaum), which provides a transition from the ancient world to a discussion of globalized and cosmopolitan citizenship in the contemporary one.

The final chapter offers some reflections on the interrelationship of mortality, politics, and political theory. In many respects, it brings together the preoccupations of previous chapters with historical remembrance and forgetting, the redemptive possibilities of politics, and the sense of loss as it appears in chapters 5 and 6. With its absurdly implausible juxtaposition of Plato's *Phaedo* and Don DeLillo's *White Noise*, it imitates and substantively inverts the content of chapter 4.

Except for chapter 6, every essay makes a case for the "usefulness" of literature in the study of political theory. This is neither a new nor an original claim, and I offer no systematic defense of it. What I do offer is a practice, and the success of my case rests on the various enactments of that practice.

Every chapter without exception presumes or argues for the significance of making Athenian political thought and democracy a presence in contemporary political and theoretical debates. I continue to believe in the moral value of participatory democracy; I continue to believe that none of its ancient or contemporary critics, no matter how intellectually powerful or politically astute they are, have offered us a form of government and culture more choiceworthy than the rule of the people, or a set of moral values more attractive than the freedom, political equality, and dignity of the citizenry as a whole and of each citizen taken separately.[18] I would insist that democracy requires the participation by the people in maintaining a political culture that constitutes them as agents and political equals, and that anything less constitutes what the ancients would have regarded as oligarchy. Thus I am not impressed by the argument that America is too democratic, though I agree that democratic rhetoric is hegemonic, often at the expense of democratic practices.

None of this is meant to ignore the transformation of scale that makes democratic citizenship (or perhaps citizenship itself) problematic. Indeed, virtually every one of the following essays explores that conundrum in one way or another. But, as I suggest in chapter 6, those transformations are playing themselves out in ways that provide spaces and occasions for a more demanding practice of democratic citizenship.

Finally, I assume here what I have argued at length elsewhere: that the origins of Western political thought[19] are constituted by a fruitful dialogue/contest/battle/struggle between Greek democracy (including drama) and philosophers who were critical of it even as they drew upon it, and that the literary memory of Athenian democracy is a crucial addition to our stock of cultural resources. The way these texts treat freedom, power and justice, individual and community, ethics and politics, deliberation and enactment, class conflict and public interest, eros and education, family and sexuality, provides an inspiration and object lesson for our reflections on politics and political theory.

III

Perhaps I should say a word about the book's title. At the most general level it poses a paradox that anticipates the juxtaposition of times and texts present in each of the following chapters. More specifically, the concept of noise was first articulated during the Industrial Revolution by an avant-garde that seized the cacophony of street, factory, and mine for artistic inspiration and political protest. Where previous eras had associated the deliberate production of percussive noise, dissonant sounds, and nonsense syllables with children's activities, madmen, and religious fanatics, these now became and were portrayed as the material conditions of everyday urban life.[20] Plato of course is associated with harmony, the rhythm of reason, unity, form, and the life of the mind.

The book's title is a play on DeLillo's *White Noise*, the subject (along with the *Phaedo*) of chapter 7. The phrase "white noise" has several meanings, all of which amplify the earlier one of noise. "White noise" is the steady hum that blocks out irregular sounds thought to prevent sleep, comfort, and the concentration necessary for workers to achieve the highest level of productivity. Later it includes artificially produced electronic sounds intended to reduce the sense of isolation workers feel in soundproof office buildings.

A second meaning derives from communication theory. Here, white noise is a random mix of frequencies that renders signals unintelligible.[21] It is too many people speaking at once without anyone's being able to hear, when speech becomes undifferentiated from other "sounds," or there is "information overload." The fear of such cacophonies lies behind the dream of undistorted communication present in Plato, Rousseau, Habermas, and Arendt.

In DeLillo's novel, "white noise" is all of this and more, and it is everywhere. It is there in the mangle of skidding carts, loudspeakers, coffee machines, and the cries of children that form a toneless system in supermarkets. It is there in what one critic calls "an entropic blanket of information from a media saturated society."[22] It is there in the hum of traffic and insects, the abandoned meanings that continue to haunt our speech, and the swarming life outside established significations that appears in non sequiturs resistant to projects of reason, enlightenment, modernization, and progress. White noise is the dark place young Wilder goes that elicits his crying jags, and the world of Silenus's wisdom and Weber's doubleness of action. White noise is the past demanding its due against the present and future, and the resentment of the aged as memory fades, agency withers, and we become shadows of our former selves. White noise is the world of Blacksmith (it is the town name, but there aren't any in it), of barns that had some purpose other than being tourist attractions, of deserted strip malls, obsolescent objects, and superfluous people. White noise is the murmur of dead souls babbling at the edge of our dreams, Rothian and Sophoclean ghosts of a past supposedly banished by our self-fashioning, the loss that cannot be acknowledged, spoken of, or even felt. White noise is the buzz that drowns out the cost of capitalism and the instrumentalizing of intelligence. It is supermarket labels that erase the origins of white man's food and the lives of people in the twenty countries that produce it. As what renders the present permeable and contingent, white noise is a threat full of possibilities.

Plato (again, as conventionally read) sees the possibility in the elimination of the threat. He wants to contain such anarchy, providing definition, form, and boundaries while escaping from the agora to the still place where philosophical reflection is possible. Yet Plato is himself becoming something like white noise, a voice below and outside the theoretical terrain, marginalized by an intellectual avant-garde but also perhaps a non sequitur that further hones and blunts the cutting edge of theory.

II

On the Uses and Disadvantages of Hellenic Studies for Political and Theoretical Life

Zeus, who guided men to think,
who has laid it down that wisdom
comes alone through suffering.
Still there drips in sleep against the heart
grief from memory; against
our pleasure we are temperate.
—AESCHYLUS, *Agamemnon*, 176–80
(Lattimore trans.)

IN WHAT follows I "use" Nietzsche's essay "On the Uses and Disadvantages of History for Life"[1] as a framework for thinking in a general way about the uses and disadvantages of classical texts for contemporary political and theoretical life.[2] I will spend most of my time engaging that essay, considering Nietzsche's idea of untimeliness and his claims for classical studies, his antimethodological method and his explicit argument, as well as the architecture and prose of his text. Mostly I will treat his reflections as he does Hellenism: as an earlier time with which we can struggle to better understand our own. In his terms I want to become a pupil of his text to become less a product of contemporary ones. But I also want to follow Nietzsche's example and treat ancient Greece as another time engagement with which we can "augment" and "directly invigorate" our activity.

I write in the belief that there is now an opportunity and a need to make what Nietzsche calls classical studies an interlocutor in contemporary debates about the quality of public life and the aims of political theory. The opportunity is provided by the challenge to historical teleologies that had consigned the past, including the Hellenic past, to the dustbin of history. The need comes from the disrepute of politics, and from the narrowing of theoretical discourse (through Marx's excision from it), both of which have contributed to what Jürgen Habermas has called "the exhaustion of utopian energies."[3]

Though most of what follows is a direct engagement with Nietzsche's essay, the concluding section offers some examples of how his timely untimeliness might augment our theoretical and political activity. In fact, the essays that follow might be thought of in the same way.

But this is not a "Nietzschean" book, even if this particular essay provides a prolegomena to it. How Nietzschean it is will be clear in the way I "use" him in discussing the three examples that conclude this chapter, as well as in the democratic sentiments present in the remaining ones. Indeed, some may regard my use of him as comforting and reassuring when it should be provocative and contestatory. Of course one person's accommodation is another person's struggle, a situation exacerbated by a thinker like Nietzsche, whose authority is deployed by people of disparate theoretical and political commitments. Perhaps there is something endemic to academic analysis that domesticates thinkers like Nietzsche, as he himself suggested about classicists studying Greece in *Wir Philologen*. Perhaps the complexity of the text also has something to do with the paradoxical enterprise that marks this essay: trying to think outside "history" as a "historical" being.

I take one of Nietzsche's principal claims to be the significance of being untimely. Yet how is one to be untimely when our own time seems to be so many times at once? More specifically, how and for whom can ancient Greece be untimely in a timely way? More specifically still, how, given the cacophonic appropriation of Nietzsche, can he be made untimely?

But then why begin this book with a detailed reading of Nietzsche's essay? Because he is both an inspiration and a rebuke to the chapters that follow. As a critic, he becomes a challenging if not skeptical interlocutor to the way I juxtapose ancient and modern texts and the political conclusions I draw from them. His essay warns against glib assimilations that encourage co-optation of the Greeks rather than engagement in a (Greek-like) struggle with them. He reminds us of how hard one must work to "use" the Greeks without abusing them by idealizing, reifying, or pacifying them.

I

Nietzsche begins his "Betrachtung" with a quotation from Goethe: "In any case, I hate everything that merely instructs me without augmenting or directly invigorating my activity."[4] The essay that follows is an elaboration of Goethe's sentiment intended, Nietzsche tells us, to show why instruction without invigoration, knowledge unattended by action, and history as a superfluity and luxury must "be seriously hated by us—hated because we will lack even the things we need and the superfluous is the enemy of the necessary" (59). There is no question but that we need history and that historical consciousness is a distinctively human achievement. But we need history for life and action, not for mere amusement or to justify self-seeking, and that requires limiting the historical consciousness lest it destroy our humanity. So we must make sure that we serve history only to the extent that history serves life.

Good teaching and real (as opposed to decorative or idle) knowledge are less matters of doctrines taught and information conveyed than of enlarging and intensifying our capacity for thought and deed. That means that any doctrine, no matter how highly it praises vigor and life, pacifies if it is expressed blandly or allowed to occupy a safe place within dominant discourse. So one question to ask of any text, theory, idea, or culture is whether it quickens the pulse, not in the interest of frivolous excitation but in the interest of energizing our sense of agency. For teaching and knowledge to accomplish this, they must be "untimely."

Each of us cannot help but be a child of our times, shaped if not nurtured by the conditions that give us physical and cultural identity. This is where we began and must begin, which means acknowledging that we live in the present even when we are most confident we have transcended it. Nietzsche accepts the implication that his essay, which will criticize his time, is nonetheless marked by it, most obviously by the very fact as well as the nature of its criticisms. Here is that acknowledgment, made near the end of the essay. I quote at length because it is a moment when Nietzsche's argument and his antimethodological method coalesce.

> In the pursuit of the perils of history we have found ourselves most acutely exposed to them; we ourselves bear visibly the traces of those sufferings which afflict contemporary mankind as a result of an excess of history, and I have no wish to conceal from myself that, in the immoderation of its criticism, in the immaturity of its humanity, in its frequent transitions from irony to cynicism, from pride to skepticism, the present treatise itself reveals its modern character. (116)

Thus his text manifests the deficiencies it inveighs against and struggles against itself. Such "inconsistencies" are not an indication of flawed logic but a recognition that even the severest critique of one's time partakes of the time it criticizes, *and* that struggle is, as we shall see repeatedly, essential to maintaining the life of a text, person, idea, or culture. If this is true, then any wholesale dismissal of one's time by some grand gesture of ennui and contempt is both dishonest and an act of self-loath-ing. That is one reason to beware of nostalgia, though, as chapter 5 will argue, there are others.

We begin as children of our own time. But if we are not to remain perpetual children, we must become "pupil[s] of an earlier time" (60). Only then can we escape the obverse of nostalgia, presentism, where what is contemporary offers itself as the culmination of what is best in the past and as the ultimate moment of self-understanding. If we can become a foster child of this earlier time and so a student rather than a mere product of our own, we can move outside the aberrations, passions, errors, and crimes that formed us. Untimeliness is the way we can "confront our inherited and hereditary nature without our knowledge, and, through a new stern discipline, combat our inborn heritage, and implant in ourselves a new habit, a new instinct, a second nature" (62). In this way we can *choose* a past in which we would like to originate instead of settling for the one in which we did "in fact" originate.[5]

Notice that untimeliness precludes both being outside the time and being located at one moment in it. It is not objectivity or neutrality but a dialectical interplay between the present and some earlier time in which the significances and meanings of each shift with the alternating light and shadow they throw on each other. Thus the two moments are not static but change their positions relative to each other in a continual process of mutual interrogation, revelation, and renewal.

If no one exists outside of time, then no story or interpretation does either. If that is so, then we produce knowledge and categories of under-standing rather than interpret a reality outside of time. Near the end of this essay, Delphic Apollo's "Know Thyself" comes to play a defining role. Yet there was another saying inscribed at Delphi, alternatively glossed as "Remember your mortality" or "Nothing in excess." While Nietzsche has reason to suppress these sayings, given the necessity of forgetting and the dangers of moderation, one implication of untimeliness echoes them: that every story and sentiment, truth and passion has a history. What is true of stories in general is, ipso facto, true of origin stories, including the one about the origin of Western civilization.

Nietzsche's notion of untimeliness undermines the metaphysics or the-ology of birth origins and beginnings. He does not so much directly deny them as remove the privileged status that accrues to them from their being regarded as natural or first. Living in two times means that, at the very least, we have dual allegiances and a distance from any single incarnation of our world and ourselves in it. No one time is originary beyond being a starting (but not ending) point to be refurbished, renewed, refashioned, or reinvented. But if we have more than one origin, and if we must derive ourselves from an alternative legacy, then no one time can be morally or culturally controlling, or represent a moment of perfection from which all that follows is a falling away or faint imitation.

Nietzsche chose ancient Greece as his earlier time. He does not think that choice simply one of many, though he never claims it is the only one or even the best one. And of course he cannot claim that the Greeks exist as a moment outside of time. Yet they do provide him with the untimely experience "necessary for understanding" his own time. And far more than understanding: "I do not know what meaning classical studies can have for our time if they were not untimely—that is to say acting counter to our time and thereby acting on our time, and let us hope, for the benefit of a time to come" (60). The challenge, then, is to be irrelevant so one can become relevant in a way that does not mimic the fashion of one's time; to explore classical texts and times for the intrinsic pleasure they bring and the virtue they reveal such that they become "useful" in an interesting way. This requires both distance and proximity, making one's own time seem distant and the other time seem present, much as Greek tragedy dramatized the Athenian present through the refracted lens of ancient myths and heroic kings.

Of course this presupposes that we really know our time enough to be untimely. We must be able to feel its seductions and share its vanities, and appreciate how it constructs its past in a narrative of identity and aspiration. Such knowledge is one thing the "Uses and Disadvantages of History" sets out to establish. But it is not the only thing.

Though I will pay some attention to Nietzsche's characterization of his own time, I am more interested in his antimethodological method, since that, even more than his argument about nineteenth-century German culture,[6] is what makes him untimely for "us." By "antimethodological method" I mean four related things. The first is the way Nietzsche keeps the interplay between the present and the earlier time vital by preventing the dialectic between them from congealing. The second thing I have in mind concerns the way the pluralizing narrative this dialectic creates is replicated by Nietzsche's "deconstruction" of various polarities that comfortably circumscribe the choices of his contemporaries: polarities such as young and old, man and animal, remembering and forgetting, enlightenment and ignorance, light and dark, truth and life. At one stroke the phrase "deadly but true doctrines" creates a quandary for those who believe in the rational foundation of morality.[7] The third is the way the text turns back on itself.

One way it does so is when a section disrupts the overall argument, a paragraph disturbs the logic of a section, a sentence upsets the expectations of a paragraph, or a word (even one as innocent as "almost") can displace the reigning sentiment of a sentence. Another way the text turns back on itself is Nietzsche's strategy of redeeming what he has gone to

great lengths to disparage (such as objectivity). At a minimum this strategy raises a question of how much of his or any argument depends on
"historical" context. More substantially, it pushes us to ask whether there
are redeeming features of what appears corrupting, and corrupting possibilities present in what is most highly valued.

The fourth thing I mean by "antimethodological method" is the way
these interruptions prevent any confident appropriation of the text and
act as incitements to keep the text useful for life. (I will make a similar
argument about DeLillo's non sequiturs in chapter 7.) "A historical phenomenon," Nietzsche writes, "known clearly and completely and re-
solved into a phenomenon of knowledge is, for him who has perceived it,
dead" (65). The same is true of a text.

In these terms Nietzsche's antimethodological method is a protest
against the compulsions of logic and history (as is Lessing's, as I will suggest in the following chapter). It is not so much that logic is some trick
and coherent stories about history are arbitrary. It is, rather, that paradox
and irony, which create spaces for interpretive agency in the essay, need to
do the same in an "outside" world committed to historical determinisms
that consolidate the present in terms of the past and thus cut off any future.

Thus Nietzsche's "method" is a test of our capacity to sustain irony.
For those who cannot, irony becomes cynicism. If he (or we) fail the test,
then his essay becomes part of the problem. If he (and we) succeed, we
will have the strength to use history for life.

II

As we have seen, humans need history and memory, but they need it to
serve life and action, not the other way around (which does not mean
that history must serve whatever prejudices are fashionable). But to live,
men must be able to forget. Forgetting is as essential for life as remembering for the same reason that darkness is as essential as light for an organ-
ism to thrive. As plants would wilt under the unremitting light of the sun,
so do men under the unremitting light of historical consciousness. A man
who never forgets is a man who never sleeps; the man who never sleeps
is a man who reacts rather than acts. The historical sense unchecked and
uncontested is fatal to living things—to a person, a people, or a culture.

The excessive cultivation and overvaluation of history is not only destructive of life in itself; it also calls forth an equally excessive, equally
destructive desire to escape history altogether. That is why for our all
vaunted self-awareness and despite our celebration of reason as the defining aspect of our nature, we cannot help envying those dumb animals and
innocent children whose nonreason we publicly disparage. Animals are

completely contained in the present. They appear wholly as what they are at every minute of their lives, while children play, unconcerned, "between the hedges of past and future." Or they do until they learn the phrase "it was," which reveals to them that existence is "an imperfect tense that can never become a perfect one" (60–61). Free from the chains of remembering, they live without the melancholy and boredom that afflict us "sophisticated" ones. In this dialectic a surfeit of history promotes the death of historical consciousness; obsessive remembering makes oblivion all the more seductive; unremitting enlightenment makes darkness seem Eden.

There is a threefold irony here. First, this dialectic means that, in crucial respects, we have the worst of both possible worlds. We suffer from a surfeit of history *and* live in the moment, since, as we shall see, objectivity makes the present the standard for all that has been and could be. Second, it means that these supremely knowledgeable men are ignorant of what their knowledge does to them. They fail to recognize how their heightened capacity for knowledge is accompanied by an atrophied sense of action and mastery. They do not realize that the more we ascend to heavenly knowledge—to objectivity, universal laws, historical narratives of progress, and full self-consciousness—the greater the chaos below and within. Third, they are unable to appreciate the fact that "[a]ll living things require an atmosphere around them; a mysterious misty vapor; if they are deprived of this envelope, if a religion, art, a genius is condemned to revolve as a star without an atmosphere, we should no longer be surprised if they quickly wither and grow hard and unfruitful" (97). Lacking such an atmosphere, men and women cannot mature. Without such a horizon to protect them from the onslaught of historical consciousness, they will wither. Stripped of illusions, they will fall into a "hopeless infinity of skepticism."

This suggests that it matters less what the illusion is than that there be one; less how the horizon is drawn than that it *is* drawn. Worst of all is having no shelter amid the storm. "Let us only make land; later on we shall find good harbors right enough, and make the landfall easier to those who come after" (116). This implies that those historical men and women whose project is dispelling illusions and erasing all boundaries are misguided. Even worse, their disregard for what they contemptuously see as parochialism and celebration of objectivity and openness leads not to generosity of spirit and universal knowledge, as they suppose, but to a defensive egoism. That is because their demystifying opens the floodgates of historical knowledge and leaves them gasping for some respite and ground. Or, to change the image, they cannot bear the weight of the world whose falseness, crudeness, absurdity, and violence they take such pride in unmasking.

What these men fail to realize is that the darkness of the unhistorical condition is the womb of the just as well as the unjust act, of freedom as well as necessity. Intent on the way man becomes man by being historical, they cannot see that he will cease being man with too much of it. Only when they acknowledge the toxicity of what they suppose to be a lifesaving drug will they be able to raise the question of when and how history can serve life rather than destroy it.

Of course Nietzsche is doing what he criticizes lovers of history for doing: dispelling illusions, challenging accepted boundaries, historicizing historicizing. That is a necessary aspect of his "method" and to be expected of one who is at least partly and initially a child of his time. But by daring to push the temper of his times further than his contemporaries, by puncturing their illusions about the value of history as they have punctured the illusions of every historical illusion, he can make them *feel* the limits of the method they glory in using on others. In his hands historicizing becomes a sobriety test for historicists as well as a way to mimic and thus make palpable the corrosive consequences that come from the fetishism of historical consciousness.

III

Nietzsche's "solution" and answer to the question of when and how history can serve rather than destroy "life" can be found in his distinctions among three kinds of history: "monumental," which exists for the man who acts and strives; "antiquarian" for the man who preserves and reveres; and "critical" for the man who seeks deliverance from his suffering.

Of the three ways history serves life, one is preeminent. "History belongs *above all* to the man of deeds and power, to him who fights the great fight, who needs models, teachers, comforters and cannot find them among his contemporaries" (67, my emphasis). To see how other men of strength and vision have triumphed over countless misfortunes enables such men of deeds to endure those changes of fortune that paralyze lesser men and their age. This man of action and power looks with contempt and distrust on those tourists of history seeking distraction or excitation.[8] Motivated not by their idle curiosity or sterile pedantry, he instead looks to the past for inspiration. Because he aims at mighty things—the happiness of his nation and mankind—he flees from resignation, habit, and apathy, from all that is petty and base. Keeping his sights on glory and honor, he himself becomes a teacher and exemplar for those searching, as he did, for what their time lacked. He will live on as they did because posterity cannot live without their protest against the passing away of generations and the transitoriness of things. He makes the world come alive while expanding the concept of man.

Yet monumental history can destroy life. By discarding "huge chunks of the past," being contemptuous of historical veracity, dealing only in generalities and approximations, simplifying motives and causes, it forces variation into a single mold. Monumental history's raison d'être is the celebration of the deeds of great men about whom stories can be told (which is the meaning of *heros* in Greek). But when "whole segments of the past" are forgotten or ignored, history comes to have a dulling sameness. Without contrasts and enemies monumental history cannot serve life because its own distinctiveness is erased in a monotonous landscape.

In the second place, history belongs to him who "preserves and reveres"; who looks back to whence he has come with love and loyalty, piously giving thanks for his sheer existence. Unlike monumental history, antiquarian history preserves life by preserving the conditions under which a people came into being. Such men see no evil or deficiency in these conditions and recognize no lack or deformity that might give them pause or leave them resentful or ill at ease. They have no sense of using the past because they have no sense of being apart from it. Their identity is fused with the city that gave them life. It is the continuity and spirit of that city that provide solace. And for them that spirit is everywhere: in the walls and gates that define its space; in the laws and regulations that define its politics; in the holidays and festivals that define its culture. At its best this veneration of the past spreads a "simple feeling of pleasure and contentment over the modest, rude, even wretched conditions in which a man ordinarily lives" (73).

Yet here, too, the past suffers even as history serves life, since a man in thrall to the history of his people sees little, and what he does see is so near and so unrelated to anything larger or more inclusive that every particular takes on the same importance. Like the man of monumental history who is in danger of submerging so much of history that the contrasts necessary to illuminate greatness disappear, the man of antiquarian history is likely to wind up doing the same because he lacks the perspective to distinguish the significance of individual events. Both are without the sense of discrimination and proportion that allows us to give the particulars of life their justice. Both by themselves make history boring.

Insofar as the man of antiquarian history regards everything old as worthy of reverence and rejects as well as persecutes everything new and evolving, the past becomes mummified. No longer animated and inspired by the freshness of the present, its piety is withering and its scholarliness merely "rotates in egoistic self-satisfaction around its own axis" (75).

But even without such degeneration there are dangers inherent in this mode of regarding history. For while it knows how to preserve life, it does not know how to engender it, or even tolerate the man who does. It paralyzes the man of action by confronting him with epithets and obstacles, weighing him down with the exorbitant sacredness of the past. Like monumental history, this history needs limit and opposition if it is not to turn in on itself, destroying its generative role and thus life itself.

Without critical history men would suffocate under the all-consuming piety of antiquarian history. If a man or nation is to live, they must, on occasion, possess and employ their strength to break up the seamless self-justifying presence of the past. One can do this only by bringing the past (and the worship of the past) before the tribunal of life. In this trial illusions are unmasked; self-legitimizing narratives are demystified; distortions, lapses, violence, and weakness are exposed.

Perhaps even more than the other ways of using history for life, this critical stance is impatient with limits on its own power. Even at its best it possesses a logic and momentum that destroy everything that stands against it.[9] That is why men and ages who serve life by judging and destroying the past "are always dangerous and endangered" (76). While this is so in every age, it is more so in Nietzsche's own.

There are many ways to interpret the interrelationship among the three modes of history. One can see them as aspects present in every age, culture, and person, though in differing proportions. Or one can conceive of them as parts of an ontological hierarchy insofar as history belongs "above all" to the man of action, in the "second place" to the antiquarian, and finally to the critics. (Nietzsche is, however, insistent that monumental history cannot "rule over" the other two.) Or they may be regarded as an evolution that culminates in a present consumed by and with critical history.

However one regards them, the central question is clear: when do we need each mode of history, and how can we distinguish the counterfeit from the real thing? It is also clear that each use of history has a degenerate form, and that each constitutes a consuming passion which, though it allows it to serve life, can become rigid and destructive when its dynamic is left unchecked and unchallenged. Finally, it is clear that Nietzsche has provided a restatement rather than a solution to the initial problem of how history can serve rather than destroy life.

It should not, given his "method," be surprising that Nietzsche offers various readings of the problem rather than a final resolution of it, and that each of his restatements provides a different angle of vision on what is at stake. Such repeated reconfiguring must be part of any "solution" because solutions always contain further questions. There can be no permanent answers or final solutions when every argument is strategic—that is, rests on a "historical" understanding of what sort of historical understanding is necessary for the life of a particular people and culture at a particular historical juncture.

There is another reason why there can be no conclusive arguments on these matters: it may be less a matter of argument than one of character. If so, the questions "How can we know when we need to forget and to

remember?" and "When and in what proportion should we honor one or
another of these forms of history?" are the wrong ones. The right ones are
"*Who* can know?" and "What sort of character must he have?" Nietzsche
makes the point first obliquely, in an analogy he draws between drama
and history, and then more directly.

The value of drama, Nietzsche argues, cannot lie solely in its conclusions. For then drama would be merely a tendentious way of reaching a
goal that might be met in other more efficient ways. Similarly, the significance of history does not lie in its propositions. Rather, it lies in taking a
familiar theme "and composing inspired variations on it, enhancing it,
elevating it to a comprehensive symbol and thus disclosing in the original
theme a whole world of profundity, power and beauty" (92–93). "Who"
can do this? Only a person of great artistic facility, creative vision, and
loving absorption in empirical data. Such a man is objective, not in the
negative sense of having rid himself of passion, but in the positive sense
found in the "inward flashing eye of the artist."

More directly Nietzsche describes this "who" as a man of health whose
powerful instincts tell him when it is wise to feel historically and when it
is not. He is a man who interprets the past with what is best and highest
in himself, since only if he puts forth his "noblest qualities in all their
strength will [he] divine what is worth knowing and preserving in the
past." And he must be a reader of oracles, since the past speaks only in
oracular terms, like the god at Delphi. Finally, he must be confident of
and for the future. "Only he who constructs the future has a right to judge
the past." Only a great end in the future can restrain what Nietzsche calls
"that rank analytic impulse which turns the present into a desert" (94).
Such a man is a founder and initiator, one who overturns all boundary
stones (in Greek, *nomoi*, which also means laws and practices). But in his
absence we must ask the original questions again, questions about what
we need, about when and how history can serve life, and about accommo-
dating the seemingly contradictory demands of monumental, antiquarian,
and critical history. We are told that every nation and man requires a
certain kind of knowledge of the past, depending on its or his goals, energies, and needs. Yet unless we know what these are and how to ask about
them, we know relatively little. But how do we choose a past and create
a second nature in a way that does not naively suppose that we are sui
generis or simply the heirs to what has gone before? And where does the
essay itself fit within the typologies it proposes and the argument it
makes? Nietzsche acknowledges that he has been exposed to the perils of
history as embraced by his contemporaries, for he is a man of his time
(though not only that). But if he is shaped by the excess of history, by the
immoderate criticism, immaturity, and transition from irony to criticism
that characterize his age, then how does he, and how does he expect us

to, escape its influence or use its energy against it? Does his work manifest the plastic power it commends? How, in sum, does *it* serve life?

IV

We know that history serves life only when men are able to forget. We know, too, that forgetting requires the presence of some limit and horizon, a mist or atmosphere, and that such a limit lies somewhere between the idolatry of the actual and unconstrained poetic invention. We also know that without respite from the constant life of reason men cannot grow for the same reason plants need darkness as well as light if they are to flourish. Finally, we know that a flood of historical knowledge drives men to take refuge in a narrow, uninteresting, and ineffectual defensive egoism. Machiavelli amplifies the point when he likens fortune to a river that inundates men unless they take proper precautions. If they build dikes and levees, the elemental forces that might destroy them can be harnessed and captured for human purposes. If they do not, they will be victims of chance and contingency. Scientific history destroys those dikes and levees. It permits a flood of historical knowledge that causes men to lose their instincts (*virtù*) and become fainthearted and insecure.

As historical knowledge streams in from inexhaustible wells that stretch back into infinity, men become sated and paralyzed by facts and possibilities, made impotent and lifeless by multiplicities of undifferentiated facts and values, and mired in verbiage. Near the end of his essay Nietzsche warns of the difficulties the first generation to be educated against history (and so themselves) will endure. He reiterates, in perhaps his most pessimistic and therefore his most challenging tone, that they will have to fight the fact that "we" are ruined for living, for right and simple seeing and hearing. Caught up in conceptual intricacies, we are blind to what is nearest and most natural to us; we become rightly suspicious of the life we lead and, more dangerously, doubt we have any life in us. "Fragmented and in pieces, dissociated almost mechanically into an inner and outer, sown with concepts as with dragon's teeth, bringing forth conceptual dragons, suffering from the malady of words and mistrusting of any feeling of our own which has not yet been stamped by words, being such an unliving and yet uncannily active concept—and word factory" (119), we suffer from a version of what Milan Kundera calls "graphomania."[10] Of course that includes Nietzsche as well as those who would be his students.

The "passion for objectivity" is, for those who wish to make history a science, a contradiction in terms. That is because objectivists aim to purge passion, which they condemn as an obstructive subjectivism. Passion creates bias; preferences are prejudices. Both are faithless to a reality that can be known only if the personality and presence of the historian are suppressed.[11] Dispassionate analysis, anonymity, passivity are the necessary conditions for the historian's authority as truth teller. But how, Nietzsche asks, can history serve life when we purge our instincts and allow it to tell its own story? How, more pointedly, can this deathlike state of anonymity and indifference possibly exist for life? The final irony is that in purging the passions, objectivists also eliminate the passion to know and be scientific.

Lacking the hunger to know, objectivists become strolling spectators of history, utterly indifferent to its heights and values, using the "knowledge" contained in their thousands of pages of tedious prose to domesticate revolutions and wars before they have any energizing effect. They are tone-deaf to Aeschylus's idea that power and agency as well as wisdom come alone through suffering. It is true that the Chorus's prayer in the epigraph of this essay is a lament and confession of bewilderment. Yet without suffering, however meaningless it may appear at the moment, nothing in the world can be deeply known, though it is true that too much suffering paralyzes action, a condition that in fact defines the overly historical man.

All of this has depressing consequences for the study of the Greeks. Objectivists believe that "he to whom a moment of the past *means nothing at all* is the proper man to describe it" (93, emphasis in original). This is the relationship that increasingly obtains between classicists and the Greeks. They mean nothing to each other.[12]

The fact that objectivity as a way of life gets angry at nothing, loves nothing, understands everything, and approaches the Greeks as if they were just one more object of study, one more historical moment among an infinity of others to be smothered in sterile descriptions that pass for serious historical scholarship, is a disaster and enraging. "It is precisely where the highest and rarest is to be represented," Nietzsche complains, "that ostentatious indifference becomes most infuriating" (93). But historical men really have no other choice. How else are they to overcome "that which presses upon [them] in too great abundance"? Their only solution is to embrace everything as slightly as possible "so as to quickly expel it again and have done with it. From this comes a habit of no longer taking real things seriously" (79).

But the leveling of all previous times is not really the equalization of all times, since (as DeLillo also suggests) everything takes its meaning from the present time, which becomes, by default or by design, the only time. And this means that objectivists are not independent of common opinion and intellectual fashion. On the contrary, they are in thrall to their time since they access the opinions and deeds of the past only in terms of whatever standards dominate the present, adapting "the past to contemporary triviality," while proclaiming any historiography "subjective" that does not accept the present as canonical. Just as clearly, Nietzsche is unpersuaded that scientific history and objectivity are means to, or themselves represent, mastery and control. Objectivists are "eunuchs" living in the "great historical world-harem" (84). Unable to make history, they study it, not for action but to promote further historical study. Studiously guarding history so that nothing comes of it except more of it, they consume all that is novel through instantaneous critiques which discard or deflate all that might provoke us. Objectivist history, then, is not proactive but reactive; not part of some world refashioning but a retreat from the relentless onslaught of information, facts, historical knowledge, and remembering.

To the degree modern man is a ready and willing student of these objectivists, he is subjectless and passionless. Learning has outward effect but no inner strength. Men have become abstractions and shadows, fearful of appearing without disguise. "No one," Nietzsche writes, "dares to appear as he is but makes himself as a cultivated man, a scholar, as a poet, as a politician" (84). Aware that he lives in a historicizing twilight, fearful that his youthful hopes and energy will not survive into the future, he is at first ironic; then, unable to endure irony, he becomes cynical, believing that as things are, they had to be, as men are now, they were bound to become.

The unrelenting historical sense encouraged and endorsed by the demand that history be a science creates such distrust and timidity that men lack the will to make history serve life. Rather, they ask history what lives they ought to lead, what they ought to do, and how they should feel. Thus they live warily, looking around to be sure that they conform to whatever self-understanding or intellectual fashion reigns. These men are spectators of their lives, not actors in it; role players in an infinite number of scripts made available to them by the triumph of history over instinct, youthfulness, illusion, and horizons.

Just when we are convinced that objectivity is an unalloyed evil, Nietzsche retrieves it from its contemporary use and his condemnation.[13] I want to say something about this retrieval, as it provides another clue to how to read his text and follow the substantive consequences of his "method," before I turn to the reasons why and how he does it.

There is something unsettling about being carried along on an intellectual trajectory with which you have come to agree (or disagree) only to have it go the other way. Nietzsche's argument/polemic does precisely that and, by so doing, makes us self-conscious about our own vulnerabilities and commitments as interpreters. (It can also lead to misology, a possibility explored in the *Phaedo* and my discussion of it in chapter 7.) More particularly, it pushes us to acknowledge the strategic dimension of argument and the way the moral and epistemological possibilities of ideas and language depend on their place in a text and world. Such a strategic dimension is not (or need not be) perversely manipulative or simply instrumentalist. It is, at a minimum, an aspect of any "use" of language. More strongly, Nietzsche's claim is that thought, to be thought at all, must attend to time and place, while acting to counter what is fashionable or agreed upon at a certain point in a text or in history. More specifically, it must hold historical consciousness, to which Nietzsche says, with uncertain irony, his age is a "justly proud" hostage.

To insist on the strategic dimension of language is to draw attention to the rhetorical quality of speech, including truth-speak. Thus Nietzsche emphasizes the way words like "objectivity," "science," "consciousness" as well as "fact" and "reality" are deployed to hypostatize the present. Like the prefatory comment that identifies one's ethnicity as a way of establishing authority for what is to follow, such words function to make the present tyrant over the future.

All that reminds us of the other side of Machiavelli's discussion of fortune mentioned above. Fortune represents an opportunity as well as a danger insofar as the absence of inherited meanings and structures makes the production of meaning (the *virtù* of the theorist and actor alike) possible. Without the unexpected and contingent there would be no space for action and deeds. History may not be a clean slate, but neither is it so written upon that we can add nothing to it through narratives that celebrate human agency and construct our lives. The space between what is and what ought to be, between the present and possible futures, gives us something to do.[14]

V

The resurrection of objectivity appears in Nietzsche's discussion of whether modern man "on account of his well-known historical 'objectivity' has a right to call himself strong, that is to say just, and just in a higher degree than man of other ages" (88). Does objectivity originate in an enhanced need and demand for justice, or is this simply a flattering prejudice, a delusion that modern man has that he possesses virtues he does not have, which Socrates regarded as akin to madness?

Nietzsche believes it is the latter. But he also believes that justice, virtue, truth, knowledge, and objectivity *could* claim our respect and admiration if circumstances were different. What sorts of claims might they have, and how would circumstances have to alter for us to accord objectivity the respect it would come to warrant?

"No one has a greater claim to our veneration," Nietzsche writes, "than he who possesses the drive to and strength for justice." Called to justice, such a man judges in utter disregard for himself. When he speaks, his voice is neither harsh nor fearful but has a matter-of-fact strength. Though he never doubts that he is a human, yet he strives to ascend from "indulgent doubt to stern certainty" (88). Never losing sight of his limitations, yet consumed by an impossible virtue he demands of himself, he must live tragically. Such a man desires truth, not as cold ineffectual knowledge or as the egoistic possession of an individual, but as a punishing judge would.

Those who possess the will to justice and the strength to be just serve truth. But the truth they serve, like the justice they strive for, is the inverse of that endorsed by the objectivist. While the latter purges passion and will in the name of neutrality toward all and everything, the former has a passion for truth and a will to justice that demands recognition of what is superior and inferior, what serves life and what saps it of vitality and beauty.

But where are we to discover or how can we create such a just man? Is he present in a part of us we have not yet discovered, in places in our culture where we have not yet looked? If not there, in some other time to which we can apprentice ourselves and so come to craft a life our time is insufficiently powerful to generate for itself? We know it must be possible to discover or rediscover, create or re-create such a man (or culture). Otherwise, Nietzsche's pessimism would not be a provocation but would foster what he most opposes: quietism and cynicism. We also know that his own text is offered as a guide. And we know that any answer to these questions must look to the Greeks for instruction and inspiration. Yet we really do not know very much about where the resources for regeneration can be found, or how precisely they can combat the eviscerations of historical culture.

Though Nietzsche provides a number of clues, they are less an answer than part of the parable with which he concludes his essay.

One clue concerns the "plastic power" of a people, culture, or person. Plastic power is the "capacity to develop out of oneself in one's own way, to transform and incorporate into oneself what is past and foreign, to heal wounds, to replace what has been lost, to recreate broken molds" (62–63). Some people and cultures have so little of this power that they die from a single experience, painful event, or subtle piece of injustice, like a man who bleeds to death from a mere scratch. But others are virtually unaffected by the worst disasters, including the committing of "wicked acts." The "innermost roots" of their natures are strong enough to appropriate things of the past. The most powerful of all can draw into itself not only from its own past but that which was most foreign to it as well, forging these elements into a volatile unity that sustains life, as Nietzsche does in his text.

Nietzsche tells us that the secret of this plastic power is its capacity to forget what it cannot subdue, and anything outside its sphere of action and life. Since we already knew about the need to forget, this does not take us very far. The problem is how to learn to forget once you have been educated to remember, how to become naive and young again. But from another point of view, the discussion of plastic power is more than a restatement of the problem. It directs our attention to the resources present in our culture and his text so that we may determine whether the asides, qualifications, non sequiturs, and turnings present in both can provide resources for our using history for life.

There is one group that can see presentism for what it is, and so possesses plastic power: the young. Nietzsche characterizes historical culture as essentially old and asserts that those who "bear its mark from childhood must believe in the old age of mankind" (101). They are preoccupied with looking back, reckoning up accounts, and seeking consolidation through remembering what has been thought and done, which for them is everything. Satiated and impotent in the present, they have no hopes for the future. They are old because history has destroyed their instincts and made them lose trust in their own reason. They have grown feeble, fainthearted, and unable to believe in themselves. They are old because knowledge has become for them mere abstractions that nonetheless have the power to make them abstract and passionless, mere shadows and poseurs who wear masks of cultivatedness and present themselves as poets, politicians, or scholars rather than as men.

The young, by contrast, are the remnants of hope. They are untimely, which we recall entails "acting counter to our time and thereby acting on our time and, let us hope, for the benefit of a time to come" (60). They are not old because they have not yet become historical beings. For the moment they are clairvoyant, able to see what their contemporaries do not see or are too afraid to articulate: historical consciousness is, for modern man, the disease, not the cure. But they also divine what medicines will work against the "malady of history" and enable us all to regain "the paradise of health" that has been lost. The antidotes—which Nietzsche calls "poisonous"—are "the unhistorical," the art and power of forgetting and enclosing oneself in a bounded horizon, and "the suprahistorical," the "powers which lead the eye away from becoming toward that which bestows upon existence the character of the eternal and stable, towards *art* and *religion*" (120, emphasis in original).

Yet this mission will be costly for the first generation who turns against the worship of history. For one thing, they will never be fully part of the future happiness of which they have a presentiment, and whose achievement they are initiating. Even worse, they cannot help but suffer from both the sickness and the antidotes even though they can, despite or because of this, legitimately claim a robust health their "grey-bearded" presentist predecessors lack. Third, they will be attacked and dismissed as uncultured, coarse, and immoderate for making the worse argument appear the better and turning the world inside out. That is inevitable since the young's "mission" is to undermine the concept the present has of "health" and "culture" while exciting mockery and hatred against these "hybrid monsters of concepts." Though its enemies will demand that youth describe themselves in terms of the "current currency of words," it can discover no concepts or slogan to describe its own nature. This, rather than being a deficiency, is a sign of its health. Rejecting such currency, it cannot be bribed; not being bribed, distracted, or corrupted allows youth to concentrate on the active power within it. Though the transvaluations they undertake may be full of trials, they will enjoy "the consolations and privileges of youth": courage, unreflecting honesty, and hope (121).

At the end of Plato's *Apology of Socrates*, the old man turns to those who voted to acquit him. To these friends he speaks informally and intimately about the meaning of what has passed. At the end of his text Nietzsche also turns with special affection "to the company of the hopeful to tell them a parable." It is a parable about the course and progress of their cure, about their delivery from the malady of history, and so about their own history, up to the point at which they will be sufficiently healthy to study history, and to employ the past in its monumental, antiquarian, and critical senses. To reach this point, they will have unlearned many things and, in the process, will no longer be an aggregate of humanlike qualities but will have "become human again." This is what will make the young laugh with hope (119–22).

But again, the question: how can we attain such a goal? What path or journey will take us there? For the "answer" Nietzsche invokes the riddling god of Delphi. That god "cries to you his oracle: 'Know Thyself.' " Yet the command is hard beyond any surface difficulties because in Nietzsche's Heraclitean reading Apollo conceals nothing and says nothing; he only indicates. But what does he indicate?

And who will take us? Who are the youth? The question seems tendentious; the youth are the young. Yet Nietzsche insists that his parable is "for each one of us." So it appears that it is not just the young but each one of us who "must organize the chaos within him by thinking back to his real needs" (122). All of us must strive for an honesty, strength, and truthfulness of character so as to rebel against the state of things in which we only repeat what we have heard, learn what is already known, imitate what already exists. Only then can we grasp that culture can and must be something other than "a *decoration of life*" (123, emphasis in original). Only then we can understand and "use" the Greeks, who themselves understood this with unique profundity.

VI

More of "On the Uses and Disadvantages of History for Life" engages the Greeks than is apparent. Indeed, they suffuse the entire essay—hardly surprising, given the claim Nietzsche makes for them. In addition to explicit references (e.g., to Delphi and Heraclitus), and identifiable though not fully explicit invocations (e.g., to the stories of Cadmus and of Thebes), there is the idea of untimeliness itself and Nietzsche's "method," both of which can be read as extrapolations of Greek tragedy. Greek tragedy represented contemporary Athenian events, figures, and issues through the refracting mirror of other places (Thebes, Argos) and other times (e.g., mythical Athens) in a dialectic of proximity and distance similar to the one Nietzsche establishes between his own and some earlier time. Similarly, performance in the theater was a way of "remembering" exclusions the Athenians had "forgotten" or banished to the margins of society. On the stage characters spoke the unspeakable and represented the foreign. Finally, one can map the rhythms of tragedy onto Nietzsche's dialectic of pessimism and agency or, more specifically, read the two-sided triumph of historical consciousness through the lens of the famous "choral ode to man" in *Antigone*. So while the final part of the essay announces a return to the Greeks, they have been a presence throughout.

Nietzsche has five specific but closely related reasons for ending his essay with the Greeks and, in the process, redeeming the extraordinary claim he made for classical studies in the beginning. The first is to offer them as a model of an unhistorical culture that was "nonetheless . . . or rather on that account, an inexpressibly richer and more vital culture." He co-opts the words of praise such as "great," "natural," and "humane" his age assigns to historical cultures like itself and reassigns them to the Greeks, who deserve them and to whom his age can *then* apprentice themselves until they truly deserve the praise they prematurely claim. Though the thought of being epigones can be painful, it is "also capable of evoking great effects and grand hopes for the future in both an individual and a nation." At least this is so if his contemporaries would regard themselves as heirs and successors "of the astonishing powers of antiquity and see in this [their] honour and spur" (103).

Second, real engagement with the Greeks can free us from conceiving of ourselves as latecomers whose purpose is to preserve with antiquarian fastidiousness what Nietzsche would not call "the Glory that was Greece." Unless one regards the power of the Greeks as a challenge to be met rather than a condition to be admired, their glory comes at our expense. What Nietzsche suggests here is that seeing oneself as the culmination of history is not, as it may seem, a form of self-praise but a "paralyzing and depressing" acceptance of weakness. It does not augment our activity but diminishes it until we can create nothing new and truthful. Unless of course we engage the Greeks in the right way.

Third, the Greeks never regarded or lived culture as if it were simply decorative. Nor did they pose an opposition between nature and convention but instead regarded the latter as a "new and improved *physis*," that is, a second nature and a new life. To be heirs of the Greeks is to use them as they used the idea of culture and, by so doing, to imitate their power. For that power was evident in the fact that they chose their natures; chose their parentage and so who they could become; chose their horizon and to forget; chose truthfulness over cultivation; chose integration of life over a division between inner and outer; and chose honesty over disguise and dissimulation. Thus they had a "true culture," one defined by the unanimity of life, thought, experience, and will.

Fourth, Nietzsche believes that his contemporaries—modern men, especially modern Germans—find themselves faced with a danger similar to the one faced by the Greeks: the danger of perishing through history. Because they never lived "in proud inviolability," Greek culture was, for a long time, a chaos of foreign forms and ideas, and their religion a battle of Eastern gods. Yet thanks to the Delphic Apollo, Hellenic culture gradually learned to organize the chaos by "thinking back to themselves, to their real needs, and so regained possession of themselves" (122).

Finally, Hellenic culture maintained its vibrancy not through a unanimity as sameness but through one that depended on variety and difference. They neither expelled what was foreign nor allowed it to triumph over them. Rather, "after a hard struggle with themselves" and through protracted application of the Oracle's injunction "Know thyself," they became "the happiest enrichers and augmenters of the treasure they had inherited and the first born model of all cultured nations" (122–23). In echoing Goethe's hatred toward anything that did not augment activity, Nietzsche is reiterating the idea contained in his "method": that the coherence of a culture or logic of an argument may kill thought and life; that warring gods need not issue in men who are paralyzed because of a mere aggregate of influence, but on the contrary can, if we follow the Greeks, become conflicts that sustain and enhance our capacity to act.

VII

One thing that unites much contemporary political and social thought is what Peter Dews calls its "deflationary" tendency.[15] It is a tendency present in analytic philosophy, the New Pragmatism, Foucault's postmodernism, Habermas's embrace of proceduralism, Rawls's "thin theory of the good," and the Cambridge historians associated with Quentin Skinner.

In varying degrees, all these represent a retreat from, if not repudiation of, what Sheldon Wolin has called the "Epic" dimension of political theory.[16]

Nietzsche's essay reminds us of how easily such deflationary tendencies sap the instinct for creation necessary for augmenting our activities and our life. The historical and historicizing drive must contain within it a "drive to construct." If it does not, if the purpose of destroying and clearing is not to "allow a future already alive in anticipation to raise its house on the ground thus liberated," then the instinct for creation (not just any specific one) will be enfeebled and discouraged (96). Historical and theoretical asceticism either removes the ground or makes it so barren that nothing can live on it.

What the essay also does is provoke a symptomatic reading of the area of theoretical convergence. Why these arguments now in this form? What is the result of accepting any one of them or the common temperament they embody? For Nietzsche (as for Marx and some pragmatists) a good idea, concept, or theory is one that augments and invigorates action and so serves "life." Thus he might historicize the historicism of the Cambridge school and ask about the consequences for political theory's ability to invigorate action when one denies the claimed originality of "monumental" thinkers while elevating to their ranks thinkers who seem to be of far less stature and interest. Are they flattening the theoretical landscape with the kind of scholarship Nietzsche thought deadening?[17]

To read ideas, concepts, or theories symptomatically is to map them onto the dialectic between remembering and forgetting, and to discern their horizon or illusions, not to unmask them but to explore what they do to the people who espouse them and the culture that accepts them. It is to trace their strategies of demystification while locating the mystifications they create in the moment of doing so.

Such symptomatic readings do not collapse theory into practice or action but challenge such distinctions for reasons analogous to those present in Nietzsche's critique of oppositions between inner and outer, abstract and concrete, surface and depth. Ideas, concepts, and theories are themselves forms of action, including ideas of historical consciousness and proper scholarship.

If we take Nietzsche's method as exemplary, a theory or text must contain a genealogy of its own construction. This involves "problematizing" the logic of its argument even as it is being deployed.

VIII

It used to be said that Nietzsche was not interested in politics, or that whatever politics he did have was reprehensible. Such assertions still surface in the context of whether and how Nietzsche is a democrat or can be "used" to develop a democratic politics, culture, or theorizing. I have no desire to join this debate here. My purpose is more modest: to offer an example of Nietzsche's influence on a work that is preoccupied with politics: Max Weber's "Politics as a Vocation."[18] This is hardly an original claim, and Weber is hardly a democrat. Indeed, he seems to share Nietzsche's contempt for democracy.

We see the influence (or, if you like, affinities between the two) in Weber's emphasis on character and his characterization of one committed to an ethic of ultimate ends. It is also present in the parallels between Nietzsche's man of justice and Weber's politician, in the importance of serving life rather than sterile excitations or petty desires, and in the need for passion and objectivity. And it is present in the Nietzschean way Weber uses Nietzsche to achieve his own untimely timeliness.

The political question for Weber is this: what sort of person does one want to have steering the wheel of history, and what is involved in doing justice to the ethical and practical demands of politics? It is in answering this question that Weber establishes his famous distinction between an ethic of ultimate ends and an ethic of responsibility.

A person committed to an ethic of ultimate ends brooks no compromise and shuns all strategic considerations. She is unequivocal and uncondi-tional in her fidelity to an ideal or way of life. The ethic demands we turn the other cheek, suffer injustice rather than commit it, conclude that failure to realize an ideal in the world is the fault of an impure world and that our sole responsibility is for "seeing to it that the flame of pure intentions is not quelched." "The Christian does rightly and leaves the results to the Lord," and moralistic politicians say the same. "You may demonstrate to a convinced syndicalist," Weber writes, "that his actions will result in increasing the opportunities of reaction, in increasing the oppression of his class and obstructing its assent—and you will not make the slightest impression on him" (120). That is because he does not care about the realities of the world and the ordinary deficiencies of people. Impatient with the moral messiness of politics, repulsed by the ethical irrationality of a world where good intentions yield evil results and, even more disconcertingly, evil means can yield good ones, she becomes other-worldly in the world. These are Nietzsche's unmaskers, those who cannot bear the weight of the world, who turn away from its crudeness and vio-lence with revulsion and contempt.

By contrast, a person committed to an ethic of responsibility allows worldly realities to work upon her with what Weber calls "inner concen-tration and calm" (115). She feels their compulsion and complexity yet remains devoted to the cause that drew her to politics in the first place. It is her attentiveness to the world that distinguishes her devotion to a cause from the devotion of someone committed to an ethic of ultimate ends. But her kind of worldliness is different from that of those faux politicians who seek power for its own sake, out of vanity and personal self-intoxication, or for the impression they wish to make on others, rather than to service a substantive principle beyond themselves. These are the men Nietzsche says have the drive to and strength for justice, those who judge in disregard for themselves. When such a man speaks, his voice has a matter-of-fact strength. Never losing sight of the limitations that mark their mortality, they nonetheless demand an impossible virtue for themselves, which is why they must live tragically. But how can a passionate devotion to a cause coexist with a sense of proportion and objectivity? This is not a problem for those committed to an ethic of ultimate ends, since they lack the second, or for those who enter politics for the sterile excitation it offers, since they lack the first. It is a problem only for those committed to an ethic of responsibility. "How," Weber asks in a Nietzschean voice, "can a warm passion and a cool sense of proportion be forged together in one and the same soul? Politics is made with the head. . . . [Y]et devotion to politics . . . can be born and nourished by passion alone" (115). There is no formulaic answer to these questions. All one can say is that one must keep one's head and balance without giving up political passion: be strategic in the interest of principle, keep a certain distance toward one's most cherished ideals, and have the objectivity to look to the political future rather than seek revenge for defeat or proclaim a righteous victory.[19] To the ancient Greeks moderation meant the tautness of a perfectly tuned string and walking a tightrope across an abyss rather than compromise. That is what Nietzsche and Weber seem to have in mind.

This tension is a response to, as well as a manifestation of, the tragic dimension of politics, and only a person who has the inner strength to bear burdens of tragedy (such as Nietzsche's just man) has the vocation for politics. The first aspect of that tragic dimension is the fact that serving one god entails offending another. Our world, Weber insists, is polytheistic, marked by a clash of values and worldviews among which one must choose, even though moral argument is unavailable. The second aspect derives from the fact that from "no ethics *in the world* can it be concluded when and to what extent ethically good purposes justify ethically dangerous means and ramifications" (121, my emphasis). The third aspect is the inevitable use of violence in politics. To use violence is to risk being used by it: to risk being overwhelmed by "the diabolical forces" it lets loose, thereby jeopardizing one's character and one's cause. Indeed, Weber argues that when people committed to an ethic of ultimate ends lose their moral orientation in the face of a recalcitrant world, they end up engaging in ultimate violence to achieve their ultimate ends without acknowledging the fact that they are "consorting with the devil" (125–26). Since I am for justice, anything I do in its name is justified. Though I am opposed to violence, my violent act is the last one because it will end all violence. The lie I tell will usher in a reign of truth.

Finally, implicit in but overlying the entire essay is the tragedy of modernity. Modernity is characterized by two forms of political corruption: bureaucracy and "the proletarianism" of politics. On the one hand, there is the depersonalism and routinization of everyday life,[20] the triumph of political philistines and "banausic" technicians who reduce politics (in Nietzsche's essay it is history) to the art of the possible and possibilities to an ordinariness that lacks all heroic dimension. On the other hand, there is the triumph of "the human machine," the masses ignorantly participating in plebiscite democracies upon which all modern politicians must depend. This machine is driven by hatred, a passion for revenge, resentment and self-righteousness, adventurism, booty and spoils. Together these forms of corruption constrict, if not overwhelm, politics as a vocation and turn the essay's argument into a lament. Indeed, their overwhelming presence moves Weber toward those who embrace an ethic of ultimate ends. The final paragraph offers evidence for this.

In it, Weber warns with a Nietzschean image of a "polar night of icy darkness," enveloping all politics and every party. What will happen, he asks, if and when we emerge from this condition? Will we be able to recover a sense of politics as a vocation, or, as seems far more likely, will politics have become an occupation rather than a calling? If so, then we may be better off engaging in a mystic flight from reality, cultivating plain brotherliness, or simply going about our work. For politics is "a strong and slow boring of hard boards." It takes passion and principle, a willingness to reach for the impossible if only to attain the possible, a sober hero to brave the enveloping corruption. "Only he has the calling for politics who is sure that he shall not crumble when the world from his point of view is too stupid or too base for what he wants to offer. Only he who in the face of all this can say, 'In spite of it all!' has the calling for politics" (128). And only he who possesses these traits has the calling to write about politics.

I said earlier that given the political realities of Weber's own time, his argument on behalf of politics shares more with an ethic of ultimate ends than with an ethic of responsibility. But this is misleading for two reasons. The first is that Weber does not see these ethics as always and necessarily opposed. There is a point where strategic considerations must stop if an ethic of responsibility is not to become unprincipled opportunism, where further compromise must be rejected if a cause is to survive as a cause. Then the two ethics converge, and the woman committed to an ethic of responsibility says, "Here I stand; I can do no other." Second, Weber is trying to establish the preconditions for "the political" independent of historical forms and forces.[21] In this sense it is untrue that he is agnostic about which cause we embrace, as most commentators and Weber himself seem to argue. In contrast to Nietzsche, his cause is politics. And it is a testament to his prescience that so many find it an unworthy one.

IX

For many of them politics is an unworthy activity, at best a distraction, at worst corrupt and corrupting. Such disaffection seems most intense among the young, who in other periods have been the repository of utopian hopes. Whatever the causes—the triumph of the liberal animus against politics, the commodification of candidates for office, particular scandals such as Watergate and Irangate, blatant partisanship masquerading as principle, increasing inequalities of wealth and concentrations of power, or the general dependency of politics on money—there seems to be a disillusionment with liberal democracy in the West almost as profound as the disillusionment with communism in the East. "Ours" seems to be an age of political cynicism.

Nietzsche's essay has virtually nothing to say about political cynicism as that is discussed in the popular and academic press. Yet he does consider cynicism as a condition of modernity in an untimely, that is, "beneficial," way. In Nietzsche's terms, cynicism pacifies and subdues the young. Like horse trainers who break horses until they are manageable, so historical-men-cum-cynics tame "the strongest instincts of youth." Contrary to contemporary characterization/caricatures of the young, Nietzsche insists that the young are "naturally" the least preoccupied with relevance and instant usefulness. Unbroken, they are contemptuous of narrow egoism, the ethic of success, and the reification of the present with its siren song of adaptation and adjustment. They, not their historically sophisticated elders, are impatient with the equation of reason with calculation, cleverness, and sobriety. What they value is the time to let ideas mature slowly, the opportunity to implant in themselves a great idea and let it grow into a greater one (115).

Cynicism is the pathology of the old (who are not necessarily the aged). It comes from their sense that they are living in a twilight of history and life, and that their youthful hopes and energies will not survive into the future. In solace they justify the process of history, denying agency in general to live with the fact of their own fading powers. They are the ones who cannot endure the ironical state that characterized the Greeks and characterizes Nietzsche's essay. Having lost their passion for life, they teach this loss as a gain, thus their celebration of objectivity and science.

And despite their qualms and fears they teach their cynicism as wisdom, saying that what was, had to be as it was, that everything now is necessarily as it is, and that the future is already contained in the present and will evolve of its own accord. In insisting that everything worth doing has already been done and all that is worth knowing is already known, the old dictate the future of the young.

This dictation is itself an aspect of their pathology. "Education," Hannah Arendt has written, "is the point at which we decide whether we love the world enough to assume responsibility for it and, by the same token, save it from the ruin which, except for the coming of the new and the young, would be inevitable."[22] Cynical men refuse to take responsibility for a world they see as imposing its will on them and so see no way to save it from ruin. Nonetheless, they impose their view of the past on the present to secure a certain future, which is what the "natural" operations of the market, the "inevitability" of globalization, and narratives of progress (or regress) also do. Cynics ignore or cannot face what Arendt and Nietzsche insist upon: that there is no human world without the risk of the unexpected, and that the future is a wager with the unprecedented.

The uncynical young despise the acceptance of what exists as necessary and natural. They want to choose their past, not have it chosen for them, and so they seek knowledge with the concentrated purpose of combating their "inborn nature" and creating a second one of their own choosing. In choosing a past in which they would like to participate rather than settling for one in which they did, and in striving to give themselves a second nature, the young seek to create themselves, as must any people who wish to remain alive.

This was the achievement of the Greeks. Because they were unhistorical, they remained perpetually young and uncynical. Any self-congratulation remained framed by a pessimism that was itself a spur to action. Despite their profound sense of mortality, of a human world constantly susceptible to the ravages of nature, the revenge of the gods, and the excesses of the great whose presence nevertheless kept the world vital, they never indulged in reticence or self-loathing. Though spectators of themselves in the theater, they were actors on the political stage outside it.

III

Hannah Arendt at Colonus

The storyteller borrows his authority from death.
—WALTER BENJAMIN

HANNAH ARENDT is one of the few contemporary political and social theorists whose reading of the Greeks invigorates and augments our understanding in the way Nietzsche commends and exemplifies. But unlike Nietzsche, who has little to say about politics conventionally understood and almost nothing positive to say about democracy,[1] Arendt, like Weber, is concerned to establish the preconditions of "the political" and regards Athenian democracy as a paradigmatic embodiment of it.

In fact, Hannah Arendt is one of the few contemporary political and social theorists for whom ancient Greece retains its hold as a point of reference and inspiration. Of the very few who think with the Greeks, she is distinctive in having recourse to the prephilosophical articulation of polis life. Where other theorists understand and judge the polis in terms of a philosophical tradition largely hostile to it, she inverts that reading, condemning the tradition for effacing the originary and in some respects still quintessential expression of freedom and power present in the practices and literature of classical Greece, particularly democratic Athens. Thus while she has much to say about Plato, it is mostly to chastise him for being antipolitical. And though she says much more in praise of Aristotle, in the end she thinks he, too, misrepresents Greek political life.

There is something perverse about this inversion. For one thing, it rests on a sometimes flat-footed reading of *The Republic*, the text that provides the principal object of her most sweeping criticisms of the Platonic project. For all of Arendt's appreciation of the theatrical and performative dimensions of Athenian politics, she is largely insensitive to the dramatic structure of that dialogue. For another thing, she seems to romanticize a society, Athenian democracy, that is utterly remote from our own, and then compounds the problem by largely ignoring or excusing what seems most illiberal and/or undemocratic about it: substantial social and economic inequalities, slavery and patriarchy, imperialist adventures, exclusive citizenship laws, the absence of rights, and the immoralism of greatness. Her relative silence about or evasion of the issues is, to say the least, frustrating.

Finally, for all her glorification of Athenian politics Arendt is maddeningly elusive about what that politics was about. "What," Hanna Pitkin asks, "is it that they talked about together in that endless palaver in the agora?" "What does she [Arendt] imagine," Pitkin continues, "was the *content* of political speech and action and why is this question so difficult to answer from her text?"[2]

This seeming perversity has led even Arendt's sympathetic critics to seek ways of marginalizing or softening her Hellenism, and less sympathetic ones to dismiss her because of her Hellenism and to dismiss ancient political thought because of Arendt.

In the pages that follow I want to look at the story Arendt tells about ancient Greece, and at why she tells it as she does. What does her Hellenism enable her to dramatize about modernity? What was it about Greece and Athens that she found so compelling and challenging, and how many of her enthusiasms should we share?

I also want to rescue Arendt from her Hellenism, and to rescue Greece and Athens from Arendt. Arendt certainly got important things "wrong" about "the Greeks" and "the Athenians." But instead of dismissing her on these grounds, I want to read her errors of commission and omission symptomatically, insofar as they reveal her uses of Hellenism. I read her this way because I regard Arendt's thought in general and her Hellenism in particular as enabling devices rather than as a set of extrapolated items of knowledge.[3] What she teaches is as much a practice of reading as a set of doctrines or specific arguments. Treating her this way seems particularly appropriate given her concerns with what thought or theories *do* and with speech as speech acts (in her sense of the phrase).

My construction of Arendt's Hellenism follows her instructions. "Let us," she writes in her essay "What Is Freedom?" "go back once more to antiquity, i.e., to its prephilosophical traditions, certainly not for the sake of erudition and not even because of the continuity of our tradition, but merely because a freedom experienced in the process of acting and nothing else—though, of course, mankind never lost this experience altogether—has never again been articulated with the same classical clarity."[4] My choice from that tradition is tragedy, more particularly Sophocles' *Oedipus at Colonus*.

Why tragedy? It is a good question given the fact that Arendt has no sustained discussion of any Greek tragedy. Yet her discussion of politics and action is suffused by the language and imagery of theater. She talks of performance and audiences, of those who play a part and those spectators who see the entire play, and of spaces of appearance as stages upon which virtuosi speak and act in compelling and revealing ways. She even suggests that the specific revelatory quality of action and speech that manifests the agent and speaker is so tied to the flux of acting and speaking "that it can be represented and 'reified' only through a kind of repetition, the imitation of mimesis . . . which is appropriate only in the drama, whose very name (from the Greek *dran*, to act) indicates that playacting actually is an imitation of acting."[5] And she regards identities as forged by various performances in which men (her word) act politically.

Moreover, Arendt implicitly connects theater, democracy, and theory in a way that defines her conception of politics and political thought. The pervasive values of performance in Greek culture, together with the special context of democracy and its institutional embodiments, meant that to be an audience was, above all, to play the role of democratic citizen. Thus the political space of democracy was established by the participatory collective audience of citizen spectators. In addition, *theoria*, which is connected to "theater," is the normal Greek for official attendance as a spectator in the political and religious rites of a city.[6] Since the Greek "to know" (*eidenia*) is semantically and morphologically cognate with the word "to see" (*idein*), tragedy helped establish and sustain the self-reflexivity that characterized fifth-century Athens. It also established a touchstone for Arendt's understanding of what political thought is. This is not to deny the significant impact on her thinking of either the philosophical tradition from Socrates to Heidegger or contemporary events. It is to suggest that her refusal to accept the designation "philosopher" may have something to do with the generalized influence of tragedy on her thinking.

In addition, Arendt's thought, for all its "optimistic" emphasis on beginnings and natality, retains a tragic sensibility articulated in Sophoclean drama. This sensibility is central to her dramatization of modernity and helps constitute the kind of political thinker she represents herself as being. And many of the central themes in Arendt's work—heroism and greatness, public and private, storytelling, judgment and impartiality, the importance of speech and action, and the unpredictability of the latter with the attendant need for forgiveness and promises—are also the subjects of Greek tragedy as text and as performance. Penultimately, the study of tragedy, including the relationship between the action onstage and the role of theater in Athenian public life, can help dramatize strains in Arendt's work and the discrepant readings of her by her critics. Thus the tension between the agonistic and the deliberative Arendt not only echoes a subject of tragedy—recall Haemon's unheeded advice to his father in *Antigone* and Oedipus's hatred toward Polyneices in contrast to Theseus's openness to persuasion in *Oedipus at Colonus*—but is replicated in the tension between what happens in the theater and what happens outside it in the assembly, courts, juries, and agora. Finally, and perhaps most significantly, reading Arendt through the lens of tragedy helps dramatize aspects of her Hellenism and thought as a whole, while that thought provides a ground by which to bring tragedy into dialogue with modernity and postmodernity.

But why *this* tragedy? I chose *Oedipus at Colonus* for many reasons, foremost being the fact that the Wisdom of Silenus she quotes from it in the final paragraph of *On Revolution* inspires her most dramatic claim about the redemptive power of politics, itself perhaps her most provocative challenge to contemporary life and thought. There is a second reason: the play brings to an end the paradigmatically tragic story of Oedipus, who, more than any other figure in Greek literature, illustrates and qualifies many of Arendt's arguments about action and storytelling. In the play, Oedipus promises to bestow a gift on Athens. Narrowly conceived, the gift is his grave, which will protect Athens against future Theban attack. Less literally, the gift, which is also Sophocles' gift to his native city, is the story of a life of endless sufferings transformed into a redemptive tale of endurance. "All sorrows can be borne," Arendt quotes Isak Dinesen, "if you put them into a story or tell a story about them."[7] "Human life," she says in a quotation to which I shall return, "because it is marked by a beginning and an end becomes whole, an entity in itself that can be subjected to judgment, only when it has ended in death; death not merely ends life, it also bestows upon it a silent completeness snatched from the hazardous flux to which all things human are subject."[8]

But this is not quite true of Oedipus. Here are the first words of the messenger bringing news of Oedipus's death:

> Citizens, the briefest way to tell you
> Would be to say that Oedipus is no more;
> But what has happened cannot be told so simply—
> It was no simple thing.[9]
> (1789–1801)

The end of Oedipus's life is no simple thing. It is, rather, a miracle and a riddle. In this it illustrates Arendt's claims about the boundless consequences of action even as it qualifies her idea of a completed life completing a story. For the story of Oedipus is retold and reconfigured in each of the disparate audiences that read or hear it. I shall return to the theme and qualification in my discussion of the *Phaedo* in chapter 7.

A third reason I chose this play is its dramatization of democracy. Arendt has been sharply criticized for her antidemocratic views[10] and yet has provided inspiration for participatory democrats. In *Oedipus at Colonus*, mythical Athens is faced with a defining test. When the city is confronted by a strange outcast and polluted refugee, the question is whether it will reject his supplications, keep him at arm's length, or provide a place and home for him, thereby honoring what is "unnatural" and "marginal," incorporating the "other" into itself.

Mythical Athens passes the test. Theseus makes Oedipus a citizen and invites him to come to Athens. But it is not clear that Sophocles' contemporaries would have, nor whether Arendt does. In both cases significant elements—restrictive citizen laws in the case of Athens, and gatekeeping functions performed by Arendt's exclusion of "the social," "the private," and the economic from politics—undercut democratic principles and practices.

There is yet another different sort of reason why I have chosen this play. *Oedipus at Colonus* is about a pariah, and Hannah Arendt knows something about that subject.[11] Of course I have no way of knowing whether or how that mattered to her. But Sophocles' drama is a play about a democracy that found a place for an exile, wanderer, and stranger.

I

At the end of a chapter entitled "The Revolutionary Tradition and Its Lost Treasure," the final paragraph of *On Revolution*, Arendt quotes "[t]he famous and frightening lines" from *Oedipus at Colonus* known as the Wisdom of Silenus:

> Not to be born prevails over all meaning uttered in words; by far the second
> best for life, once it has appeared, is to go as swiftly as possible whence it came.[12]

This wisdom was forced out of Silenus by King Midas, who, having hunted a long time for this companion (some sources say teacher) of Dionysus, finally captured him by getting him drunk. Though Silenus was at first sullen and uncommunicative, refusing Midas's request that he tell him what he considered man's greatest good, Midas pressed him, expecting that Silenus would name the king's achievements of status and wealth. With what Nietzsche calls "shrill laughter," Silenus retaliates against Midas's coercion, with words as shattering as they are unexpected. Here is Nietzsche's version of Silenus's wisdom: "Ephemeral wretch, begotten by accident and toil, why do you force me to tell you what it would be your greatest boon not to hear? What would be best for you is quite beyond your reach; not to be born, not to be, to be nothing. But the second best is to die soon."

How is it possible to live with such wisdom? What could possibly redeem human life in the face of it? How are we to avoid hatred of the world, self-contempt, bitterness at existence, or exhausting resentment after hearing it? If life is merely the beginning of death and the interim pain and excess, better to end it before it begins.

Nietzsche tells us that it was out of the need to avert their eyes from the full realization of such a paralyzing vision that the Greeks invented the Olympian gods, "imposing a world of art between themselves and the world of suffering, casting a veil of beauty over the abyss." The gods are a conscious self-deception.

For (the early) Nietzsche it is tragedy that allows the Greeks to look at and look away from the abyss. Drama interposed itself between the blinding darkness of Silenus and the normal that veils it, allowing only an indirect light into the theater to remind the onlookers of the Dionysian sources of their energy and power. At the same time, the magnificence of tragedy's poetry and the greatness of its heroes transform while incorporating darkness into a thing of beauty. For him drama redeems life against the Wisdom of Silenus.

For Arendt, politics does, though as we have seen, it is a politics of art and theater. In her gloss on the Wisdom of Silenus, she says that Sophocles "let us know through the mouth of Theseus, the legendary founder of Athens and hence her spokesman, what it was that enabled ordinary men, young and old, to bear life's burden; it was the polis, the space of men's free deeds and living words, which could endow life with splendor—*ton bion lampron poieisthai*" (*OR*, 285).

How is this possible? How did the polis and how can politics bear such a weight? Does it, must it, can it, play a role in the contemporary world analogous to the one Arendt claims it played in Athens?

I want to construct an answer to these questions in four steps. The first situates the Wisdom of Silenus in the play as a whole. The second relates the play to Arendt's ideas about politics and action. The third moves to a discussion of Greek tragedy and its relationship to what Arendt does argue and what she might or should have argued. The final step looks at the Wisdom of Silenus in a modern context by offering some concluding remarks about Arendt's Hellenism.

II

Here is the Wisdom of Silenus with its political elaboration:

> Not to be born is best of all:
> when life is there, the second best

to go hence where you came,
with the best speed you may.
For when his youth with its gift of light heart
has come and gone, what grievous stroke
is spared to a man, what agony
is he without? Envy, and faction,
strife and fighting and murders are his,
and yet there is something more that claims him,
old age at the last, most hated,
without power, without comrades, and friends,
take up their dwelling with him.
(1411–23)

If anyone's life proves Silenus wise, it is Oedipus's. Given Laius's and Jocasta's disregard of the prophecy that Laius would die at the hands of his son, Oedipus should never have been born, and if born should have died before he killed the man at the crossroads, who was his father, and unknowingly received his mother as a wife. And who has endured more than Oedipus, each living day adding to his burden? He wanders the earth a blind old beggar, exiled by his sons and city, dependent on the kindness of strangers, supported only by a girl as vulnerable as he. The Oedipus we see at the play's outset must hide until he can discover the sentiments of those who see and are powerful; he must flatter when necessary, plead for food, a place to rest, or assurance of security. And he is not an exile just from Thebes, but from all that is natural. For he has committed horrific transgressions. When Oedipus asks the chorus of old men whether Theseus will care enough for a blind man to come himself, they assure him that Theseus "surely will when he has heard your name. . . . Your name, old man, has pierced the ear of many; were he asleep or slow to move, yet when he hears of *you* he will come quickly to his place" (320–23).

Oedipus's sufferings resurface every time he answers the question "Who are you?" Innocent questions—such as, From what city are you? Who are your parents? What brought you here to this place or to this pitiable state?—cause him to relive his sorrows in answering them. So when the Chorus pushes him to recount his sufferings and tell his story again, he resists, asking them not to press their inquiry, saying, "I am your guest; you were kind to me. Do not lay bare my sufferings; they are beyond shame" (213). Yet his helplessness and need to appease force him to comply.

The ode's opening line—"Whoever it is that seeks to have a greater share of life" (1394)—echoes the concluding lines of Theseus's first speech: "For I am very certain that I am a man; such as I have of tomorrow no greater share than you [Oedipus] have" (646–47). Despite their disparity of age and appearance, of power and standing, both are subject to the mutability of fortune; both participate in what Arendt calls the "frailty of human affairs," with its unpredictability of action and the unyielding opacity of events and circumstances. Oedipus was once a prosperous and honored king, as confident and capable then as Theseus is now.[13]

Theseus's exchange with Oedipus enacts this otherwise abstractly stated equality. Annoyed by what he regards as Oedipus's excessive anger, Theseus chastises the old man. Instead of passively accepting the rebuke, Oedipus rebukes the king in return. "Rebuke me when you understand, and not till then." Instead of getting angry at Oedipus, Theseus accepts the criticism: "Tell me then. True, without knowledge I should not speak" (677–78). This from a king to a beggar. Later, Theseus offers to make Oedipus a citizen of Athens and invites him to choose whether to return to the city with him or to remain at Colonus. "Oedipus, I submit to your judgment. It shall be as you choose."

It is clear that Athens in the play is not a democracy. And there is a way in which the community between the onetime king and the present one rests on a sense of shared elite privilege. Nonetheless, Theseus is, in P. E. Easterling's phrase, a "proto-democratic king" and, I would add, an idealized democratic citizen. He is respectful of those without power, giving them choices and inviting their judgments. He is willing to be persuaded and to take criticism as well as give it, and he backs up his promises even when it means taking risks. One can trust him and speak frankly to him despite his power because he does not stand on ceremony or demand obeisance. And his piety reinforces his readiness to identify with outcasts and strangers. Yet this does not distract him from acting decisively when the occasion demands. In this he stands opposed to Creon.

If he were not forewarned by Ismene, Oedipus could easily have been taken in by Creon's words, by his protestations that he comes in peace (though with armed troops), and that he is too old to fight a war and too respectful of Athenian power to provoke one. If we did not know better, we might be convinced that Creon is deeply moved by the plight of Oedipus and the vulnerability of Antigone, and that inviting them to return to Thebes is as much an act of kindness as a politically useful one. But we know why he wants them to return. Oracles have said that the existence of Thebes depends upon Oedipus's returning to his native land. We know from Ismene that he will not be allowed actually to live in Thebes, only near it; that the Thebans will not let him be his "own master" but will seek to "own" him (445–46), and that they will even forbid his being ritually covered by Theban soil upon his death. Their concern is all for themselves and their predicted sufferings, not at all for his past and present ones. And this, we learn, is typical of the way he has been treated. For when Oedipus wished to be exiled, the city did not grant his desire. But when "my anger was sated" and "living in the house was sweet to me," then did they banish him. And they did so less because of the curse upon him or out of respect for the gods than because of a lust for power. The soft words of those who banished him are like chalk scraping a blackboard.

It turns out that even while Creon is talking, his men have kidnapped Ismene, and so his words are, in effect, war by other means. Theseus chastises Creon for this. What Creon has done—ignoring the laws of Athens and justice, taking what he wants by force, abusing hospitality, dragging suppliants away—dishonors the gods, Theseus, Athens as a city, not to mention Thebes and Creon himself. "I," Theseus asserts, "would have known how I ought—a foreigner among citizens—to conduct myself" (1066–67).

Yet it would be wrong to push the contrast too far. Recall Theseus's comment about the mutability of fortune and the fact that Oedipus, the onetime king, illustrates it. Oedipus reiterates the point: "All mastering time confounds; all that seems permanent in human life is not; the strength of our body dies, trust dies, friends become enemies, enemies friends. What is sweet turns bitter and then back again" (695–99). But Oedipus does more than illustrate these shifting tides and contraries; his life and character embody them. The sacred grove that is Oedipus's final resting place belongs to the Eumenides/Erinyes who are at once violent virgins, terrible to name and so fearsome they leave men speechless, and sources of life, benign and holy. This double aspect is present in Oedipus's great teacher, time. Time destroys the strength of the body and the city, loyalty and faithfulness. But it also generates new life in the endless succession of nights and days in which the most unexpected can happen.[14] (Arendt calls such occurrences "miracles" because they emerge unbidden, unannounced, and against all logic and empirical evidence.) This double aspect parallels Zeus's own genealogy, in which the highest principle of order and harmony is intimately and necessarily connected to a primitive violence from which it emerges, and which it only imperfectly manages to repress.[15] It is present, too, in a choral ode in *Oedipus at Colonus* that Bernard Knox judges to be "the most moving and beautiful ode in praise of Athens that was ever written." At the same moment the ode celebrates Athenian strength, power, and beauty, the pastoral images that frame it also suggest death and loss.[16] This double aspect applies to Oedipus: he, too, is frightening to see but bestows great benefits on those who rightly honor him.[17]

The lines of the ode that immediately follow the statement of Silenus's wisdom constitute a lament by the chorus of old men for their lost youth. As they look back upon it, they see it as a time of confident strength when many friends and comrades sustained them in whatever afflictions or trials they encountered. In those days they had seen less evil and were less burdened by the sorrows that multiply cumulatively as the compass of life stretches beyond the bloom of youth. The longer one lives, the more horror one experiences: horrors of war, civil strife, murder, and faction. The Chorus goes on to liken old age to an implacable enemy and nature to an assaulting army against whom one is fated to lose. In these images and at this moment there is no refuge, no redemption, no hope; here and now Silenus is right.

The reference to civil strife and faction has a more concrete referent when, at the ode's conclusion, Polyneices appears to enroll his father in support of his attempt to oust his brother, who had seized power and sent him into exile. As we have seen, Oedipus rejects the suit, cursing those sons who drove him out and now want him back when it suits their purposes. When Oedipus refuses Polyneices, and when Polyneices, who knows that his father's refusal means the failure of his enterprise and a death sentence on himself and his brother, refuses to call off the expedition, these choices seal the death of Laius's line of Thebes and of Antigone. All that remains living is the story of Oedipus's life.

In the end it is this story that matters. What Oedipus has endured, the countless sorrows of his life, will live on as a testament to the power of his struggle with the conditions of his existence as they are both given to and chosen by him. This indefatigability is Oedipus's gift to mythical Athens as it is Sophocles' to contemporary Athens.

We know from early on in the play that Oedipus has a gift for Athens: his tomb in the sacred grove at Colonus will shield Athens from her enemies. Yet there is another gift he bestows: the story of his life and its ending.

Near the end of the play Oedipus recovers his power. The stumbling, blind old man who has lived so many years as a helpless beggar becomes an actor in the drama of his life. Approaching death, he becomes a guide and leader, instructing others, not only in particular and at the moment, but in the larger significance of his life. Once crushed by the gods, he is now exalted by them. The end of his life is miraculously also a beginning. Silenus is wrong.

Yet there is even more to the gift than this. For what we see and hear is Oedipus not simply living the story of his life, but participating in the telling of it. Unlike the Oedipus of *Oedipus Tyrannos*, this one insists that what he did—killing his father and marrying his mother—was done in ignorance, that his failing was intellectual rather than moral. He never denies that he should have to pay for his transgressions. But he insists that the suffering he has endured for so long has more than compensated for them. Oedipus persuades the Chorus: "Many of the ills that were his, all uncalled for; may God in justice exalt him again" (1784–85). In so doing, he shapes the story of which he is the subject.

Of course Oedipus cannot be the author of his life, since that life is not yet over. Because everything one says and does constitutes who one is, one's identity can be fully known only when one ceases to speak and act. "Human life," Arendt writes, "because it is marked by a beginning and an end becomes whole, an entity in itself that can be subjected to judgment only when it has ended in death; death does not merely end life, it also bestows upon it a silent completedness snatched from the hazardous flux to which all things human are subject" (*LOM*, 164). In the case of Oedipus the end remains shrouded in mystery. But we know he has found respite from this "hazardous flux"; his wanderings are, at last, over. He has found a home and rest among his now fellow Athenians.

But these conclusions are too easy, too comforting, too dependent upon an uncritical view of Oedipus, as if his view in the play is also the play's view. And it is too sanguine about Silenus's power and so the task for tragic politics. In the larger view Oedipus acts like the unpersuaded Furies of Aeschylus's *Oresteia* and shares certain traits with Silenus.

Let me begin by looking at the Polyneices scene. Now, Polyneices is hardly guiltless. It was he who, when he had power, drove Oedipus into exile. And he, like Creon, seeks to turn the oracle concerning Oedipus's power to decide the fate of Thebes to his own advantage. Moreover, his initial response upon seeing his father is one of revulsion rather than pity. Yet Polyneices is not another Creon and does not deserve to be treated as one, as he is by Oedipus. He comes unarmed, poses no threat, and is, as Oedipus was (but Creon was not), a suppliant who seems somewhat sincere in his sympathy for his father's and sister's plight and acknowledges his own role in it.[18] Moreover, both Theseus and Antigone speak against Oedipus's refusal to even hear Polyneices. Theseus must remind Oedipus that he has an obligation to a suppliant, such as he had just been, and that no one is forced to act merely by listening. Antigone pleads with her father to remember his own parentage and so the family curse he is about to perpetuate. (In effect, she is also pleading for her own life.) She reminds him of the excess that drove him to self-blinding, implying that he is being blind to the present one; she argues that even if Polyneices wronged him, he is still his son, his blood, and of his nature, and so Oedipus, even if wronged, cannot justly punish him.[19] All this persuades Oedipus to listen or, more precisely, to tolerate Polyneices' speaking.

For perhaps good reasons nothing Polyneices says convinces Oedipus or assuages his fury. All the old man's past resentments and hatreds explode at this moment and at this son. But the son as object is less significant than the explosion; the question of whether Oedipus is "just" in his denunciation is less significant than the fact that his gathering sense of his own power, his recognition that the previously hostile gods now favor him, and his realization that the fate of Thebes is in his hands allow him to reassert himself and avenge the slights he has suffered. In this case time has not healed the wound; it has made it fester. The passing years may have taught Oedipus that his self-blinding was an excess, but the character who did that deed is reemerging before us.[20] Age mimics youth: Oedipus is still Oedipus.

From one point of view Oedipus's passion for revenge establishes a parallel with Silenus. If we think of Oedipus as being held captive by his poverty and dependence, couldn't we then regard his turning against his (perceived) captors and sentencing them to death as analogous to Silenus's revenge against humankind?

To the degree that Silenus's wisdom is heard with particular acuity by the old, as the ode indicates it is, then *Oedipus at Colonus* is also a play about the revenge of the old against the young, the past against the future. The old become what Oedipus has been for most of his adult life: feeble, defenseless, led and directed by others, and (as happens still) resentful of those who have power over their lives, even when it is used for their "benefit."[21]

It is this intractable Oedipus who is called by Zeus to his death after the scene with Polyneices. The kind of man Oedipus has become suggests the limitations of C. M. Bowra's conclusion about *Oedipus at Colonus* that "the gods are not after all indecipherable; they reward the just."[22] But it is not clear that Oedipus is just, despite his exaltation by the gods. Heroic, yes; larger than life in his loves and hates, certainly; but moderate, reasonable, judicious? Hardly. To the degree that Oedipus is both just and unjust, his condition restates the peculiar volatility of his identity as a blind seer, polluted innocent, suppliant savior, and one whose intense passions both bring the world alive and destroy it.[23] Though tragedy's space of performance lies at the center of the city, the metaphysical space where Oedipus is buried lies on the outskirts. The hero, Sophocles implies, Pericles proclaims (in describing the Athenians), and Arendt argues, stands outside conventional judgments of right and wrong.

Bowra is misleading for another reason, this one having to do with Antigone's exclusion from the burial. Though everyone except Theseus is excluded, Antigone's has special significance. She is "our eyes and ears as well as Oedipus's," someone "with whose vision we sympathize."[24] Deborah Roberts has argued that burial at the end of tragedy is a kind of closure because it marks the end of life for the dead and punctuates the lives of survivors, bringing different mourners together in a communal act and setting socially constructed limits on the potentially unlimited expression of grief. If this is true, then the frustration of a mourner with whom we identify compromises, modifies, or undercuts the closural force

of burial for the other characters and for the audience. This means that
the play ends with a mystery, or, better yet, it concludes, appropriately
enough and as Lacan suggests, with a riddle. Oedipus's gift, Shoshana
Felman writes, glossing Lacan, is not that of a solution but "the paradoxical gift . . . of the enigma of his own death."[25] In the play and to Arendt
the discovery of who one is and what one has done appears only in retro-
spect. "We know," Bernard Williams writes, "that in the story of one's
life there is an authority exercised by what one has done and not merely
by what one has intentionally done."[26] That is why Weber characterizes
the world as "ethically irrational," and one of the reasons why forgiveness
plays such an important role in Arendt's discussion of action.

All this suggests that Bowra has simplified the play by domesticating
its contradictions, as Arendt may have done of the story of Oedipus. Here
is Oedipus speaking to Theseus:

> O dearest son of Aegeus:
> only the gods know neither age nor death;
> everything else all-mastering time confounds.
> The strength of earth, the strength of body, dies;
> trust dies; distrust comes into blossoming.
> The same breath does not blow from man to man,
> constant in friendship, nor in city toward city.
> It may be now, it may be later, sometime
> the sweet turns bitter, and then again to friendship.
> If now the way is bright between you and Thebes, uncounted time
> in course will breed uncounted
> nights and days, shattering with the spear
> those right hands presently clasped in harmony.
> The cause will be so slight!
> At that time my body hidden in earth and sleeping
> will coldly drink their hot blood,
> if Zeus be still Zeus and if Zeus' son
> Phoebus speak clearly.
> But it is not pleasant
> to speak the words that should be undisturbed.
> Let me stop where I began; do you only keep
> the pledge you gave me and you will never say
> that you received as dweller in this land,
> a worthless fellow, Oedipus—
> unless the gods shall cheat me.
> (695–716)

If everything changes, if all of nature, human activity, and history are
subject to reversal or disenchantment, if even the strongest social bonds

can be loosened and faith dies, then how can one be sure anything matters? More pointedly, of what use is Oedipus's pledge and promise, since it depends not only on Theseus's keeping his word but on the secret's being passed on to his successors? The best you can do, what one *must* do, is to believe in the power of human commitment, hold steadfast to friendship, and honor supplicants. But you can never be sure. The best you can do is to wish and to pray, and even prayer is uncertain. Twice in the speech human resolve is halted by the gods; unequivocal assertions are followed by qualifications, absolutes by conditionals. It is like the rhythm of Nietzsche's prose.

III

What adds dimension to Oedipus's death and the play's end is that this play is also an ending for Sophocles. *Oedipus at Colonus* is his last work, written at the very end of his life. Moreover, he was born at Colonus, so the story of an old man finding a home there may have had special meaning for him. And we know something about the historical context in which the play was written and then performed, though one can never be sure about the meaning(s) the drama had for any particular audience.

There is good reason to believe that the play's reference to and display of faction and civil war at mythical Thebes had a contemporary resonance, since Athens had experienced an oligarchic coup in 411 and was still living with its aftermath in 406 B.C.E. when the play was written and Sophocles was eighty-nine years old.[27]

There is also reason to believe that the play is an epitaph for Athenian power. Though Athens was still undefeated when the play was written, her lands had been laid waste by Sparta, which is why the play's reference to olive trees "may well have moved the play's first readers or auditors to tears."[28] By the time the play was first performed in 401, four years after Sophocles' death, Athens had experienced starvation and capitulation. The disunity and diminished power of the contemporary city stand in marked contrast to the myth of Athens and of Theseus in the play.

Theseus is the legendary unifier (*sumoichistes*) of Athens. The play presents him as worshiping in the local deme as well as the city proper and honoring Poseidon in both his aristocratic and democratic representations. Because the city is unified, it is capable of swift, decisive action and uses its power, not for empire or glory, but to defend innocents and suppliants against impious aggressors.[29]

Text and context indicate that the play is also about Athenian democracy. Theseus was not only the legendary unifier of Athens; he was also coming to represent the founding of Athenian democracy. The democracy

dramatized in the play and embodied by Theseus is characterized by openness to persuasion, fearlessness, the sharing of authority and responsibility, decisiveness, a sense of justice involving mutual respect and reciprocity, a shared sense of human fallibility that issues in what Blundell calls
"spontaneous pity," the use of force without boastfulness, a defense of
the weak, and, most centrally, a capacious understanding of citizenship.

Though Oedipus's transgressions make him a profound threat to the
"normal" boundaries of a social and political order, the Athenians accept
him now as they did the Erinyes before him. They recognize the necessity
of honoring what is terrible and wondrous, of incorporating what is extraordinary and heroic into the everyday, and of giving place to what
seems foreign and alien. It is when they do so that they are portrayed as
united and powerful, in contrast to Thebes.

The play suggests that if the Athenians are to profit from Oedipus's
presence, each generation must continue to display the virtues of the idealized city that welcomed him. From Theseus to the democratic leaders of
Athens, due respect and remembrance for the secret tomb must include
the reciprocity and friendship initiated in the play and necessary for citizenship. And insofar as the demos itself actively participated in the governing functions once monopolized by leaders, the responsibility as well
as the power falls to them as well. The question and the challenge is
whether contemporary Athenians have met this test.

It is not clear that they have. They had accepted restrictive citizen laws
and had traditions of autochthony to legitimate them. Froma Zeitlin has
argued that Athenian tragedy posited Thebes as the "other" place, where
Athens plays out in the confines of the theater the dangers it seeks to
avoid outside it. One of these dangers is the inability to establish a "viable
system of relations and differences either within the city or without, or
between the self and any other." Incapable of incorporating outsiders,
Thebes is unable "to generate new structures and new progeny."[30] But in
this play the contrast is between mythical and contemporary Athens, and
the issue is whether Athens is becoming Thebes, a prospect particularly
repugnant given Thebes's role as Athens's implacable enemy during the
Peloponnesian War.[31]

IV

It was the polis, Arendt claims, that "enabled ordinary men, young and
old, to bear life's burden." In this space of men's free deeds and living
words, life was endowed with meaning, significance, and beauty. In it men
redeemed themselves, defying the paralyzing Wisdom of Silenus.

If politics alone redeems us against this wisdom, then it is the most important activity of all, since without it we would have no reason or will to live. "As long as the polis is there to inspire men to dare the extraordinary, all things are safe; if it perishes everything is lost" (*HC*, 206). It follows that maintaining the preconditions of polis life takes precedence over the specific content of that life. It also follows that the first task of a political people is to ensure that the space for action and speech they enjoy is passed on to their posterity. It was the inability or unwillingness of the American founders to do this that led to what Arendt regards as the Revolution's failure.

But this still leaves us uncertain about what kind of politics it is that can redeem human life, and what kind of redemption Arendt is endorsing. We know what (Arendt's) Plato thought the redemption of politics entailed, but we also know that she repudiates the philosophic "solution" to the frailty of human affairs.

Politics requires and presupposes the existence of a public realm, what Arendt calls "the space of appearance," where men speak and act before each other. The aim and consequence of their doing so is not, as we might expect, to accomplish some objective such as passing a piece of legislation, protecting their interests, increasing their wealth, or assuring their security, but to be seen by others. She opens the chapter "Action" in *The Human Condition* with the following quotation from Dante:

> For in every action what is primarily intended by the doer . . . is the disclosure of his own image. Hence . . . every doer, in so far as he does, takes delight in doing; since everything that is desires its own being, and since in action the being of the doer is somehow intensified, delight necessarily follows. . . . Thus, nothing acts unless [by acting] it makes patent its latent self. (*HC*, 175)

Acting in public gives us a sense of being alive and powerful. It provides an opportunity for us to communicate who we are, to manifest that style of action and traits of character that make us distinctive. And it is a way of inserting ourselves into history, announcing ourselves so that others must take note and notice of us.

In *The Life of the Mind*, Arendt argues that this "urge toward self-display" is a quality of all living beings. All "make their appearance like actors on a stage" with other creatures to play with and spectators who recognize their existence. Though the stage is common to all, it seems different to each species and, in the case of humans, to each individual. Thus what appears in the shared space of speech and action depends upon the perspective or standpoint of the spectator (*LOM*, 21–23).

Since the public realm is "permeated by a fiercely agonial spirit" (*HC*, 41), where everyone is constantly trying to distinguish himself from others and to "show through unique deed or achievements he was the best of all," it is not clear how political life is possible, let alone redemptive. How can citizens be competitive and cooperative at the same time? How is a plurality of unique beings possible, and why is it desirable?

For Arendt, a *political* community, as opposed to the ersatz politics of a Platonic city or a liberal state, requires the contentiousness of strong-willed individuals who also appreciate how the world they share makes their individualism possible. "Human plurality," she writes, "the basic condition of speech, has the two-fold character of equality and distinction" (*HC*, 175). If men were not equal, they could not understand each other; there could be no politics or community. But if they were not distinct, if they did not bring a unique perspective to bear on the world they continually reenact through speech and deed, there would be no need to speak and so no need for politics. The fact that everything that appears in public in what Arendt calls "the space of appearance" can be seen and heard by everybody, that others see what we see and hear what we hear, assures us of the reality of our world and ourselves as actors in it (*HC*, 50). That reality is not vitiated by the fact that each of us sees it from a distinctive perspective—that truth is, as we now say, constituted discursively—since it is the nature of political truth and reason to be based on what appears to me and to us. It *is* vitiated by preoccupation with private life and by philosophic speculation.

To distinguish oneself presupposes the presence of others from whom one is distinct and against whose deeds and words one understands and measures one's own. Since each is engaged in a similar enterprise, all are actors and audience, performers and spectators in turn. As this implies, there must be a certain agreement on shared understandings, judgments, and practices[32] if the agonistic politics is to have meaning. If men go too far and fail to recognize any limit in their drive for glory, they will lose everything, including the polis and their chance for earthly immortality, which drove them to act in the first place. Paradoxically, it is agonism itself that makes such mitigation possible, because with it each is intensely alert to each and to the preconditions their striving for glory requires. This suggests how and why one could cooperate with one's competitor and depend upon those one seeks to outshine.

The polis exists to combat the frailty of human affairs, and it does so by multiplying the occasions upon which men can win immortal fame, and by being a form of organized remembrance. In the first instance it enables men to do permanently though "within certain restrictions" what was otherwise possible only infrequently: "make the extraordinary an occurrence of everyday life" (*HC*, 197). In the second instance, the polis increases the chance that a deed deserving of fame will in fact be remembered. Elsewhere and less equivocally, Arendt says that the polis "assures" the mortal actor that his "passing existence and fleeting greatness will never lack the reality that comes from being seen, being heard and generally appearing before an audience of fellow men" (*HC*, 197–98).

For the polis to turn back the Wisdom of Silenus and provide a stage for great actions, the public realm must "transcend" the life span of mortal men. Lacking such transcendence, "no politics, no common world, no public realm is possible" (*HC*, 55). It was for "the sake of this public realm and the chance it afforded to men to show who they inexchangeably were and out of love for the body politic that made immortality possible, that each was more or less willing to share the burdens of jurisdiction, defense and administration of public affairs" (*HC*, 41)—to be political in our sense.

Politics, which is what gives meaning to human life, is a world of appearances. Politically speaking, what appears *is* the world, not some pale imitation of another world beyond it. The political does not lack firmer ground or more efficient organization, and it is not, as Plato's parable of the Cave seems to indicate, a shadowy place lacking splendor and beauty. It is, rather, a world rich with tone and texture. Worldly men are, in Nietzsche's phrase, "superficial out of profundity."

Since the political realm has its own integrity, problems that arise in it must be solved in its terms. The philosophical tradition regards this as unacceptable. Its siren song lures men into renouncing action, with its boundlessness, unpredictability, and irreversibility of outcome, and into rebelling against the outrageous fact that we are not in control of our actions, of "who" we are, and so of the stories told about us. The remedy is to substitute making for doing, politics as craft for politics as performance, and a metaphysics of truth for perspectivism. Then we will be able to see that behind the obvious multiplicity of the world's appearances, and behind the equally obvious plurality of man's faculties and abilities, there exists a single measure of validity and goodness. Grounded in a realm outside politics, immune to the instabilities and conflicts that leave men unable to understand and control what they do and how they live, it would clean up the messiness, the pretensions, and the deficiencies of worldly existence. In this world there would be no place for Oedipus and so no place for *Oedipus at Colonus*, no place for tragedy as sensibility and institution.

From one point of view, "the" philosophic tradition offers itself as the answer to Silenus, and we will see one way it does so in chapter 7. But from another point of view, it is, and understands itself to be, complicit with him, as in Plato's recognition that, from a worldly point of view, philosophy is a kind of death. Arendt regards this antipolitical vision of redemption as a snare and self-defeating. "The life span of men running toward death," she writes in a passage that might well serve as an epigraph for DeLillo's *White Noise*, "would inevitably carry everything human to ruin and destruction if it were not for the faculty of interrupting it and beginning something new, a faculty which is inherent in action like an ever-present reminder that men, though they must die, are not born in order to die but in order to begin" (*HC*, 246). Philosophers find the risk of the miraculous too unpredictable and either work against it or remove themselves sufficiently from the world of appearances that it cannot touch them.

By purging tragedy, philosophy generates an antipolitical vision of redemption. It does so by positing a stark opposition between the utter chaos of the Dionysian and the perfect harmony, unity, and order of the Apollonian so that only the latter can redeem the former. In these terms plurality, perspectivism, agonism, worldly life, action, and of course politics itself can only be seen as dangerous and life-threatening. In these terms, performance, theater, and drama are distractions, since there can be no mediation between the Dionysian and the Apollonian.

Against this Arendt sides with politics and drama, the world of appearances and opinion, with truth as negotiation among competing viewpoints, and with a notion of redemption that retains tragedy as institution and sensibility.

V

Reading Arendt through the lens of tragedy illuminates her political thought, while her thought dramatizes aspects of tragedy in ways that bring it into dialogue with modernity. Of course the lens illuminates the limitations and missed opportunities as well as the depth of her thought. Similarly, her political theory draws attention to aspects of tragedy she ignores, and which make it both a more relevant *and* a problematic interlocutor in contemporary considerations of modernity.

Arendt talks about "the Greeks" despite her celebration of distinctness, and about "the Athenians," even when, as in her discussion of Thucydides, there is a question of whether one can (any longer?) talk about "the" Athenians. Moreover, she seriously misrepresents "Greek" attitudes toward biological reproduction and turns warnings about conflating private and public life into polarities "the Greeks" themselves would not have recognized. Finally, she makes pronouncements about the prephilosophical literature she invokes that ignore the multiple voices present, say, in the *Iliad* (which she reads as a straightforward endorsement of the heroic ethic), or indeed in *Oedipus at Colonus*.[33]

Certainly the absence of qualifications and multivocality in a thinker who insists on plurality and distinctions should make us wary of the textual basis for her various claims about the Greeks. But is such absence also a reason to dismiss her Hellenism as a distraction from what she "really" wanted to argue or should have argued? Let me answer this first by suggesting parallels between Arendt's political thought and tragedy she did not articulate, and then turn to aspects of her Hellenism we do find in her work.

Though Arendt's idea of judgment owes much to Aristotle and Kant, it has Hellenic parallels in the performance conditions of tragedy. Theater provided a place and moment when citizen spectators could judge refracted versions of themselves onstage. In *Oedipus at Colonus* the chorus of Athenian citizens are judges in the disputes between Creon and Oedipus, and between Polyneices and Oedipus, like their counterparts in the audience who were jurors in the law courts. The Chorus's judgment of these cases becomes "a test not only of their moral character but of their democratic potential as prototypical Athenian citizens."[34] In addition, the dramatic festivals were themselves competitions in which ordinary citizens judged the plays and awarded prizes. If we consider all this, and if we regard each play as a point of view on issues, people, decisions, and cultural practices, and think of how many plays each year and over a lifetime an Athenian citizen witnessed, we can imagine the development of something like the "enlarged mentality" Arendt distills from Kant's discussion of taste. The possibility of impartiality, of seeing the world from other points of view, of "going visiting," to use her phrase, to develop a capacity for independent judgment, is an aspect of the theatrical experience.

This suggests that we can understand Arendt as I think she understood herself, and as the tragedians certainly thought of themselves: as political educators of democratic citizens. "Theater," Carol Dougherty has written, "functions as a second agora, or public space, in which the community at large can discuss its political options."[35] But these options are considered in a more comprehensive form than the urgency of decision present in the Assembly Council or courts allow. In this form, tragedy, like Arendt, sought to understand the conditions of action but did not, any more than she does, prescribe particular acts. Tragedy and Arendt both seem less concerned with solving problems than with deepening our understanding of them, whether those "problems" have to do with empire, leadership, war, and democracy (as in Arendt's *Crisis of the Republic*), or with those larger cultural accommodations and exclusions (as in her *Human Condition*) that function as unproblematic conditions of collective life. In both instances each dramatizes the "unboundedness" and "unpredictability" of action. To quote Vernant again: "In the tragic perspective, acting and being an agent has a double character. On the one side, it consists in taking counsel with oneself, weighing for and against and doing the best one can to foresee the order of means and ends. On the other hand, it is to make a bet on the unknown and incomprehensible and to take a risk on a terrain that remains impenetrable."[36] "Because an actor always moves among and in relation to others," Hannah Arendt writes, "he is never merely a doer but always and at the same time a sufferer" (*HC*, 190).

Arendt shares this tragic sensibility with the Greek dramatists. It is a sensibility that appears in the narrative of modernity she tells in *The Human Condition*. The story of Oedipus, who was confident of his ability to solve any problem and of his powers of discernment, yet was nonetheless shadowed by some evil twin so that he never quite knew what he was saying or doing, is paralleled by that of the scientific and technological pretensions that she regards as defining modernity. If we think of Oedipus's blindness not as a physical condition but as a metaphorical or even political one, then it makes perfect sense that some of Arendt's most profound reflections on modernity appear in a collection of essays entitled *Men in Dark Times*.

One can even think of Arendt as imitating the impartiality she admires in Homer, Herodotus, and Thucydides. True, she says the social ontology that made such impartiality possible, especially the assumption that greatness is instantly recognizable, no longer exists. The antipolitical traditions that have shaped modernity have made greatness, like power, a dirty word. Yet she does believe that there is something like political greatness found in quite different historical occasions, such as the American Revolution, the Russian Soviets, the French Resistance, and, no doubt, had she lived long enough, Polish Solidarity. In this regard one could say that she, like Herodotus, wished to preserve "from decay the remembrance of what men have done," and prevent "the great and wonderful actions of Greeks and Barbarians from losing their due portion of glory" (*History* 1.1).

One can also view the tensions in Arendt's work through the lens of tragedy. Critics have noted a strain, even a contradiction, between an associative, communal, democratic, deliberative Arendt, who admires the episodic revivals of political freedom, and an Arendt "captured" by the Greek model of greatness, heroism, agonism, and aestheticized politics. Mostly, they praise one Arendt or the other, wishing that she were not so committed or arguing that she really isn't that committed to the stance they find unpalatable.

This tension is dramatized by the tragedians. The question of what to do with what Bernard Knox calls "the heroic temper" in a democracy was, if not the text, then the subtext of many plays. The question of how one is to reconcile the agonism necessary for politics, including democratic politics, with the need for deliberation parallels the question of how one "fits" figures like Oedipus, who give life meaning precisely by their excess, into a community of political equals. The issues are not posed merely onstage; they are posed in the contrast between the dramatic and historical space of the play, between its content and its context of performance.

The balance of proximity to and distance from contemporary issues afforded by the theatrical experience provided a place and time for the Athenians to become spectators of themselves. Attaining a certain distance from the press of decisions and events provided an occasion for a reflectiveness impossible in other public settings. In saying this, I do not want to underestimate the intensity of audience response, particularly if Nietzsche is right about tragedy's removing the veil covering the Dionysian abyss. Nor am I suggesting that Greek tragedy is a morality play where the audience celebrates its superiority to the partial and distorted perceptions of those onstage. Pity yields to fear since any of us (and any city) could find ourselves in the position of Oedipus, not because we will kill our fathers and marry our mothers, but because success and power leave us confident of our ability to solve problems "because we can't see the problems we cannot solve." Certain that he understands the conditions of his life, Oedipus in *Oedipus Tyrannos* was "unable to recognize any dimension of his life's meaning other than the one he already knew." In this sense "he denied the possibility of tragedy until he was overwhelmed by it."[37] This is, I think, Arendt's view of the modern condition.

VI

Arendt is a dramatist of modernity who no more aims to return to ancient Athens than Sophocles aimed to return to the Athens of Theseus. But what, then, is the point of her Hellenism (especially her celebration of politics), and does her use of it explain, even if it does not justify, her reading of the Greeks?

Arendt's Hellenism is equal parts aspiration, remembrance, and recognition. We may still use words like "action," "power," "politics," and "freedom," but we do not understand their full meaning because we lack the experiences from which they spring, or cannot recognize those experiences for what they are when they do appear. If we could restore access to the polis, the full significance of those words and corresponding experiences would become clearer to us.[38] And we can gain such access because the "polis" is less a physical entity or specific historical configuration than an ever-present possibility, even under the inhospitable conditions of modernity. The polis, Arendt writes, is "not the city-state in its physical location; it is the organization of the people as it arises out of acting and speaking together . . . no matter where they happen to be" (*HC*, 98). It is, we might say, a generative myth or a kind of monumental history to

inspire and augment contemporary politics and theory. The fact that
Arendt ends a discussion of the French Resistance (which itself ends a
book on the American Revolution permeated by recurrent historical manifestations of people acting and speaking together) with a quotation from
Sophocles suggests that she believes that the experience of politics still
has the capacity to redeem men from the Wisdom of Silenus. Indeed, one
could read her work as an imitation of (her) Homer and Thucydides, as
telling a story about such experiences to sustain us in their absence.

But such redemption must be political, not antipolitical, for the same
reasons she insists on a distinction between a *political* community and an
antipolitical one, represented, she believes, by Plato's *Republic*.

If we want a sense of what a world without politics and with Silenus
triumphant would be like, we can look to Arendt's portrait of totalitarianism (aspects of which recall Nietzsche's indictment of modernity in chapter 2). For Arendt, totalitarianism represents an extreme manifestation of
developments present in modernity as a whole. As such, it fosters and
responds to a radical loss of self, a cynical, bored indifference in the face
of death or catastrophe, a penchant for historical abstractions as a guide
to life, and a contempt for common sense along with a dogged adherence
to traditions that have lost their point, if not their hold.[39] But the very
triumph of Silenus comes from the desire to erase his wisdom altogether,
absorbing mortality into the marching columns of a thousand-year Reich.
Politics is the struggle against a wisdom that cannot be defeated because
it "reminds" us of our mutability and the enigmatic quality of situations
or lives about which we have accumulated unwarranted certainty. For
Nietzsche, Arendt, and perhaps Sophocles, the continued contest against
this "fate" spurs us to action and gives life its energizing passion. I think
something like this dialectic is present in Weber's view of politics as both
a heroic activity and the long, slow boring of hard boards.

Arendt is no more nostalgic for ancient Greece or Athens than
Nietzsche was or, for that matter, I am. Her project is, as she puts it in
her most Hellenic work, *The Human Condition*, to consider that condition "from the vantage point of *our* newest experience and *our* most recent fears" in order "to think what *we* are doing" (my emphasis, *HC*, 5).
In these terms her Hellenism, like Nietzsche's, is an attempt to think
through the present without being presentistic.

Moderns have not only lost their capacity to understand the full meaning of words like "politics" and "freedom"; they have also lost their capacity to think politically. Arendt insists that she is not a philosopher but
a political thinker, and the word "political" makes a difference not only
in what she thinks about but what she takes thinking to mean. Indeed, one
aspect of her political use of Hellenism is deconstructing the philosophical
tradition's version of it, thus pluralizing the ways to see "the Greeks."

Arendt, like Nietzsche, uses her Hellenism as a provocation. She seeks, in George Kateb's words, "to press the past into the service of establishing the strangeness of the present,"[40] to make the everyday seem anomalous, thereby opening up the present for real thinking, if not real political struggles. We have come to talk in clichés—"language codes" is what Arendt calls them in *Eichmann in Jerusalem*—and no one can think in clichés. Her desire to deconstruct outworn notions and categories may explain her own protean identity, the difficulty critics have in pinning her person and her ideas down.

It is because Arendt is a political thinker and polemicist that words like "deliberative" misdescribe her project, and why she is sometimes suspicious of rigorous standards of logical consistency. "Deliberation" is too pallid a word to describe the way she enacts in her own work the agonism she finds in the polis. As for the rigors of logic, Arendt praises Lessing because he "rejoiced" in what distressed philosophers—the fact that "truth when uttered is immediately transfigured into one opinion among many"—and went so far in his "partisanship" for the world to "sacrifice to it the axiom of non-contradiction, the claim to self-consistency" (*MDT*, 27–28). It was this that allowed him to be a writer who "anticipates dialogue with others," as I think Arendt herself does.

One of the central themes of *Oedipus at Colonus* is that of teaching and learning. The play presents Oedipus as someone who has been taught by his long sufferings, by the passage of time, and by some quality of mind and temper that has made him capable of grasping the lessons of his life.[41] Yet he is, for all his learning, a learner still. His exchanges with Theseus and the Chorus are ones of reciprocal teaching and learning and remain so until his life is over. Even then he continues to teach, not didactically but in the way Apollo's enigmatic oracles do, illuminating the landscape of human life without mapping it, so that we remain interlocutors in what that life is and how it should be lived. That is his and Sophocles' gift to Athens. It is also Arendt's gift to us.

But finally one must admit that there is a tempered romanticism about Arendt's Hellenism. She did believe that ancient Greece contained "thought fragments" that could be pried loose from the depths of the past. In these terms (taken from Walter Benjamin), she is a pearl diver whose aim is not to resuscitate the past or renew extinct ages, but to introduce crystallizations of rare beauty and profundity into the lives we share with each other.

IV

Aristophanes in America

"Democracy" on sale half price

"Theory" everything 50% off

"Philosophy" 33% off

—Sale signs at Loehmann's dress shop, Miami, Florida

THIS ESSAY is animated by a question whose answer seems perfectly obvious. The question is, can television, particularly television comedy,[1] play the role in contemporary American democracy that Old Comedy played in ancient Athenian democracy? And the perfectly obvious answer is of course not. Ancient drama was a highly specific, if not unique, historical occurrence. When we examine its context of performance, which we must to understand its "content," as we elaborate its place within a designated time and space as part of a vast conglomerate of religious ritual and civic festival, the claims dramatists made to be the political educators of their audience, and the way in which that audience coincided with the civic order of citizens who originated, regulated, and judged dramatic competitions, the juxtaposition my question poses seems far-fetched at best. The same conclusion presents itself if we begin with the historical specificity of television. Think of how different our world is from that of the ancient Athenian, politically, religiously, socially, economically, and culturally, or of those huge transformations of sensibility and scale that established the context for "television." Just imagine setting a classical Athenian down in New York or Los Angeles. It is itself a pretty promising comedic premise.

One can hardly ignore the significance of such disparities, which means that insofar as I do, I can only ask the reader for a certain suspension of disbelief and a willingness to play along much like what Aristophanes asked of his audience. And though I will make something of an argument, my purpose, like his and that of the TV comedies I examine, is more interrogatory than constitutive. Though Aristophanes seems to think that ridicule, parody, and mockery had ethical import, and that the comic poet was the political educator of his fellow citizens, he does not claim that humor constitutes a politics or an ethics. The point, rather, was to laugh at those who confidently assumed they knew what morality was, at those political leaders who were sure of their wisdom and power, and at those social conventions and cultural practices that were assumed or claimed to be "natural." Of course for Plato this lack of respect for authority was part of the problem, which is one reason why he is so unrelenting in his criticisms of comedy in *The Republic* (which is not to deny that there are comic elements in that text).

There is a delicious irony in the fact that what Plato regarded as the height (or depth) of popular culture, namely, Aristophanic comedy, we now regard as "classic" and so part of high culture. Clearly, works of art move up and down the cultural ladder. So do genres, as is evident in the case of movies that have become "film" and "cinema" with baroque theories and intertextualities of their very own. All this suggests two questions that I can only raise here: how do such transformations take place, and is there any reason to suppose that television comedies such as *Seinfeld*, *In Living Color*, *The Roseanne Barr Show*, *The Honeymooners*, or *The Simpsons* will climb a similar ladder?

In the case of comedy, cultural respectability is a trap. Tragedy invites and can easily bear the weight of serious analysis. But comedy is highly susceptible to the disease of didacticism because it seems to disintegrate under the scalpel of academic attention. E. B. White called this the "Frog" problem, which seems particularly appropriate in the case of Aristophanes, who titled a play *The Frogs*. Analyzing comedy, White suggested, was like dissecting a frog: both die in the process of displaying their innards.[2] On the other hand, there is something comical about academics scurrying to make Aristophanes into a philosopher in drag (which is not so different from what I am about to do), or insisting that he offers a double message, one for the refined and sophisticated (i.e., us) and one for the unwashed masses.

In what follows I want first to say something about the cultural climate in which Aristophanic comedy was produced, the performance conditions of that production, and the content of the plays, which can be understood only in terms of that climate and those conditions. More specifically, I will be concerned about the relationship between democracy and comedy, and the role of the comic poet as political educator of his fellow citizens. Second, I will turn to the critics of television and their charge that it is a form of antipolitical education that corrupts democracy, and then criticize the critics, not because I think them wrong, but because I think their attitude toward television (which some are quick to say they seldom watch) is self-fulfilling and therefore politically suspect. My critique of the critics is intended to provide some space for thinking about the ways in which television might become something other and better than it seems necessarily to be, and to reintroduce the juxtaposition between Aristophanic and TV comedy present in my initial question. Finally, I will elaborate this juxtaposition by suggesting that if Aristophanes were to find himself in New York or Los Angeles, he would be a writer for *The Honeymooners* or *The Simpsons*.

I

The relationship between theater and politics in Athens was quite different from what it is for us. A playwright did not create a drama and seek to have it produced for an audience that would exist only at the moment of performance. Nor was the play a piece of writing destined for individual consumption by private readers. The audience, which in this respect largely coincided with the civic order of citizens, was already constituted, and the poet applied for permission to appear before it.[3] There was a preliminary selection determining which text would become a play and a subsequent contest: prizes were awarded by a jury chosen from the general public according to procedures analogous to those used for deciding membership in the Boulē (council). This meant that theater was a communal time and place even when representative aspects of that community were being subjected to ridicule and critique. It also meant what contemporary critics find so hard to accept—that ordinary citizens voted first prizes to plays that were highly critical of their own leaders' policies, foibles, and cultural accommodations such as those concerning gender and class.

But to speak of theater as a whole elides the differences between tragedy and comedy and begs the question of whether comedy did indeed have practical consequences outside the prescribed festive celebration of which it was a part.

Theater provided a place and time in which the assembled citizenry saw itself represented onstage confronting issues such as leadership and authority, democracy and empire, generational and sexual conflict, the relationship between oikos and polis, gods and humankind, wisdom and madness, power and freedom, ingenuity and transgression, nature and convention, as well as the place of drama in public life. But the form of representation and so the way those issues were considered were different in comedy and tragedy. As we saw in the previous chapter, tragedy relied on stories from heroic myth, emphasizing dire personal and social events that had befallen heroines and heroes, families and dynasties in the distant past, mostly at places other than Athens, mostly in highly stylized language. Comedy, by contrast, was firmly anchored in the present and in Athens was openly topical about its objects of ridicule—militarism, greed, litigiousness, Socrates, the Sophists, war with Sparta, Cleon, Pericles, education, the gullibility of the demos, patriotism, and the glory of the past. Except when parodying the conventions of tragedy, its language was colloquial and its choice of linguistic and musical registers and subjects much wider. While a tragic hero was likely to meet a horrific fate as the result of an equally horrific transgression, the comic "hero" was likely to be a farmer or artisan who was merely trying to "make ends meet." And while tragedy encouraged its audience to reflect in the most general way on issues of agency and fate, reason and passion, comedy's satirical depiction of Athenian democracy was designed "both to arouse laughter and to encourage reflection." Like a modern topical cartoon, it humorously distorted reality to draw attention to gaps between truth and lies, principle and practice.[4]

Though a tragedy might speak about an otherwise unspeakable act (such as incest), or a character in it might question the gods, it was comedy that was free to engage in types of ridicule audiences regarded as illicit in public life. Because comedy was allowed or even encouraged to indulge in forms of personal ridicule and flout otherwise common standards of propriety, it was the quintessential expression of parrhēsia, frank and honest speech unintimidated by power. To a degree impossible in tragedy, comedy ridiculed gods and politicians, generals and intellectuals, mocked the demos's favorites and its critics, all the while exulting in verbal abuse, uninhibited sexuality, and repeated references to excrement and flatulence.

James Redfield has argued that tragedy is "a partial art" that calls forth its antitype, "Old Comedy."[5] While tragedy brings home the limiting conditions of human freedom, comedy mocks these constraints. The cultural forms that tether human possibilities to the earthly realities of everyday life are ridiculed in a way that reminds us that culture is something invented and can be renewed and recast. In *The Wasps*, the judicial process is likened to a game that could just as easily be played with cooking utensils; in *The Birds*, the hero decides to conquer the air rather than other cities; in *The Akharnians*, he opts for making a separate peace with Sparta and then makes fun of his compatriots who self-destructively keep fighting; in *Lysistrata*, the women take over the city; in *The Ecclesiazusae*, the question is raised as to whether the Athenian assembly could make women men if they so desired. After all, why should nature be a limit? If the Athenians have the power to make every sea and land a highway of their daring, and conceive of themselves as an island and then act in the world as if they were one—proposals made by Thucydides' Pericles—then what is to stop them from voting to make women men?[6]

In what sense was Aristophanes the political educator of Athenian democracy? There are two questions here. The first concerns whether the audience brought its theatrical experience (whatever that might be) to their participation in other political venues, or, more broadly, whether comedy had any substantial political consequences. The second concerns the ways in which these consequences could be termed "democratic."

Many commentators believe that Old Comedy was necessarily conservative, since whatever anarchic, transgressive, and liberatory impulses might be present in the plays were domesticated by the "controlled environment" of state-sponsored religious rituals. In these terms comedy seems more carnival than a prelude to an action, more a letting off of steam "than a challenge to conventional hierarchies." Because of this, whatever vision of renewal comedy might offer remained a mere vision since it "lacked any programmatic" dimension. Add to this a nostalgia for a "simpler time," and comedy could not pose a viable alternative to the inequalities embedded in city-state life.[7]

Part of this skepticism about comedy's having radical consequences outside the carefully patrolled context of festival and theater may stem from skepticism about democracy and the capacity of the *hoi polloi* to make intelligent judgments. (It is a skepticism mirrored by leftist critics of television who see it as a vehicle of the capitalist class controlling the unwitting masses, and by conservative critics who see the medium as further debasing an already contemptible popular culture.) While it is true that the playwright had to please the judges and audience, it does not follow that pleasing them meant flattering them, or that they could not appreciate mockery of their own foibles and excesses. Nor is reaffirming traditional values quite so conservative if those values are democratic and if, as I shall argue, they include a tradition of collective self-critique.

Nonetheless, the argument is a useful corrective to any presumption that we know what an Athenian audience took away from a dramatic performance (though the argument has its own presumptions about this). No one can be sure whether Aristophanic comedy had any effect on Euripides' reputation or the fate of Cleon, for example. Indeed, Cleon was voted the generalship soon after the judges awarded first prize to *The Knights*, in which he is viciously lampooned. Nor, given the bivalent meaning of *skoptein* and its cognates—to joke with reference to play, fun, and humor, and to mock or deride in ways that dishonor—can we be certain that ridicule did not exacerbate rather than heal divisions within Athens (presuming what is not obvious, that such healing is always positive). In a culture as shame-oriented as ancient Greece, the derisive dimensions of laughter were volatile indeed.[8] The skeptical argument also sharpens the distinction between an immanent critique of Athenian democracy as found in Aristophanes and a transformative one present in *The Republic*. And it reminds us that Aristophanes' plays must have meant something very different to their original audience from what they do to all subsequent audiences and readers.

But it is not obvious that Aristophanes is nostalgic for some simpler time. Old Education, Aeschylus, and the rustic Strepsiades are subject to as much ridicule as New Education, Euripides, or Socrates. More important, there is evidence that comedy was expected to and did have substantial impact on Athenian democracy. There is, to begin with, Plato's harsh and persistent criticism of what comedy does to the citizenry. And of course Plato and Xenophon thought Aristophanes' caricature of Socrates helped shape the animus against him.[9] Then there is the fact that Aristophanes was awarded a crown by the city after the performance of *The Frogs* in 405 B.C.E. for having given it good advice. In addition, Cleon's lawsuit against Aristophanes makes little sense if comedy had no political consequences outside the frame of theater and play. Moreover, the fact that the liberty of comic ridicule was suspended by law (from 440/39 to 437/36) suggests that it was regarded as something more than lighthearted entertainment.[10] Penultimately, there is the sheer implausibility of the idea that theatrical experience could be tightly compartmentalized, both because laughter is often uncontrollable and because other posited compartmentalizations in Athens (say, between public and private) are far more porous than official designations indicate.

Finally, there is the poet's claim, acknowledged by the city, that he was its political educator, not in the sense that Plato's Guardians were or Plato himself perhaps hoped to be, though Old Comedy, like *The Republic*, exposed the demos's tendency toward self-deception and confronted the artifices of a political system that tended, as all political systems do, to naturalize its practices. Rather, Aristophanes offered advice by way of parodying the city's favorite leaders, giving some issues more salience than others, articulating shared resentments or a general malaise, pressuring for reconsideration of policies already adopted or minority views previously rejected, and in general providing a stage on which the tensions, instabilities, and transformations of democratic life could be dramatized, mediated, and explored.[11]

One could say that comedy was aporetic in the sense that it "transferred the last word to the audience who were left to enact [their] own part but a little more reflectively than before."[12] In this sense comedic political education could help its citizen audience think about what they were doing and what others were doing to them, sometimes in their name, always for their supposed benefit.[13]

Still, none of this directly addresses the question of how much and whether comedy extended and deepened democratic practices and culture.[14] Suppose we think of democracy as an ethos[15] that includes a form of governance of, by, and for the people, and an egalitarian constitution of cultural and political life. A democratic ethos encourages the sharing of power and responsibility, presuming both that the former can enhance the latter (but without the naive expectation that it necessarily does), and that the sharing of power is a prerequisite for dignity as well as self- and mutual respect. A democratic ethos is suspicious of hierarchies, especially but not only political ones, and is prejudiced against claims to authority by actual or potential elites. Similarly, democrats may treat political leaders with respect, but ultimately the people are the government and leaders are more advisers and competitors for public stature than august representatives of the state.[16] A democratic ethos presumes that political knowledge is constituted discursively rather than deductively, that at the very least it requires the contributions of high and low, and involves sometimes heated debates among people who may differ intensely about what they should do and who rightly constitutes the "they." A democratic ethos can tolerate some economic inequality as long as it does not compromise political equality or legitimate moral or significant social inequalities. Penultimately, a democratic ethos is a social process through which fixed identities and naturalized conventions periodically confront their conventional status. This does not mean that people can shed such conventions easily, or that simply naming them as conventional could or should be liberating. It does mean that social and cultural conventions are modes of performance, instantiated in thousands of small and large actions in ways that elude full cognitive disclosure. Finally, a democratic ethos assumes that democracy is as much a politics of disturbance as a form of government and order.

In what ways does Old Comedy exemplify and define such an ethos? We know that conservatives disliked it, that it was exceptionally inclusive in subject matter and audience, and that comic fantasies and inversions of the norms provided a vision of things as they used to be, or should and could still be, against the weight of the status quo.[17] Then there is the additional fact that while tragedy at its origins was patronized by tyrants, comic drama was officially accepted into the Dionysia only in 486 and into the Lenaea about forty-five years later, suggesting that it was the product of "democratic patronage."[18]

In addition, comedy was a cultural form of political accountability. Here is Jeffrey Henderson:

> The precise effects of comic ridicule and comic abuse are impossible to gauge.
> But surely no prominent Athenian imagined that the laughter of the *demos*

at his expense could possibly do him any good, and the better the joke the less comfortable he would be thereafter. For this very reason the *demos* institutionalized the comic competitions. In return for accepting the guidance of the "rich, the well-born, and the powerful" it provided that they be subject to a yearly unofficial review of their conduct at the hands of the *demos'* organic intellectuals and critics, the comic poets.[19]

Moreover, comedy helped sustain the egalitarian constitution of political and cultural life. In *The Clouds*, for example, everyone becomes a spectacle for everyone else: the Chorus and characters onstage; the characters who, stepping out of their roles, talk directly to the audience about themselves as actors and refer to the theater in Athens; "Aristophanes," when he comes forward to address the audience in the parabasis, and the audience when he looks out at them. No one escapes being part of the spectacle; each is in turn seer and seen. Each moment of superiority, of laughing at others and ridiculing their foibles, is reversed as if Aristophanes was, in the context of theater, imitating rotation in office that was distinctive to Athenian democracy.[20]

Penultimately, Old Comedy helped constitute a tradition of self-critique in which various practices and cultural accommodations basic to Athenian public and private life were called into question. An example of such self-critique is present when Thucydides' Pericles criticizes the convention of giving Funeral Orations that required and entitled him to do what he is about to do, thereby dislodging the practice from the tradition that legitimized it. Such problematizing of what is also enacted (which is also present in Socratic philosophizing) is an aspect of the restless daring the Corinthians tell us (in Thucydides 1.70) typifies their Athenian enemies. "To describe their character in a word, one might truly say that they were born into the world to take no rest themselves and to give none to others" (Crawley trans.). A few pages later, the Athenians echo those words in the course of boasting about their daring patriotism at Salamis. (The restlessness is brilliantly parodied by the twitching of the flea-infested Strepsiades in the opening scene of *The Clouds*.)

Finally, Aristophanic comedy does not simply endorse such daring and self-critique but provides a stage on which "conservative" and "postmodernist" excesses are both ridiculed. Thus *The Clouds* dramatizes the costs of the displacements democratic politics may demand, and which it otherwise celebrates. Consider, for example, the way the play treats the opposition between town and country, upper and lower classes. Strepsiades comes from a lower-class farming background, while his wife comes from an aristocratic family linked to Pericles. The birth of their son exacerbates these differences as they fight over his name. They finally compromise on "Pheidippides," meaning cheap aristocrat. But this solves nothing when the son is instructed to honor his parents. How can he when they come from different classes and ways of life? The only solution, which the son adopts after his sophistic education, is to *dishonor* them both. Here the fluidity, egalitarianism, and hybridity of democratic culture has a darker side: dispossession, confusion, and loss of ground.

By the fourth century, the growing specialization of culture meant a separation between popular and elite culture, seriousness and humor, education and entertainment. As popular theater developed into a form of entertainment, the new genres of rhetoric and philosophy took over the paideutic function that drama, including comedy, had once possessed.[21]

II

Given all this, comparisons with television can only be absurdly tendentious. There was a time before the triumph of industrial capitalism, consumer culture, and the commodification of leisure when one could find less tendentious parallels between ancient and modern *theater*.[22] Before nineteenth-century state building and industrialization, churches, lodge halls, and community centers were sites for theatrical productions designed to make occasions such as weddings and holidays more festive. The new commercial theaters that replaced them "needed no special occasion nor ritual activities" to justify their existence. Such performances, George Lipsitz argues, "became commodities sold to strangers for an agreed-upon price rather than collective creations by communities enacting rituals essential to group identity and solidarity." Unlike previous conditions and Athenian drama, performers in these theaters lacked direct ties of kinship, propinquity, and history with their audiences.[23] The new audiences did not share a history, reciprocal responsibilities, or obligations.

Lipsitz is careful not to tell a moralizing story of decline. Thus he recognizes how the new commercial theater created a kind of social space for working-class men to escape the surveillance of moral authorities and institutions, and for women to escape parental supervision and patriarchal domination. This theater also encouraged audiences to pursue personal desires and passions outside their socially prescribed responsibilities and, because of the audience's unfamiliarity, provided a cover for feelings and emotions that could be aired without explanation or apology.[24] Nonetheless, he regards the new theatrical forms as creating the "psychic conditions for the needy narcissism of consumer desires,"[25] and goes on to argue that by "establishing commodity purchases as symbolic answers to real problems," the new theater laid the basis for a commodity culture "where advertisers and entrepreneurs offer products that promise to bring pleasures and fulfillment." Though nineteenth-century theater may have emerged in part as a rebellion against sexual repression, "its greatest long-term significance lay in shaping the psychic and material preconditions for Americans to shift from a Victorian industrial economy to a hedonistic consumer one." It is precisely the triumph of this culture, with the material conditions that accompanied it, that makes comparisons with ancient theater seem so far-fetched.

But what about the idea of television as a form of democratic political education? Like Greek drama, television is, in Neil Postman's words, "our culture's mode of knowing itself. Therefore, how television stages the world becomes the model for how the world is properly staged."[26] But this "stage" is a mass medium that constitutes a spatial and temporal organization of collective life no longer linked to the sharing of a common locale and face-to-face dialogue. To talk about contemporary public spaces, we need to rethink both the idea of space and publicness in a way that reflects the complex interdependencies of the modern world with its highly mediated forms of communication.

Moreover, contemporary democracies are liberal or representative rather than participatory. There is no rotation in office, selection by lot, or absence of semipermanent elites with their own corporate interests. Democracy now does not mean maximum self-rule (unless it is maximum "feasible" rule) and the mutual accountability of citizens, but a mechanism to ensure some degree of accountability of rulers to the ruled. Indeed, one could argue that even this minimal notion of democracy has been eroded in the past twenty years as American society has grown more and more inegalitarian, more divided by extremes of wealth and poverty, and more systematically dominated by corporate power. Insofar as this has meant increased power for elites bent on appropriating the conduct, knowledge, and procedures of public life, it is the inverse process of the democratization Jean-Pierre Vernant traces when he describes the evolution of democracy in classical Athens.[27] In any case, what seems clear is that since very few of our citizens actively share in the opportunities and responsibilities of power as Athenian citizens did, they can hardly bring the experience of direct participation in politics to the watching of television. Still less does television seem to provide the occasion and the place to reflect on public life with the depth and comprehensiveness present in Greek theater.

Television is frequently blamed for the attenuation of even this pallid form of democracy, as well as for the corruption of public discourse generally. Some thirty-five years ago, Newton Minnow called television "a vast wasteland" (pinpointing situation comedies as the worst offenders). Television, he and his fellow critics claimed, was vulgar and one-dimensional rather than complex and edifying; sordid, prurient, and mean-spirited rather than uplifting and realistic. More recently, television has been

named as a significant cause of the erosion of social capital, civility, and
deliberative democracy, of the trivialization of private and public life, and
of political voyeurism's replacing political judgment.[28] For such critics
television is and must be a form of antipolitical education that corrodes
democracy. There are eleven elements to this general condemnation.

1. Television transforms citizens into consumers, political freedom and
power into consumer sovereignty, and the public sphere into a realm of
media manipulation and spectacle.

2. In its quest for ratings, television homogenizes culture,[29] in effect
imposing a form of censorship on what can be produced. Cable does not
substantially change the situation, since the parts imitate each other rather
than offer real alternatives.

3. Television fosters and represents a closing in and down of public
spaces. Given VCRs and pay-per-view, there is no need to go out to the
movies. Given the Home Shopping Network, there is less reason (mostly
for women) to go out in public and be in the company of, if not in conversation with, friends.[30] At the same time, television penetrates the home,
helping to order domestic space, leisure time, and family identity, all of
which are reconfigured around commodities and possessions rather than
ethnicity or class. Finally, it colonizes intimate areas of gender and personality by exacerbating anxieties about sexuality and personality, all in the
interests of selling products.[31]

4. In this world of private men and women the good life is the consuming life. Unable to think as citizens, they regard public responsibilities as
distractions from and intrusions on the world of banal utopian visions
where all needs are instantly met, conflict is nonexistent, and poverty has
evaporated into thin air.[32]

5. Television fosters political cosmeticians, image managers, spin doc-
tors, and ad experts who sell candidates as they do other products. Almost
all candidates are now bound to the commercial form and are presented
as commodities. Indeed, television is the means by which democracy is
absorbed by the market, producing what Mark Danner calls "democracy
commodified," a hybrid implicit in Loehmann's sale sign. Given this, is it
surprising that people are cynical about government?[33]

6. Television worships power and devours those who have it. On the
one hand, it displays obeisance to the sacred offices of the state.[34] But on
the other, it subjects holders of power to a contemptuous scrutiny that is
more voyeuristic than substantive.

7. Television makes the workings of power invisible. This is as true of
its own form of power as of the larger structures of power in which it
participates. In presenting itself as providing direct, unmediated, instantaneous reports of events as they are occurring, television obscures the fram-
ing force of the medium—for instance, the way stopwatches organize the

images that constitute "the news." It also obscures its own place within a capitalist economy—for instance, the unprecedented corporate consolidation of the media during the Reagan and older Bush administrations.[35]

8. Where television does not misinform or underinform us about its own power and complicity with the dominating economic and political powers of our time, it distracts us from power's effects by substituting what Pierre Bourdieu calls an "imaginary participation," which is "only an illusory compensation for the dispossession people suffer to the advantage of experts" and professionals.[36] This pseudopower is symbolized by the "remote control" that allows people (usually men) to change the world by changing channels.[37]

9. Television news precludes thoughtfulness, depth, and analysis.[38] It relies on sound bites in which images compete with each other for ninety-second slots and leap from one issue to another in a way that flattens all distinctions and differences. By moving instantly from protests in Bosnia to football in Brazil, from floods in California to spelling bees in Pennsylvania, from research on the AIDS virus to an outing of the royal family, it eliminates hierarchies of significance; each fragment is related to another only by the medium itself.[39]

10. Television is ahistorical and presentist. In his study of the medium's coverage of the Ethiopian famine, Michael Ignatieff shows how its "brief, intense and promiscuous gaze"[40] provided viewers with no opportunity for historical background and no reason to think one would be relevant. It was not only that television ignored the food shortage until it became a famine of epic proportions and so worthy of voyeuristic coverage, but also that, absent any analysis of imperialism and colonialism, the crisis appeared to be a natural phenomenon outside of history and politics. Thus real human suffering was seen as an elemental unmediated moment of connection between human beings outside of time, power, or ideology.

Domestically, television (along with other mass media) has turned us into political amnesiacs. This memoryless public is an essential element in the structure of political passivity that sustains "megastate power."[41] Media politics makes the present the definition of reality. The present itself is merely an arbitrary arrest of sound, motion, and fashion, and the future is simply the next successive image. Because television cannot convey the historical depths of events and the political implications of those events, it ignores history and turns politics into a Nintendo game. Nietzsche's concern about memory and forgetting becomes a nonproblem.

11. As part of the privatization of public life television is a significant factor in the decline of the rich associational life Tocqueville thought essential to combat the susceptibility of individuals to the quiet despotism of an administrative state, and of what Robert Putnam, building on Tocqueville, calls "social capital."[42] The loss of social capital has meant

a loss of citizen trust (the proliferation of lawyers and security guards is evidence), of willingness to keep agreements, of reluctance to cheat strangers or to give or take bribes, and of encouragement of good citizenship in one another by unofficial means, all of which is essential to democratic self-government. Not only does the centrality of television privatize public life in a way that undermines social capital; the speed of the medium as represented by MTV promotes superficial relationships rather than deep friendships, or political allegiances and expressive associations at the expense of substantive ones.

There is a great deal to be said for this critique of television. Yet it is an exaggeration and itself antipolitical insofar as it assumes a technological determinism, supposing that the medium *is* the message, and that the aggregate of such messages does and must define the quality of public life. More than that, it is self-fulfilling and demonizes television rather than allowing it to be seen as a problematic whose contradictory forces and democratic possibilities need to be explored rather than peremptorily foreclosed.

This is not meant to deny that the medium contains a powerful cultural logic, or that regarding it as a neutral instrument to be used for good or ill is superficial. But the challenge is to specify the medium without reifying it, to see it as a cultural form embedded in historical and material practices and shaped by decisions taken by particular groups in specific circumstances. This means studying television both as a vehicle of corporate capitalism and as a generator of forces that move outside or even subvert the hegemony such capitalism seeks to assure. It also means, following Marx on religion, looking at how television salves the wounds and disappointments of daily life, and at how its power may be symptom and sign of our powerlessness. "Even if we could safely dismiss every program on television as artistically worthless," George Lipsitz writes, "we would still need to understand the ways in which television presents the illusion of intimacy, how it intervenes in family relations, how it serves the consumer economy, and how its hold on the viewing audience is related to the disintegration of public resources, the aggravations of work, and the fragility of interpersonal relations that characterize our lives."[43]

Once we see television as part of a larger cultural dialectic, it becomes possible and necessary to ask whether television invented the superficiality and triviality of public discourse, political sloganeering, and distracting pageantry that define our public life, or has become dominant because of that development. If we could transform the vulgarity and shallowness of the medium or even eliminate it altogether, would that restore or let flourish a more acceptable form of discourse? Do charges of television's being antidemocratic nostalgically ignore the parochialisms, hierarchies, and exclusiveness present in previous forms of public life and communication, as one might argue in regard to Habermas's story about the rise and decline of the public sphere?[44]

It also becomes necessary to look more closely at the assumption that what corporate sponsors and television executives or producers want to communicate is what is in fact communicated: that, in Todd Gitlin's phrase, the medium "operates hypodermically," injecting the proper ideas into the unsuspecting bloodstream of the masses. Like those critics who suppose that Aristophanes wrote for two audiences—the sophisticated few who recognized his real intentions and the gullible many who did not—critics from Plato to Adorno, Postman, and Habermas assume that the masses are manipulable fodder for elite control through the latter's domination of the media.[45] But there is evidence that the effects of programming are more various and dispersed and the audiences more savvy than this,[46] which means that we need to know how programs are read rather than just what is watched. "Preferred readings," Stuart Hall writes, do not preclude "oppositional ones."[47]

III

While these responses qualify and complicate the critique of television, they do not, nor are they intended to, undo it.[48] What they do is to provide interpretive space for thinking about the ways in which television might become something other and "better" than it seems necessarily to be, or, more precisely, about the possibilities of television as a mode of democratic political education. And that opens the door, if only slightly, for reconsidering the apparent absurdity of comparing Old Comedy with television sitcoms.

For the door to stay open or open wider it is necessary to find opportunities for contemporary citizens to experience the pleasures and possibilities of sharing power and responsibility, and for them to bring such experiences to the watching of television.

Such opportunities are present in multiple sites of citizenship, both formally and informally defined. They exist in various environmental, human rights, and gay liberation movements, in women's health collectives, union organizing, mobilization of the poor, and the frequent complex negotiations in multiethnic neighborhoods that generate vibrant effective local political associations. Of course one must be careful not to romanticize civil society and social movements by assuming that their politics will be wholly congenial. And one must avoid assimilating even such neighborhood politics to the Greek polis, though the idea of "the parallel polis" generated by Václav Havel and Václav Benda—along with Hannah Arendt's suggestion, noted in the previous chapter, that we think of the polis not in its physical location or historical configuration, but as "the organization of the people as it arises out of acting and speaking together"—does provide a language for seeing some analogues.[49]

But even if many of our fellow citizens bring some form of political experience to the watching of television, what about bringing the experience of watching television to that political experience? For reasons already adumbrated, any conclusions on the subject must be highly speculative, which will not of course stop me from offering some.

IV

In many respects stand-up comics such as Eddie Murphy, Phyllis Diller, George Carlin, Richard Pryor, Margaret Cho, and Chris Rock, each of whom appears on television regularly, would fit comfortably in the world of Aristophanic comedy. They, like he, violate the normative taboos against toilet talk and vulgarity, give ferociously self-deprecatory first-person accounts of sex and sexuality, and refer to orgasms and flatulence, genitalia and fantasies with casual abandon. Such violations of "decorum" seem especially shocking in the case of younger women comics, which suggests how much a double standard remains in effect. (To watch the very different reactions of most men and women to these comediennes is itself pretty funny.) Then there is the willingness to say what is unsayable in other contexts and polite company about corporate greed and military posturing, the personal peccadilloes of politicians, and the romanticizing of marriage, parenthood, and family values (epitomized in Roseanne Barr's gum-chewing nasal proclamation that she is a "Domestic Goddess").

The lampooning of cultural icons and political rituals, the ridicule of what have unobtrusively become banal solemnities legitimating suspect power, and the mocking of national narcissism and government manipulation echo Aristophanic comedy. (As the reaction to Bill Maher's comments on September 11th suggests, there are limits to this, as there were in Athens.) These comics unite high and low entertainment with edification in a way that reminds us of Simon Goldhill's claim that Athenian democracy was the precondition of comedy, and Nicole Loraux's argument that the reverse was also true.[50]

Nowhere is comedy's informally sanctioned privilege more obvious than in the "handling" of racial issues. With very few exceptions, comedy allows a frankness of expression found nowhere else. On the comic stage people are willing to see their carefully screened racial attitudes exposed and mocked. Whether it is Richard Pryor's parody of white walking and white talking, Margaret Cho mimicking her overly protective, fiercely achievement-driven Korean mother, or Archie Bunker explaining the nature of "the coloreds" or "the Hebes," comedy can present forbidden sentiments in public and perhaps unite (an admittedly self-selective) audience in laughter at its own prejudices.

But situation comedies as a genre seem to deal with comfortable emotions and easy issues in a highly stylized format. Anything that disturbs their formulaic bromides is erased within an hour or half hour. All divisions between sexes, generations, races, and classes dissolve in what David Marc calls "a whirlwind resolution" that provides a "tantalizing illusion of structural order in family, community, nation, and cosmos."[51] Nothing illustrates the erasure of dissonance better than *Hogan's Heroes*, a comedy about Allied prisoners in a World War II prisoner-of-war camp that manages not to mention Nazism or Jews. From this show to *Ally McBeal*, sitcoms are populated by generic protagonists and static characters whose principal role is spouting one-liners.

Of course there are exceptions that seem to share some of the aims and sensibility of Aristophanic comedy. The cartoonish characters on *Third Rock from the Sun* often reveal something provocative about the "real world" their more realistic counterparts do not. When we laugh at the Solomons, it is because the absurdities and shifting boundaries of their lives mimic ours, which means we wind up laughing at ourselves.[52] Then there is *The Roseanne Barr Show* on same-sex relations, generational conflict, teen pregnancy, obesity, and working-class life generally; *Beavis and Butt-Head* on the infantilization of culture (including television); and *Absolutely Fabulous* on the vacuity of consumerism and parental authority.

But I want to focus on two sitcoms that are different in mood and content and appear at very different moments in the development of television, popular culture, and political life. The first is *The Honeymooners*, the second, *The Simpsons*. Pompously put, one is modern, the other postmodern.

Writing about Aristophanes, David Konstan argues that "[w]here society is riven by tensions and inequalities of class, gender and status, its ideology will be unstable, and literary texts will betray signs of strain involved in forging such refractory materials into a unified composition."[53] *The Honeymooners* can be read in these terms. It enacts while trying to expunge television's role in papering over the bitter divisions that surface in consumer heaven, and that very process was dramatized by the contradiction between it and the show of which it was, for a number of years, a segment.

Most viewers were introduced to *The Honeymooners* as part of a variety show whose overall tone and frame could not have been more at odds with the life of Ralph Kramden. The show began with an overproduced dance number that seemed equally inspired by Busby Berkeley and Las

Vegas. At its conclusion, Jackie Gleason made a leering entrance dressed in ostentatious finery that paid unembarrassed obeisance to his nouveau richness. When it came to booze and broads, this man lived like a king with a banner proclaiming, "How sweet it is." Following his royal entrance, Gleason did five minutes or so of stand-up and then asked for "a little traveling music."

The journey was multilayered: from Manhattan to Brooklyn;[54] from present success to a Depression-era past, when Gleason left school to become a pool hustler in a working-class neighborhood like the one in which *The Honeymooners* is set; from Farouk-like royalty to the wounded machismo of a fat guy who drives a bus; from ostentatious display and conspicuous consumption to "a barebones flat the likes of which this consumer medium has not seen since."[55] The flat is barren not only of material comforts but of social and psychological ones as well—all this despite the name of the show. The Kramdens' poverty was present in what was in their apartment and what was not: in the antiquated oven and icebox that barely worked, and the nonexistent telephone and television. Such technological backwardness suggests people whom time and progress have passed by, who are cut off from others and forced to turn in and on themselves. This claustrophobic atmosphere, compounded by the absence of children and a bedroom and the choice of static camera positions, recapitulated their endlessly repetitive lives.

All attempts to open up this world fail miserably. They try to adopt a child, spending all they have to decorate their apartment to impress the adoption agency, only to have the charade demeaningly exposed. After they go to such lengths to pretend to have what they do not and be what they are not, the iceman cometh to demand payment on an overdue bill. Their hopes destroyed, they lapse back into a world without a future. No new beginnings or culture of self-help here.

Ralph's get-rich-quick schemes—glow-in-the-dark wallpaper, developing uranium mines on the Jersey shore—are no more successful and no less desperate. He is stuck in a dead-end job that brings him neither the material rewards nor the social recognition he craves. Though full of bluster, he is intimidated by the powerful and wealthy. The few moments when he tells someone off are always based on a false premise that forces him into an abject apology later. In all other situations he stands before them hat in hand, looking down at the floor, overly earnest and fawning, as if enacting the stereotype of the slave. For this sycophant with a hair-trigger temper there is no American dream; Horatio Alger might as well be a beer label.

The show is built around two unspoken ironies: its title and his work. As I have already suggested, there is nothing honeymoonish about the show, despite the deus ex machina endings of "Alice, you're the greatest." The moon we hear most about is the one Ralph threatens to send Alice to when he is in one of his typical rages. Indeed, the threat of domestic violence is omnipresent. Ralph's attempt to be master of his house (in contrast to his obsequiousness in the presence of his "betters") is continually frustrated by Alice, who remains "terrifyingly calm" and thoroughly unintimidated in the midst of his fury. Her "Now, listen to me, Ralph" is both motherly and caustic, advice as well as insult. Then there is his job as a bus driver. The idea of a man as impatient as he is driving a bus in Manhattan traffic is both frightening and funny. It is hard to know what would be worse: riding with him or being a pedestrian anywhere near him.

Finally, Ralph is a prime candidate for an early death. Dangerously overweight, constantly frantic, volatile, frustrated, and disappointed, he is heading for a stroke or heart attack. If one were to enumerate the victims of modernity or capitalism, then Ralph Kramden would be high on the list.

But this is all frog dissection. The show is often hilariously funny, particularly when Ralph hatches some plot with his sewer-tending pal, Ed Norton. Norton is everything Ralph is not: self-satisfied, with an oblivious calmness that enables him to slough off life's insults and focus on what really matters—food. Moreover, there is some opening up of and to the world: a (disastrous) trip to Europe, Raccoon Lodge meetings, an appearance on a quiz show, and a classic train ride.

Though I can imagine Aristophanes writing for *The Honeymooners*, I am convinced, on the flimsiest of evidence, that should he come down (or more likely up) to earth, he would be a writer for *The Simpsons*, and not only because the patriarch of the family is named Homer. (*The New Yorker* had a cartoon of Rembrandt's *Aristotle Contemplating the Bust of Homer*. You can guess which Homer it was.) Like Aristophanic comedy the show is anarchic yet pointed, sophisticated, and raucous, anti-intellectual in an intellectual way, subversive and caustic about the excesses of its own subversions. As with Aristophanes' comedies, the issues are serious—greed and the passion to consume, nuclear power safety and corporate responsibility in general, the erosion of community and local control, the dangers of the therapeutic state, self-help programs and moralistic religiosity, high culture and television itself—while their treatment is farcical.[56] Finally, *The Simpsons'* distrust of power remote from ordinary people, its suspicion of intellectual pretense (as when Mensa tried to establish a Plato-like utopia in Springfield), and its mocking of institutions, practices, and cultural forms that pretend to be natural recall Old Comedy.

Homer Simpson is the Strepsiades of his generation. Like Strepsiades, he is ineptly self-interested, manipulative and greedy; he has low and vulgar tastes, tries to cheat his creditors, is infinitely gullible, and has to deal with a "difficult" son. Homer's vision of the good life is a day in the hammock or owning a used grease concession. He is forever wanting things he'll never have, scheming to get them only to fail miserably (which is why one critic thinks Homer's struggle owes as much to Ralph Kramden as to "the poetry of Aristophanes").[57] Yet, like Strepsiades, Homer loves his family and, in his own morally bumbling way, is superior to those who proclaim their superiority.

The Simpsons has a cartoon within its own cartoonness that brilliantly satirizes the popular culture of which it is a part. *Itchy and Scratchy* is its name, and it is every parent's nightmare. Full of the gratuitous violence that politicians rail against, it has episodes entitled "The Last Traction Hero" and "Remembrance of Things Slashed"; it portrays a Disney-like theme park divided into Torture Land, Explosion Land, Search Gas Pain Land, and Unnecessary Surgery Land, with a state-of-the-art chemical dependency center for Mom and Dad to visit while the kids destroy everything. In one episode, *Itchy and Scratchy* writers are running out of themes, so they produce a show about running out of themes. In another, a panic about ratings leads to the creation of focus groups and co-optation of new trends (such as rap music) to keep the clichéd show on for a bit longer. Others are devoted to the cartoon industry, suggesting a self-reflectiveness also present in Old Comedy.[58]

The Simpsons does something Old Comedy did not need to do and *The Honeymooners* did not do: it preempts the blunting of its satire by the commercialized nature of the medium. To the annoyance of the Fox network, it mocks television commercials and the way their mere existence (let alone their explicit content) frames and thus blunts the program's irony.

The Simpsons has certainly had an impact on the "outside" world. Elementary schools tried to ban Bart Simpson T-shirts, and George Bush attacked *The Simpsons* in his 1992 State of the Union address, telling Americans they should be more like the Waltons than the Simpsons. (A week later *The Simpsons* responded that they themselves were like the Waltons since they were also living through an economic depression.) But of course Bart's contempt for authority is as American as Tom Sawyer's or Huck Finn's, and while *The Simpsons* does indeed mock the idealized portrait of the 1950s family and the self-righteousness of the Religious Right, it ultimately endorses the family, as ragtag as it may be, and, almost uniquely on television, recognizes the importance of religion in American life.[59]

But in what ways, if any, can we say that *The Simpsons* contributes to the political education of democratic citizens?

It is a good question. It is a good question because present circumstances suggest that while political satire is booming (the people who count such things say it has increased fourfold in the past decade), politics isn't. Late-night comics like Leno, Letterman, O'Brien, and Maher, to mention only those on network television, are full of biting jokes that skewer the persons and pretensions of politicians. Yet almost all of the jokes are devoid of ideological content and social commentary of the sort found in Old Comedy. The question is whether once politics has become a form of entertainment, forms of entertainment (which Old Comedy certainly was) can be political. The question becomes even more pointed when political figures appearing on late-night talk shows fawn over the host rather than the other way around, as was once the case. The next president, David Letterman boasted, goes through me. It was a joke, of course, but not much of one.[60]

What *The Simpsons* can do and what Aristophanic comedy almost certainly did was to make the assumptions of the culture visible in a way that brings politics and power back into the realm of social agreements and out of the realm of an unchangeable order of things. Thus *The Ecclesiazusae* challenges the natural differences between young and old, beautiful and ugly, men and women. Why should the young and attractive have easier access to sexual pleasure? Why shouldn't the old be given sexual privileges? Why should only men have political power and not women? If you believe in equality, why stop with equality among male citizens? What is it about women that debars them from sharing such power? Even if the Assembly cannot eliminate biological differences—*if* biological is what they are—why shouldn't it alter the meaning of those differences by equalizing the functional advantages associated with them?[61] *The Simpsons* raises similar questions about capitalism, religion, mass media, and inequalities of status, intelligence, and power.

It is a good question for another reason. If, as some critics such as Jedidiah Purdy charge, our culture is one of irony, and that irony erodes what Robert Putnam calls "social capital," then *The Simpsons* may be part of the problem. Purdy thinks the danger in irony is that it is less a way of conveying hidden meaning than an undermining of meaning altogether, and that the refusal to believe in the depth of relationships or trust the truth of speech or the sincerity of motivation leaves us putting scare quotes around our lives. Purdy thinks this has led to an alienation and indifference that encompass a passive acceptance of things as they are. All of this, he argues, is represented by *Seinfeld*.[62] Perhaps it is. But *The Simpsons* is not *Seinfeld*, and demographics suggest they have significantly different audiences, the former cutting across ethnic particularities in the way the latter does not. Moreover, *The Simpsons* is less ironic than satiric in precisely the way Old Comedy was.

Even then there are many forms of irony and many instances in which irony can be a way of investing something with insight and feeling. And there are good reasons to resist the possibility and desirability of the purified language Purdy seems to oppose to irony. Finally, irony might even make political deliberation possible. If being ironic means having some distance from one's views, then it allows argument to be something other than people simply repeating their views at increasingly high decibel levels. If that is the sense in which *The Simpsons* is ironic, we should be thankful.

V

The great Marxist critic C.L.R. James thought television would be an art of the people and for the people; that it would, precisely because of the kind of medium it was, be able to dramatize the infinite complexity of modern life in "the manner of the Greeks." Television (as well as film, comic strips, and radio) could, he believed, "shake the nation to its soul" as Aristophanes did to the soul of the Athenians.[63]

With few exceptions (*Roots* might be one), this has clearly not occurred. As now constituted, television continues to sustain a presentism in which memoryless citizens are made politically passive. This social and economic "fact" must be the beginning of any study of television as a cultural phenomenon. But after noting the fact and acknowledging the lost opportunities it represents, one must also acknowledge that it need not always be that way, that television is a more diverse medium than its critics recognize. We need, as Stanley Cavell put it some years ago, to think of television as a "question,"[64] and to develop criteria of judgment and political critiques that are not simply mechanical applications of principles developed for other arts that, unsurprisingly, reveal television to be a miserable failure. Indeed, by recognizing the falseness of television's claims merely to represent the real world, we can move beyond the rather astonishing circumstance that, as Alexander Nehamas has noted, the "greatest part of contemporary criticism of television depends on a moral disapproval that is identical with Plato's attack on . . . poetry."[65]

More particularly, while it would be absurd to claim that *The Simpsons* "shake[s] the nation to its soul," it has played a significant interrogatory role in our public life. It does not, any more than Old Comedy did, provide solutions to particular problems or offer directives to ameliorate injustice. But it does, as Old Comedy did, make fun of contemporary institutions, culture, and social practices in ways that might lead citizens to think differently and even act differently. More certainly, it will make its audience laugh at themselves in ways that maintain some space between our identities and our public commitments. In that alone it might help keep America whole, not to mention the frog.

V

The Politics of Nostalgia and Theories of Loss

Is this the promis'd end?
—KENT, in *King Lear*

O<small>N</small> February 18, 1970, Michael Eugene Mullen, sergeant first class, Sixth Infantry Division, was killed in Vietnam. As the eldest son of Peg and Eugene Mullen, he had been expected to inherit the Iowa farm that had been in the family for five generations. For the Mullens, Michael's death seemed the death of the future, as such deaths did for so many Vietnamese and Americans. They disrupted the continuity of life, uprooting them from the ground that had defined their lives. At least in our civilized times, the young are not supposed to die before the old, and parents are not supposed to outlive their children. Except of course in times of war.

For the Mullens, particularly Peg, finding meaning in their son's death became a way of life. At first that meant reconstructing the specific circumstances of his death: how did he die? At what time and place? Who was with him? Did someone hold and comfort him as he faced his final ordeal? No detail, however incidental or ordinary, could be left out as Peg tried to connect the story of his short life that she knew with the story of his death that she did not.

But the army stonewalled. They evaded her questions or answered them dishonestly. And they had good reason to since Michael Eugene Mullen had been killed by drunken American gunnery; he had died by what the army called "friendly fire." In a war noted for its euphemisms this may have been the most perverse, since it allowed the army not to count Michael's death as a casualty of war. In the gruesome game of body counts, his didn't count at all.

Driven by grief, outrage, and loss, Peg, like many others of her generation, became politicized. She began to organize Iowa farm families against
the war. The Mullens took out a half-page advertisement in the *Des
Moines Register* on April 12, 1970. On page 5 of the news section there
was a half-inch-high banner black headline:

A SILENT message to the fathers and mothers of Iowa

and then below it in smaller boldface type:

We have been dying for nine, long, miserable years in Vietnam in an unde-
clared war . . . how many more lives do you wish to sacrifice because of your
SILENCE?

Off to the right of "SILENCE" was a small black cross, and beneath it,
the epitaph "Sgt. Michael E. Mullen—killed by friendly fire." "Then,"
says C.D.B. Bryan, from whom I take these details, "came the crosses."[1]

Row upon row of crosses, fourteen rows containing forty-nine crosses each,
a fifteenth row with twenty-seven and space left open for more. Their ranks,
so starkly aligned and black against the bleak white page, suggested a photo-
graphic negative of some well-kept battlefield cemetery viewed from afar.

"These 714 crosses," a legend explained, "represent the 714 Iowans who
have died in Vietnam." Near the bottom left-hand corner of the page
was printed, "In memory of Vietnam War Dead whom our son joined on
February 17, 1970."

Peg not only became politicized; she simultaneously became "theoreticized" in the sense that the loss of her son generated a passion to find
meaning in his death by asking increasingly comprehensive questions
about the nature of our public life. Naturally enough the questions began
with a demand for details about his death. But they soon expanded in
scope into questions about the Vietnam War and war in general, about
patriotism and democratic accountability, and eventually to questions
about American political culture and political realism. It seemed that only
complete knowledge of the structure that shaped her son's life could provide solace for the absurd circumstances of his death.

I do not mean to romanticize Peg Mullen (or the 1960s), though I do
admire her persistence and politics and share her sense of loss. Her relent-
lessness could be wearying, while her obsessive preoccupation with Michael's death unnerved even members of her immediate family. There is,
naturally enough, more than a little rage and desire for revenge mixed in
with her grief.

Still less do I mean to argue that when Peg became theoreticized,
she suddenly became a philosopher. Obviously she never wrote anything
remotely like *The Republic*, and while the loss of her son politicized

her life, the loss of Socrates (as *The Seventh Letter* tells it) depoliticized Plato's. Still, it is worth recalling that Socrates was in the streets
rather than in the academy, and that the conversation in Book 1 of
The Republic is about everyday matters in everyday language. Indeed,
one of the interlocutors defends a notion of justice as helping friends and
harming enemies, which Socrates critiques by raising questions about
how we can distinguish our "true" or "real" friends from our false and
seeming ones.

My point in beginning with Peg Mullen is threefold: she represents a
response to loss without nostalgia; her reaction to Michael's death suggests why and how personal, political, and epistemological dimensions
of loss are more than contingently related though less than necessary;
and, most significantly, her story can be read as a parable about the emergence of political theory in classical Athens and its reemergence in otherwise disparate historical settings. At a minimum it reminds us that people
were and are driven to theorize by a need to make sense of a world that
suddenly appears out of joint as they themselves come to feel displaced
in it. More generally, I want to argue that while philosophy may begin
in wonder that things are the way they are (Aristotle), may be a preparation for death (Plato), or may be the acceptance of finitude, much political theory begins with loss. Loss animates it as an enterprise and forms
its problematic.[2]

To claim that political theory emerges and reemerges from a sense of
loss does not tell us very much unless we can specify how particular
theorists understand and represent that loss. Do they present it as an
aberration in a trajectory of progress, or as endemic to "the human condition"? What rhetorical or poetic devices, what metaphors or prophetic
intonations do they use to dramatize the loss they confront and promise
to move beyond or redeem? Do they embrace, indulge in, or resist nostalgia, counsel accommodation, endorse revolutionary praxis, or posit
some purer realm unsullied by the messiness or undisturbed by the frailty
of this world?

Why does loss so often haunt even the most utopian theoretical visions?
Unlike functionalist discourse, which assumes that loss can be erased
without a trace, Freud suggests that oblivion is not an irremediable absence but a presence absent only from itself, a veiled surface sheltering
what would only have been repressed, the crudely healed scar of an ampu-
tation forever memorable[3] like the cherry-choke tree on Sethe's back in
Toni Morrison's *Beloved*. Is that the case with political theories?

We also need to know how various theorists (Plato, Machiavelli, and
Marx, for instance) pictured, then responded to the absences and erasures
loss represents, and what filled the spaces in life and thought left
empty. How did they confront narratives of inevitable decline (or indeed

progress) of fate or history that would have made their theoretical endeav-
ors futile?

Finally, we need to know not only what is lost but who loses what
and who loses most. Peter Laslett writes about a "world we have lost,"
a world in which "the whole of life went forward in the family, in a circle
of love, familiar faces, known and fondled objects, all to human size."
Robert Wiebe tells a similar story about late-nineteenth-century
America, which he calls a "distended society." Nationalization, industrialization, mechanization, and urbanization led to a profound sense of
"dislocation and bewilderment." As men inadvertently shaped a world
that required them to range farther and farther from their communities,
"they tried desperately to understand the larger world in terms of their
small, familiar environments,"[4] to master a now impersonal world using
the customs of a face-to-face community.[5] While such stories, as I suggested in the previous chapter, can easily encourage a nostalgia that un-
deremphasizes how inscribed hierarchies of class, race, gender, ethnicity,
and religion operated in a now romanticized, naturalized past, they need
not do so. In the mid-1970s, historians such as E. P. Thompson, Lawrence Goodwyn, and Herbert Gutman saw nostalgia not as a pathology
of reaction, as Hofstadter and Schlesinger had twenty years earlier, but
as a legitimate way of being in the world. Tradition could contain and
encourage a critical perspective or spark of rebellion against the omnipo-
tence of the present. Here, nostalgia is not a symptom of ignorance and
backwardness but a retrieval of a preindustrial, precapitalist culture as
a source of political radicalism.

The knowledge of what is lost and who loses what and most cannot be
just about losses publicly recognized, as the above stories are. It must
include those that cannot be acknowledged as present and so cannot be
lost or grieved over. Judith Butler writes about preemptive loss and a
mourning for unlived possibilities. "If this [homosexual] love is from the
start out of the question, then it cannot happen, and if it does, it certainly
did not. If it does, it happens only under the official sign of its prohibition
and disavowal."[6] Her argument challenges us to identify circumstances
where loss is effaced, to ask about absent presences, and to distinguish
between loss and constitutive absences.

In what follows I want to offer four such narratives of loss: the synchronic (Homer and tragedy); the philosophic (Plato in *The Republic*);
the perspectival (Machiavelli's *Prince*); and the diachronic (Marx and
modernism). Each narrative tells a story about theory and loss, and each
tells us something about the power and danger of nostalgia. None is
purely what I say it is, and not all are given equal space. This is especially
true of the last, which is most familiar.

II

In pre-Platonic Greek thought loss is generally conceived synchronically (from the Greek *sun*, meaning "along with, in the company of, or side by side," and *chronos*, meaning "time") rather than diachronically. Though the life of man is likened to the cycles of nature ("hero" is related to words having to do with the seasons),[7] there is no notion of a historical process analogous to a natural one. And despite the fact that Hesiod describes a Golden Age from which his own has degenerated, and figures from Nestor (in the *Iliad*) to the orator Demosthenes refer to earlier better times, there is no initiatory moment outside of history that might provide a transcendent moral ideal to be recaptured or redeemed.[8] Because there was no sense of processes such as capitalization, disenchantment, or degeneration, there could be no redemptive moment when loss would be made good and the tragedy of human agency erased.

With no significant idea of afterlife (except in certain mystery cults), what counted was what men did in this one; and what counted in this life was excellence in words and deeds. Only the brilliance of one's achievements, especially on the battlefield, and the courage shown in the face of death could give one a second life on the lips of men. It was honor and glory that gave meaning to life and defined the human condition. Since the gods were immortal, they were immune to the ravages of old age and the finality of death. It was the intense Greek awareness of both that heightened their sense of beauty and their equally intense sense of loss. In choosing a short, glorious life, Achilles preserves his virility and strength; through death he becomes fixed in a beauty of an unending youth.

But the *Iliad* is a poem of loss: of men and cities, of friends and family, of life itself. Achilles poses this logic of loss and recompense in the starkest terms: life for song, home and old age for *kleos* (fame, glory, renown). "Achilles," Simon Goldhill writes, "can only carry into battle on his shield a representation of a social world he cannot take part in," but that we are reminded of by his foil Hector.[9]

There are of course moments of respite and relief: Hector with his wife and son, the reconciliation scene between Priam and Achilles, instances of ransom and recognition of guest friendship. But they just make the sense of loss all the more acute and unbearable.

By the epic's end the world is in flames. Hector has been killed; his city will soon be sacked and destroyed. Achilles has finally avenged the loss of his beloved Patroclos, but that, he knows, is prelude to his own death. Loss is victory's companion; death and weakness shadow mastery and strength. We are all equal in the end, Achilles complains. Even the greatest of Greek warriors and the son of a goddess confronts the pathos of death, the sudden change from the brightness of life to meaningless existence, from the joy of friendship and the responsibility of family to forsaking and being forsaken by them. Like Michael Eugene Mullen, these men die far from home and family, and no one, not their comrades nor their loved ones, can help them or make good their loss.[10] That is why the funeral games, a ritual of loss in Book 23, along with the mourning for Hector in Book 24, constitute an epitaph for everyone in the epic as well as for those mortals hearing of their deeds in song. The last line of the *Iliad*, "Such was the burial of Hector, breaker of horses," really is the end.

But not quite. The deeds of heroes live on as long as there are bards to tell their stories and audiences to hear and think about them. For example, one of the most vehement controversies about the *Iliad* concerns the episode where Odysseus, Phoinix, and Ajax come to offer Achilles recompense for Agamemnon's insult in hopes of inducing him to rejoin their ranks and reverse their flagging fortunes. Achilles rejects their offer with a violence of, and to, language that is unique in the epic, and he goes so far as to contemptuously dismiss the heroic ethic of which he is the supreme exemplar. No gifts can compensate for such an insult; no glory is worth a life if he like any other man dies in the end. Though this scene is distinctive for its intensity, it is, nonetheless, typical in the way it draws its readers/listeners into evaluating *kleos* with Achilles and makes us active participants in the "debate" he is having with himself and the three ambassadors about what sort of life is most worth living.[11]

The synchronic nature of loss and gain in the *Iliad* means that endings are also potential beginnings. For as death stalks life, so life is present in the living traditions of storytelling. Just as there are no necessary beginnings—the *Iliad* starts in the middle, and tragedians reinterpreted mythic traditions that were themselves polyvocal—there are no final endings, and those that are "forced," such as the deus ex machina in Euripidean plays, merely serve to emphasize the artificiality of an order that appears out of nowhere. Works like the *Iliad* and the *Odyssey* satisfy not only our desire for an ending but also a desire for the not-ending, the unendable, at the same time.[12]

The *Odyssey* is a story of a homecoming (*nostos*, from which "nostalgia" comes), which immediately sets it against the ethos of the *Iliad*, where Achilles rejects his *nostos* in favor of immortal glory.[13] Though home is the objective of Odysseus's journey and the end of his story, yet the end of the story is not the end of the journey, despite the fact that we have every reason to expect it to be. Having revealed himself, taken Penelope to bed, and had his revenge on the suitors, Odysseus engages in one more act. In the words of Margaret Anne Doody: "Having regained his own house, Odysseus leaves it to venture into the fields to find his humble father, the farmer, digging, in a tattered and dirty chiton." In contrast to the trials of Odysseus's journey home and the heroic ferocity of his revenge, Laertes is antiheroic. It is not just that he is, in terms of the poem, something of an embarrassment, but that he "casts our minds to the future, in which Odysseus himself will no longer be the middle-aged hero he is now, but an old man without the strength of arm to bend his bow."[14] Though there is a parallel scene in the *Iliad* where Priam and Achilles look upon one another's beauty as the latter remembers his father and so his own mortality, Priam is a majestic even if pitiable figure. Not so Laertes.

Perhaps the fullest articulation of synchronicity in Greek literature can be found in what is commonly known as the "choral ode in praise of man" in *Antigone*. The first thing to say about the ode is that it is not in praise of man but concerns what is strange and alien about human beings. I quote at length from the Grene translation:[15]

> Many the wonders, none
> is more wonderful than what is man.
> This is it that crosses the sea
> with the south winds storming and the waves swelling,
> breaking around him in roaring surf.
> He it is again who wears away
> the Earth, oldest of gods, immortal, unwearied, . . .
> (368–74)
>
> The tribe of the lighthearted birds he snares
> and takes prisoner the races of savage beasts
> and the brood of the fish of the sea,
> with the close-spun web of nets.
> A cunning fellow is man. His contrivances
> make him master of beasts of the field
> and those that move in the mountains.
> So he brings the horse with the shaggy neck
> to bend underneath the yoke;
> and also the untamed mountain bull;
> and speech and windswift thought
> and the tempers that go with city living
> he has taught himself, . . .
> (376–89)
>
> He has a way against everything,
> and he faces nothing that is to come
> without contrivance.
> Only against death
> can he call on no means of escape;

but escape from hopeless diseases
he has found in the depths of his mind.
With some sort of cunning, inventive
beyond all expectation
he reaches sometimes evil,
and sometimes good.

If he honors the laws of earth,
and the justice of the gods he has confirmed by oath,
high is his city; no city
has he with whom dwells dishonor
prompted by recklessness.
(393–408)

The Greek *deinos* (strange, wondrous) and its cognates refer both to that which inspires awe, such as technical ingenuity, intelligence, mastery, resourcefulness, and daring, and to that which inspires dread, such as the monstrous, evil, self-annihilating, and violent. These double meanings are played out in the ode (as well as in the ode's place in the play as a whole).

Human beings alone can master nature and use her for their own purposes. They are not, as animals are, passive "victims" of nature's imperatives or at the mercy of oceans, winds, and brute strength or dependent on nature's largesse. Their ingenuity harnesses nature's creatures and power; they plow the earth with oxen, trap birds and fish to eat, build shelters to protect themselves against the elements, invent medicines against disease. More than that, they have taught themselves language, thought, and civic virtue, creating cities that provide power, camaraderie, and a space for law and justice. Only death thwarts their power; only against death is human ingenuity helpless. And even death need not be the end. Those men fallen in war, Thucydides' Pericles tells his compatriots, "offered up their bodies for the common good and took for themselves that undying praise and that most distinctive tomb—not the one in which they lie, but the one in which their fame remains to be eternally remembered in words and deeds on every fitting occasion" (2.43).[16] Recall Hannah Arendt's argument from chapter 3 that the polis "is the space of men's free deeds and living words which could endow life with splendor—*ton bion lampron poieisthai*."

But then there is the other meaning of *deinos*. Humans may tame the sea, but they cannot tame their own passions. When men use nature to enhance her offerings, they assault her; mastery over nature and nature's creatures is a constant temptation to tyranny, as suggested by the fact that Antigone is likened to a bird and Creon seeks to yoke her (as well as others) as men do animals. How much pride can man take in his self-taught language, his reason, and his civic virtue if he has also "taught" himself how not to listen, how to turn such achievements to his own selfish purposes, using them, as Creon does, as instruments of oppression and violence?

Humans are the only creatures of nature who are unnatural in the sense of re-creating themselves against as well as with nature. This means that their home, their city, the place of justice, freedom, and power, is also a "sign" of their homelessness. We are unnatural, too, in the knowledge of our own mortality, which means that for us death is a traveling companion and haunting double. Thus our greatest achievements—freedom and knowledge—leave us absent to ourselves, necessarily divided and multiple, unsettled and unsettling. The question is whether we can acknowledge our condition without melancholy, nostalgia, or resentment.

There is another dimension to this doubleness. It is played out not in *Antigone* but in *Oedipus Tyrannos*. Michael Janover has argued that the "ailments" of nostalgia, in the sense of the pain of homesickness, exist in an "uncanny proximity to their converse, the pains of homeland." From this perspective not only are we sick when away from home; we can be sick of our home, of the places, times, and selves that seem to constitute a given identity. Such self-fracturing, such disgust with being too much at home, too much oneself yet paradoxically "not at all at one with oneself," describes the story of Oedipus. Such pains of longing for another place, another time, or another self can, for all the dangers of romanticism and resentment, "also be the refracting lenses of constructive critique." This is especially so given the indelible message of the play: that there is no innocent past to return to.[17]

In the *Iliad*, loss is endemic to the human condition. In it the inequalities evident to us in the treatment of Thersites, the dependent status of women, and the often lethal disparities of prowess pale before the shared recognition of mortality. We may well regard the heroic ethic as murderous and self-destructive. Indeed, the *Iliad* itself regards it that way even as it projects and instantiates it. Yet there is something to be said for a response to human finitude that avoids melancholy and nostalgia, ressentiment and redemption.

Though tragedy, as represented by the choral ode, also linked achievement and loss, the themes of the play together with the conditions of its performance give wider opportunity to human action.[18] However transgressive our achievements may be, we are capable of an agency not present in the *Iliad*. In this regard one could say that tragedy exists halfway between the pretheoretical self-contained world of epic and the transformative aspirations of Platonic philosophy. If drama does not envisage overcoming this world to produce new values, new men, and a new order, it does believe that things as they are—particularly Athenian political life—might be otherwise and better.

In the case of tragedy the issue of who loses is more prominent and so politicizes the idea of synchronicity and "the" human condition. Though it is not clear whether such prominence altered political practice, tragedy dramatizes loss by depicting its consequences for women, slaves, and barbarians. At least in the confines of the theater and dramatic festival the excluded and closeted appear on stage. In this space and moment the defeated survive; the indigestible, unassimilated and cross-grained, and otherwise effaced possibilities have at least a shadowy presence. And while it is true that a tragic sensibility precludes the idea of redemption, the beauty of its poetry provides a redemptive moment by transforming suffering and loss into a story of human endurance. In this respect at least, political theory carries forward a bardic tradition. Theorists, too, are singers of songs even if the hero is Socrates rather than Achilles and the audience is philosophers rather than the *aristoi* or *demos*.

III

Plato is thought to have ended all this because his rejection of tragedy and epic in the name of an ontologically grounded morality transmogrifies synchronicity into a toxic vision of the human condition. To leave the Cave is to ascend from the everyday world with its fleeting appearances, clashing opinions, and moral confusions to one in which moral and political judgments are univocal. In terms of *Antigone*, one could say that Plato believed that Creon had the right instincts but the wrong character and insufficient knowledge to accomplish what he intuitively knew had to be done. Order and harmony are indeed the goal of politics, but they cannot be found in or founded upon the world as presently constituted and understood.

Though much can be and has been said for this reading of *The Republic*, I believe it underestimates the continuities between epic, tragedy, and philosophy while overestimating Plato's rejection of synchronicity. An alternative reading of the dialogue suggests how Plato displaces synchronicity by incorporating its rhythms and sensibility into philosophical dialogue. This process of displacement is Plato's response to a loss which, not unlike that of Peg Mullen, is at once personal, political, and epistemological.

Sheldon Wolin emphasized the continuities between epic and theory in his discussion of "epic political theory." In Plato, epic theory has three dimensions. First, it imitates the heroic aspiration of achieving some memorable deed whose greatness will live on in the stories men (and women) tell about it. But here the theory is the deed. "If the great words failed to be translated into reality," Wolin writes, "if society could not be made into the image of the world, the world might endure nonetheless as a memorial to the aspirations of thought." Thus theory provides a "pattern of the good society which cannot be erased by forgetfulness or destroyed by history,"[19] and the tradition of political theory becomes a form of story-telling. Second, as this suggests, epic theory is an attempt to redeem in thought what is denied in practice. In these terms, *The Republic* is a meditation on and response to Plato's failure at Syracuse, and Plato is a theorist out of frustration rather than aspiration. Finally, the epic dimension of theory refers to its transformative ambition to recast all social relationships, revolutionize our conception of knowledge, and provide a new vision of the destiny of the human soul.

While *The Seventh Letter*[20] provides evidence for Wolin's argument that *The Republic* was, in part, a response to Plato's failure at Syracuse, the *Letter* also suggests another factor: the Athenian treatment of Socrates. In the *Letter* Plato says that the idea of the philosopher-king came to him because of the harassment of Socrates by his oligarchic friends and relatives and the trial and conviction of Socrates by the restored democracy. It was because of this that he drew back from entering Athenian public life. (Though Plato vaguely alludes to other deeds that deterred him, the treatment of Socrates is the only one specified.) That his erstwhile political allies, far from leading Athens out of injustice, were leading it further into it, and that the restored democracy, though surprisingly moderate, nonetheless condemned his friend and teacher to death despite the fact that he had "at the time when his accusers were themselves in misfortune and exile . . . refused to have any part in the unjust arrest of one of their friends [Leon or Salamis]" made all political alternatives seem hopelessly corrupt.

"The more I reflected upon what was happening," Plato writes, "on what kinds of men were active in politics, and upon the state of our laws and customs," the more he realized "how difficult it is to manage a city's affairs rightly." Indeed, the corruption of the city's laws and customs "was proceeding at such amazing speed that whereas at first I had been full of zeal for public life, when I noted these changes and saw how unstable everything was, I became . . . quite dizzy."[21] This did not stop him from reflecting on how to make the city more just, though it did make him wary enough to wait for the ideal moment. But after further reflection and perhaps continued disappointments, he reluctantly concluded that "all existing states are badly governed and the condition of their laws practically incurable, without some miraculous remedy and the assistance of fortune." Since it was only from the "height" of true philosophy that he was able to discern what the nature of justice was and how far existing states fell short of it, he decided that the "ills of the human race" would be perpetual until "either those who are sincerely and truly lovers of wisdom come into political power, or the rulers of our cities, by the grace of God, learn true philosophy."[22]

In this story political theorizing emerges from a sense of loss analogous to that suffered by Peg Mullen. In both cases personal loss is also political and epistemological: political in the sense that America and Athens forfeited their moral claim to patriotic attachment; epistemological in the sense of a felt need to discover the truth behind shifting appearances. For Peg as for Plato, the dizzying quality of events pushed them to seek firmer ground for belief and action.

As *The Seventh Letter* makes clear, Socrates' death convinced Plato of the irremediably corrupt status of Athens. By abandoning its moral principles to the extent of killing the man who best exemplified them, the city lost its bearings. Thus Socrates' death signified a twofold loss: that of a moral exemplar, teacher, guide, and friend; and the removal for Plato of an opportunity for honor, power, and achievement. Together they created not only a sense that something irretrievable had been lost and the world diminished by it, but a pervasive sense of loss in excess of anything in particular.

How did Plato or, rather, how does *The Republic* respond to this sense of loss? It does so in three ways. The first, which conforms to the conventional reading of the dialogue, generates a contrast between a political domain of unreality, deception, mutability, and loss and an ultimate changeless reality in which loss is a noncategory. The second represents the way in which a synchronic relationship is established between the conventional reading and elements in the text that challenge and interrogate it. The third is represented by a displacement of synchronicity into dialectic and dialogue.

The first response to loss is to create a world that would never kill another Socrates. This is the world ruled by philosopher-kings, themselves "selfless instruments of timeless truths."[23] In this world Socrates would be vindicated and avenged largely at the expense of democracy. Indeed, the ideal state with its harmony, unity, and naturalized hierarchies founded on moral certainty seems a virtual inversion of what we know about Athens, especially as it is presented in the portrait of democracy in Book 8.

Yet vindicating and avenging Socrates seems to require his erasure. For the Socrates who is conducting the dialogue would be superfluous, if not dangerous, in the society that *The Republic* creates. We know that Plato went to Syracuse in the hopes of turning a tyrant into a philosopher-king. But we also know, or have reason to believe—based on what "Socrates" says in the *Apology* and *Crito*—that Socrates would never have gone to Syracuse and would not endorse the idea of a philosopher-king. Nor is there evidence in these early dialogues that Socrates had anything like a theory of the forms or the view of moral certainty that is entailed by it.

The second response speaks to the paradox of a vindication that is also erasure. Here Socrates continues to do in death what he did in life: talk to everyone he meets about the choices they have made and do not know that they are making. Here his death dramatically frames the themes and urgency of the dialogue. Socrates' loss is a constantly felt absence drawing the search for understanding and knowledge forward, exploring alternative narratives in which his death can be given meaning. In these terms, Socrates lives on in the dialogue with the interlocutors, with Plato, and with us.

In this voice loss does not generate visions of redemption and certainty. For all of Socrates' clear endorsement of moral principles about virtue's being knowledge, about accepting injustice done to one rather than committing it, "he" is aware of the contingent nature of every moral claim. Political theory is not a preparation for death or a gesture of contempt toward the world of becoming. It is the carrying on of talk, speech, and dialogue without end. The abjuring of endings is suggested not only by what seem distracting interruptions (as when Socrates says his argument is just to please the interlocutors, or that he will say only what the occasion requires), but by the ending of Book 1, the beginning of Book 5, and the concluding Myth of Er.[24]

The significance of aporetic dialogue lies in the possibility that while we do seek closure, we also seek the continuation of life that the inconclusiveness of dialogue represents. So we come to endings only to defer them by finding ways for the talk to begin again. Endings are about power; to subscribe to an ending—the end—is to subscribe to power of some kind.[25] To resist such endings is to resist the power to stop the dialogue (though under some circumstances silence can be eloquent). If the real ending is death, then resistance means life: of a text, its readers/interlocutors, and its argument. In these terms Socratic political theory as embodied in this second voice is not a preparation for death but an affirmation of life.

If my argument about the two voices in *The Republic* has merit, then the synchronicity banished in the first voice reappears, not so much in the second alone, as in the tension between the two. As with Homer and *Antigone*, achievement is shadowed by transgression, gain accompanied by loss. The gains: intelligence, rationality, intellect, certainty, and with them redemption against the vicissitudes of becoming; harmony and order, goodness and justice, and the achievement of community. Yet against this assertion of mastery and hope is the insufficiency of mortals, which guarantees the incompleteness, if not the futility, of the quest. But "insufficiency" begs the question insofar as it ignores the loss and erasure

"Platonic" philosophy demands: citizenship, friends, family, the body, the pleasures of particular places and people, the texture of ordinary recognitions and loves.

What synchronicity exists in *The Republic* is subject to philosophical interrogation as it obviously is not in epic and tragedy. Homeric heroes live on in the stories of glorious deeds passed on from generation to generation. The reality of those deeds, their "ontological" ground, depends upon a world of comrades and friends, of action and publicity, and of singers whose formulaic retellings were this-worldly, however much inspired by the Muse. Characters could protest against the injustice, even absurdity, of the heroic ethic as Achilles does in Book 9 of the *Iliad*. But there was no other ethos for him to embrace, no other superior life available to him as there is for philosophers in *The Republic*. And though Achilles may envy the gods their immortality, he knows and even prides himself on the fact that he, not they, must pass the ultimate test of courage when encountering death. Because mortals exist in time and places with others, synchronicity literally defines the human condition. The question is whether this itself represents a falling away and insufficiency to be remedied. Certainly there are ways in which *The Republic* suggests it is: that the frailty and darkness of life as exemplified by politics can and must be redeemed for men to have an end to what Plato calls "the ills of the human race."

IV

Like Plato, Machiavelli became a theorist by default. Though one cannot imagine the former seconding the latter's declaration that he loved his country more than his soul—not only because care of the soul trumps patriotism for Plato, but because he advised foreign princes—both were driven to theoretical reflection by a sense of loss that was at once personal, political, and epistemological. The personal aspect was Machiavelli's being forced out of office, thereby being denied access to the realm in which he felt most alive. Political loss had a general as well as specific aspect. The general one concerned the tenuous status of republicanism not merely at the moment and in Florence, but in the face of emerging political forms of monarchical states. The specific one concerned the disarray of Florence and Italy as a whole. Ravaged by petty quarrels, random violence, narrow ambition, and an interfering church strong enough to prevent common action but too weak to create the conditions for it, both were incapable of maintaining their liberty. The loss was epistemological in the sense that men had forgotten how to gain political knowledge and what was distinctively political about it.

As was the case with Plato these crises induced a dizziness that para-lyzed understanding and action. Here is J. H. Plumb on politics in Renais-sance Italy:

"Horror waits on princes," wrote Webster, the Elizabethan dramatist for whom the bloodstained annals of Italy had a compulsive fascination. Cer-tainly, the way to power was strewn with corpses; men murdered their wives, wives poisoned their husbands, brother slaughtered brother, family raged against family, city sacked city. In 1402 the chief members of the ruling house of Lodi were burned alive on the public square; at Bologna in 1445 the peo-ple, enraged by the slaughter of their favorite family, the Bentivoglio, hunted down their enemies and nailed their steaming hearts to the doors of the Benti-voglio's palace, as a token of their love. Yet Bologna was a tranquil city com-pared to many, and even bloodless when matched with Foligno; there a noble—Pietro Rasiglia—cuckolded by his prince, took his vengeance. He flung his faithless wife from the turrets of his castle and killed two brothers of the Prince. Retribution rapidly followed. The whole Rasiglia clan, men, women, and children, were butchered and chopped up; their joints, hung like meat, were paraded through the streets. Of course, the ghoulish chroniclers liked to heighten the horror, and their macabre imaginations rioted in sadistic fantasy. [Plumb is not doing too badly either.] Yet all allowances made, poli-tics became a murderous game in which death in bed came only to the skillful or the lucky. The savagery used by men in pursuit of power was due to the nature of society and the prizes which it offered.[26]

Here is the opening of Machiavelli's famous chapter 25 on Fortuna in *The Prince*:

It is not unknown to me that many have held, and still hold, the opinion that the things of this world are controlled by Fortune and by God, that men with their wisdom cannot control them, and on the contrary, that men can have no remedy whatsoever for them; and for this reason they might judge that they need not sweat much over such matters but let them be governed by fate. This opinion has been more strongly held in our own times because of the great variation of affairs that has been observed and that is being observed every day which is beyond human conjecture. Sometimes, as I think about such things, I am inclined to their opinion. Nevertheless, in order that our free will not be extinguished, I judge it to be true that Fortune is the arbiter of one half of our actions, but that she still leaves the control of the other half, or almost that, to us.[27]

Given such unprecedented, relentless, rapid, and violent changes, many are tempted by intellectual and political fatalism. Now Machiavelli does not dismiss this view out of hand. In fact, he admits his own susceptibility to it. Yet he does not give in to it because doing so would ensure it was true, since there is always a self-fulfilling dimension to political beliefs. A theory, or at least a political theory, does not merely describe the world but carries prescriptive force in the sense of creating an imaginary future that either invites or discourages theoretical and political agency. Nor is Machiavelli willing to join those who, because so much seems beyond human control, give up the idea of control altogether. A demand for mastery is so easily disappointed that endorsing it becomes a recipe for cynicism and passivity. The challenge, then, is to accept contingency without a longing for certainty, to explore the moral possibilities of politics without endorsing an antipolitical moralism.

Machiavelli likens fortune to a river whose elemental power threatens to overwhelm every obstacle unless one takes the precaution of building dikes and levees. If rightly constructed, these not only will limit nature's destructiveness but can even turn its elemental power to creative purposes. This image implies two things: that fortune presents opportunities for as well as dangers to the exercise of human power (*virtù*); and that fortune is not just external natural forces but includes the adequacy of human responses to it. The domination of Fortuna then signifies human failures.

What then are Machiavelli's precautions against the domination of Fortuna? Wherein does his theoretical *virtù* lie? How does he propose to provide men with the intellectual and political wherewithal to act in the face of this seemingly implacable rush of events without falling into the destructive dialectic of mastery and abasement? He has, I believe, five related strategies: the use of realism; a critique of moralism; an antinostalgic reading of the past; a proposal for and definition of political knowledge; and the substitution of renewal for redemption.

The first precaution Machiavelli takes is his use of realism. To say that Machiavelli uses realism as a strategy to shore up human agency and direct the elemental forces of nature (including a prince's passions for power and glory) means that he is no realist. This is not to deny that he had a pessimistic view of human nature; believed that the ends justify the means; regarded violence as a necessary dimension of politics; saw politics as a limit on morality, rather than vice versa; thought politics involved disguise and deceit; insisted that a single-minded commitment to goodness, rather than bringing success, brought failure; endorsed the significance of will and passion in politics; claimed intentions or the state of one's soul were largely irrelevant political considerations; or thought that in politics men needed to rely on the instincts of a fox and the animal power of a lion. It is to insist, in the first instance, that we need to be leery in our assertions about someone who advocates disguise, deceit, and changing with the times. It is, in the second place, to remember that Machiavelli advocated views that qualified this realism. For instance: that men could become republican citizens and so better than their nature;

that only a few very extraordinary ends justified any means; that one should use violence and cruelty economically; that his critique of morality was (I shall argue) a critique of moralism; that his insistence that politics requires disguise and fraud draws attention to the rhetorical and theatrical dimensions of political activity; that his division of goodness and success must be reconciled with the way he comes to insist that the prince must moderate his excesses so as to maintain his power and ensure glory, thus providing prudential grounds for morality; and that emphasis on will and passion (as with others of his ideas) is not limited to realists.

What I am arguing is that realism is Machiavelli's strategy for getting himself heard against the competition of others and allaying Medici suspicions. One way of doing both was to make what he said seem necessarily true and obvious while insisting that the means by which such obvious truths were discovered—such as extensive study of the past and an ability to see from high and low—were not. In this regard consider the lengths to which Machiavelli goes, in the "Dedication" to *The Prince*, to distance himself from those self-indulgent advisers who lard their advice with rhetorical embellishments. By contrast he has "neither decorated nor filled it [his work] with fancy sentences, with rich and magnificent words, or with any other rhetorical or unnecessary ornamentation" (78).[28] His own rhetoric denies that he has any; *The Prince* is simply a reflection of reality. Thus the words he uses represent the facts of the world. No interpretation intervenes to distort his mapping of the political forces and/or presentation of choices a prince must make. His competition may need copious references to ancient authority to establish their own. But he does not, which is why he has exactly two such references in the entire *Prince*. His authority comes from verisimilitude. His talent is packaging such truths in a terse, easy-to-read tool kit for princes on the go.[29]

Consider in this regard the utter confidence evinced in chapter 2. In a few brief sentences Machiavelli maps the political terrain. "All states and all dominions . . ." he begins, and the rest of this very short chapter divides all the political regimes that ever existed into a few categories.

The second precaution Machiavelli takes is a critique of moralism, as exemplified by Weber's ethic of ultimate ends. Moralism is the declaration of absolutes in a world of contingencies, a dogmatic idealism indifferent to political realities, and an otherworldliness that has corrupting influences it does not acknowledge.

Moralists say "never" and "always." They are committed first to the purity of their intentions and state of their soul and are only secondarily, if at all, concerned with the consequences of their righteousness.[30] At the level of abstract principle at which they think, they need not ask how the morality they embrace came into the world. If they dared to ask, they would be forced to acknowledge that great states are almost always founded on violence, and that without the existence of such states moral life could not be lived. It would then follow that it is self-contradictory to criticize what makes morality possible on moral grounds. Politics must be a limit on morality before morality can be a limit on politics.

Moralism includes the fetishism of ideals. If one writes to be useful rather than to just spin out intellectual fantasies, one must be attentive to how truths and ideals can be made effective. This means that truths and ideals must arise out of the political world itself. If they do not, if the imagined political societies are only wishful thinking, they can never come into existence, though the desire and belief that they can will have real deleterious political consequences. "For there is such a gap between how one lives and how one ought to live," Machiavelli famously writes, "that anyone who abandons what is done for what ought to be done learns his ruin rather than his preservation; for a man who wishes to make a vocation of being good at all times will come to ruin among so many who are not good. Hence it is necessary for a prince who wishes to maintain his position to learn how not to be good, and to use this knowledge or not according to necessity" (126–27). As several commentators have pointed out, Machiavelli is not recommending that one abandon altogether what ought to be, but insisting that any political vision must be accountable to and for the world it seeks to transform. Nor is he advocating being evil. Rather, he insists that when necessity requires it, a strategic use of not being good is the only way to make goodness real. Any prince who refuses to abide by these dicta will lose his power and likely increase the evil and violence in his city.

Much of this critique of moralism and idealism is present in Machiavelli's judgment of Christianity.[31] Like idealism, Christianity is otherworldly but ignores confronting the worldly implications of its unworldliness. For instance, its counsel of humility promotes passivity and subjection to authority, thereby leaving the worst men free to dominate politics and discouraging "good" men from trying to alter whatever political circumstances happen to exist. This not only increases the immorality of human life; it also insulates political miscreants from (conventional) "moral" reproach. The language of Christian virtue, in promoting respect for existing authority, allows the rich to present themselves as the wise protectors of the people's liberties and encourages the poor to accept this self-serving self-presentation.[32]

Despite its otherworldliness, moralism provides a reading of the past that legitimates certain attitudes toward the present and expectations about the future. In its hands history becomes a morality play where good and evil battle for supremacy. States like Rome and Sparta, or figures like Brutus and Romulus, are either pure or corrupt, righteous or damnable. The result is a nostalgia that reinforces the passivity already made attrac-

tive by the dizzying pace of change. It is against such nostalgia that Machiavelli offers a political (in Nietzsche's terms, a monumental) reading of
the past, a specific idea of political knowledge, and the notion of renewal
as a political response to loss.

The problem is not that people ignore the past, but that they are in
thrall to a sanitized version of it. Some are titillated by past deeds and
actors as if they were watching a play that had little import beyond the
moment of performance. Others aestheticize the past in the double sense
of admiring its literature and art while ignoring its politics, and purging
politics of power so it can be viewed as a work of art. By depoliticizing
ancient societies, they separate politics and culture, education from political education, in the way the ancients themselves did not even when their
self-presentation might indicate otherwise. Still others philosophize the
ancients: again, the double sense of only reading philosophers and reading
them as philosophers, even when they were responding to political crises.
In these terms, imaginary republics such as one finds in *The Republic*
become even more rarefied. As Claude Lefort reminds us, "the classical
search for the best government proceeded from the experience of and the
critical reflection on corrupt regimes." For Machiavelli, "the assumptions
of the ancient philosophers have come to justify new forms of corruption." Still others worshiped the past as constituting a new religion, not
in the pagan civic sense Machiavelli commends but in a Christianized
secular sense. Thus Greece or Rome, Athens or Sparta, or the Roman
Republic becomes a transcendent moment of perfection compared to
which we mere mortals are utter failures.[33] We unworthy ones cannot
hope to compete with such achievements. Better to let things be as they
are and take pleasure in the contemplation of a greatness that is totally
beyond our ken.[34]

It is against such paralyzing nostalgia that Machiavelli offers a political
reading of the past.[35] That reading has critical and constructive moments.
The critical one begins with a denial that the inferiority of the present is
a necessary and permanent condition. If one learns the "right" things
from the past, the present can become its equal or even surpass it, given
that the past did not have itself to study. Since human nature is largely
constant and the central questions of public life recur in every epoch, the
past becomes a repository of political experiences for the present. What
this implies is that any dismissal of one's own time in some grand gesture
of ennui or contempt is a foppish luxury.

To indulge in such posturing is to embrace a debilitating self-loathing
while encouraging a corrosive cynicism. Such melancholic displays are
a pathological response to loss analogous to the one Freud analyzes in
"Mourning and Melancholia." There he describes the melancholic as
someone who so fixates on an actual loss that it promotes a profound

impoverishment of the ego. That is because melancholics engage in self-flagellation, proclaiming their moral inferiority and worldly incapacities. Such impassioned self-abasement seems so excessive, so radically dispro-portionate to what occasioned it, that the patient seems delusional. But, Freud insists, if we look further, we find that while the most violent of their self-condemnations does not fit them, it does fit someone else whom the patient loved or may still love, so that the self-reproaches are masked accusations against a lost love object. More than that, the melancholic's sense of loss eventually expands beyond the death of a loved one to in-clude every situation in which the "patient" feels slighted, neglected, or disappointed.[36] In political terms, the nostalgic's contempt for his age is an act of aggression and resentment, a pique and irritation at not being more honored.

The constructivist moment involves a narrative of Roman history that contests the reigning one, and the creation of true fictions that exhibit the principles of successful action in the past to enable similar ones in the present.

Machiavelli had his own ideal to compete with those imaginary repub-lics he scorns in *The Prince*. His ideal is Rome. But not the Rome of contemporary humanists who presented the Roman Republic as a harmo-nious community guided by the wisdom of the Senate. His ideal Rome was full of social divisions and class antagonism, and these, not unity and order, are what made Rome great. Those who celebrate the intrinsic virtue of Roman institutions or the virtuous nature of her citizens ignore the role such quarrels played in avoiding tyranny and license, as well as con-testing an authority that would, left to its own devices, have become too petrified to adjust to the times. In this narrative the usual story of the agitations of the people destroying an otherwise peaceful and good city are seen to be self-serving *and* politically naive.

Machiavelli's writings are full of stories about successful and unsuccess-ful actors and ventures. Such stories are playlets that dramatize events while distilling the principles of action operative in them. The point of these dramas is to teach not just precepts of right action but the political sensibility that made those actions and actors successful (barring com-pletely unforeseen strokes of fortune). And the past is essential for such teaching, since the present lacks inspiring examples of *virtù*. The combina-tion of this arduously gained knowledge of great deeds of the past to-gether with extensive experience of the present is the gift Machiavelli of-fers to Lorenzo in the form of *The Prince*.

The claim Machiavelli makes here, that political knowledge comes from the ability to inhabit two times, is complemented by his claim that it also requires the ability to inhabit two places. Here is the famous passage in the introduction to *The Prince* where Machiavelli likens himself to a landscape painter.

> Neither do I wish that it be thought presumptuous if a man of low and inferior station dares to debate and regulate the rule of princes; for just as those who paint landscapes place themselves in a low position on the plain in order to consider the nature of the mountains and high places, and place themselves atop mountains in order to study the plains, in like manner, to know well the nature of the people one must be a prince, and to know well the nature of princes one must be of the people. (78)

Because the prince occupies one position only, his power is also his powerlessness, since he lacks the double perspective that would enable him to change with the times and sustain his position. For the same reason he lacks the crucial political knowledge of the impressions he makes on others and they have of him. In these terms, political power and political knowledge require the ability to look down from on high and up from below, in contrast to the morally and epistemologically privileged position ascent and height have in *The Republic* and the Christian theology of heaven and hell. The epistemological implication is that political knowledge is built up discursively rather than deduced from a metaphysical, theological, or ontological premise. The equally radical political implication is that those who are low have a part of political knowledge as essential as the part held by those who are of higher status.[37]

This does not mean Machiavelli is a partisan of the people. Though he praises their virtues, his commitment is neither to them nor to the prince but to their mutual recognition of the shared dependency that is the ground of political power. To the prince Machiavelli promises power and glory. But to get that, he must moderate some of his excesses, for the same reason performers modify their performances to receive the applause they crave. So the prince must be moral or rather be seen to be moral, or at least not too immoral, if he is to be successful—a not inconsiderable limitation when appearance is the only thing that counts. To the people Machiavelli teaches two things: that the prince's dependence on them means they have more power than they know; and how to make political rather than moralistic judgment of princes.

There is a sense in which the dual perspective that defines Machiavelli's notion of political power and knowledge extends to his idea of founding. That sense can be explored in terms of Hannah Arendt's characterization of Roman politics. At the heart of that politics, from the beginning of the republic until the end of the imperial era, stands the conviction of the sacredness of foundation. Unlike the Greeks, for whom the founding of a body politic was a common occurrence, the Romans saw foundation as the "central, decisive, unrepeatable beginning of their whole history, a unique event."[38]

Founding figures prominently in Machiavelli's thought as well, and the Roman founding is the one that matters above all others. At one and the same time he perpetuates the sacredness of foundations in the Latin sense of religion (re-ligare, meaning "to be tied back, obligated, to the enormous, almost superhuman, and hence legendary effort . . . to found for eternity")[39] and undercuts it. The founding story he chooses to tell (there were alternatives) is that of fratricide. On the one hand, the killing of a brother dramatizes, as does Brutus's killing of his sons and Lucretia's suicide, the sacrifice great republics require. Yet fratricide is also a story likely to provoke skepticism toward sacredness, given Augustine's use of fratricide as a reason to condemn the pretensions of Rome and politics generally. Thus while the founding is necessary, it is not a moment of perfection and unity to be revered. What can it mean to be "tied back" and "obligated" to such a legendary founding? This attitude toward foundation is consonant with three other aspects of his thought: his rewriting of Roman history to emphasize the role of division and conflict in sustaining Roman power; the cynical way he tells the story of Numa's pretending to cavort with a nymph[40] as a strategy to establish religion in Rome; and his insistence on the inseparability of good and evil.

If good and evil are inseparable, there can be no apocalyptic endings any more than there can be pure beginnings, and redemptive narratives are read out of politics. Of course Machiavelli is no more above using the language of redemption when it accomplishes a worthy end (witness the last chapter of The Prince) than he is above advising the prince to use whatever means necessary to establish and maintain his power.[41] But the invocation of the Christian prophecy of the Second Coming in that chapter in an appeal to the Medici has the same distancing effect that the story of fratricide and the origins of Roman religion has in the founding mythology. What is notably absent in Machiavelli is any narrative of redemption, any story of final deliverance and perfection, atonement and harmony, salvation and moral certainty.

What Machiavelli offers in place of redemption is the idea of renewal. One reason for Rome's longevity was her ability to deal with those crises that threatened the disintegration of the city. That she was able to deal with them in ways that exorcised corruption while invigorating the citizenry had to do with her institutions, the virtue of individuals produced by them, and their ability to remind their compatriots about what it was they shared that made their liberty and power possible. Such reminders did feature recourse to the founding myth. But given the substance of that myth, any invocation of community, let alone brotherhood, would be highly problematic.

One can think of renewals as replenishing and reviving civic virtue through continuous rearticulations of origins that respond to the exigencies of changing times. Though such renewals are most dramatic where the city's existence is in the balance, Machiavelli's idea of it is more extensive in two respects. To begin with, because politics is at every moment poised on irresolution, each decision is a form of renewal, not necessarily because of what is decided, but because the very act of decision reaffirms and exemplifies the liberty of a free people to decide for themselves. Second, there is the sense in which renewal is an appeal to the culture institutions create from the actual but varyingly corrupt practices those institutions now sanction. While the Romans and Machiavelli emphasize institutional politics, institutions, like the prince, have a propensity to become ossified unless there is a way of reconstituting them, of having something like a Jeffersonian revolution every generation. Some of this flexibility was provided by the mixed nature of the Roman constitution itself and its provision for extraordinary powers in times of crisis. But some of it came from the political culture, which was at once fuller and more formless than even these emergency powers.

Machiavelli's notion of renewal allows for the significance of appeals to common origins without reifying them, to foundations that acknowledge those conflicts communities write over in their subsequent history, and to beginnings that must be begun again. In this he recognizes the need for invoking the past in a political way that forestalls nostalgia and narratives of redemption. Lacking a story of inevitable progress or decline, he restores the idea of synchronicity while emphasizing the political dimension present in its Greek meaning.

I have argued that Machiavelli uses realism as a way of establishing his theoretical bona fides and allaying Medici suspicions. I have also suggested that he is sympathetic to the sense of futility that came on his contemporaries in the wake of the wildly fluctuating vicissitudes of fortune. Though one must always be alert to the strategic dimension of Machiavellian thought, especially in *The Prince*, there seems to be an element of desperation to his realism there, as if he needs to reassure himself as much as his compatriots that there are still spaces for political and theoretical *virtù*. Given the unanticipated consequences of our deeds (what Weber called the ethical irrationality of the world), exaggerated by particular historical circumstances, there is a question of whether politics, particularly republican politics, is possible (which is why Francisco Guicciardini regarded Machiavelli's republicanism as utopian). Think, for instance, about the degree of mastery and accuracy of prediction necessary to realize Machiavelli's advice about well-used cruelties and economical use of violence. Suppose, for instance, that a virulently imperialistic fascist regime were to come to power in Russia. Would we then look back at 1989 as a disaster? Does not Machiavelli's advice require a degree of foresight that, if we looked too closely, would intimidate action in the way he wishes to avoid?

If this reading has any merit, Machiavelli's realism is born of desperation as much as of confidence, is as much a prophecy of hope and an act of faith as evidence of mastery and control. It is also a readmission, however inadvertent, of the tragic synchronicity of the choral ode against the philosophical tradition's efforts at erasure.

But it would be too unperspectival to leave matters here. For despite a resonance with Aristotle, Machiavelli asks a new kind of question: do division and conflict necessarily and always signify corruption, or can they be a sign of political and intellectual vitality?

Here is Claude Lefort:

> For the thinker, is the experience of conflict not a source of endless questioning? For the political actor, is it not a reason for accepting ultimate indeterminacy, whenever he is confronted with the requirements of judging and acting? For the city, is it not an incentive for his historical creation?[42]

V

Peg Mullen, Plato, and Machiavelli all attest to the profound disorientation that attends loss. Plato in his reaction to the treatment of Socrates and Machiavelli in his response to the pace of change admit to feeling dizzy and momentarily incapacitated. Neither gives in to those feelings (nor does Peg Mullen, for that matter), unless one reads *The Republic*'s philosophical rejection of politics as doing so. But Machiavelli does something more: he enables us to see why even such rapid changes are or must be seen to be opportunities for *virtù*; and he allows us to see his susceptibility to the lure of nostalgia and redemptive hopes in the face of such transformations before insisting that they lead to political disaster.

In some respects Marx's famous description of capitalism as revolutionizing economic and social life, creating constant uncertainty by dissolving every relationship while preventing any new ones from solidifying, reads like a gloss on Machiavelli's discussion of Fortuna.[43] Yet for Marx, Machiavelli's turn to Rome is itself a kind of nostalgia. Here is Marx in *The Eighteenth Brumaire of Louis Napoleon* on the distraction of republican rhetoric in the French Revolution.

> The tradition of all the dead generations weighs like a nightmare on the brain of the living. And just when they seem engaged in revolutionising themselves and things, . . . they anxiously conjure up the spirits of the past to their service

and borrow from them names, battle slogans and costumes in order to present the new scene of world history in this time-honoured disguise and this borrowed language. Thus Luther donned the mask of the Apostle Paul, the Revolution of 1789 to 1814 draped itself alternately as the Roman Republic and the Roman Empire, and the Revolution of 1848 knew nothing better to do than to parody, in turn, 1789 and the revolutionary tradition of 1793 to 1795.[44]

The leaders and parties of the Revolution performing "the task of their time in Roman costume and with Roman phrases" diverted attention from the mundane sobrieties of commercial reality surrounding them.

Marx's rejection of Machiavelli's political use of the past is possible because he erases the problem of Fortuna that haunted Machiavelli with the process of dialectical materialism. It is true that the vividness of Marx's description/evocation of capitalism's human costs is unsurpassed. But the synchronicity present in *Antigone*'s choral ode is effaced by a narrative of historical progress in which God's curse on Adam and Eve—that they and all their progeny are fated to enmity, sexual inequality, and unceasing, unproductive, and unrewarding labor—is redeemed by capitalism and communism. In this diachronic narrative, loss and pain, alienation and contradiction, are redeemed by the certainty of a better future. As we shall see in chapter 7, even death seems to dissolve in a vision of agency where men and women are able to integrate identity and activity, being and doing, in demystified form. Here change means liberation and renewal,[45] and the idea and expression of loss become delusional and pathological.[46] To the extent that one loses a sense of loss in Marx and Enlightenment thought generally, to that extent the story I have told about political theory belongs in the dustbin of history.

Until quite recently neoliberals and globalizers extended this narrative not so much by standing Marx on his head as by rewriting his final chapter. Thus Victor Nee has argued that it is state socialism that is an outdated transitory mode of production whose internal contradictions have led to capitalism. It is state socialism, not capitalism, that "appropriates surplus directly from the immediate producers and creates and structures social inequality through the processes of reallocation."[47] But the Fukyamian moment has largely passed. Despite its apologists, globalization as process ideology, where corporate giants have "the technical means and strategic vision to burst old limits—of time, space, national boundaries, language, custom, and ideology,"[48] is increasingly seen as politically disabling. The existence of unaccountable corporate power and the dizzying pace of change it demands have left men and women with a sense of loss analogous to that discerned by Wiebe and Laslett in the previous century.

Two things complement these developments of late-twentieth-century capitalism. The first has to do with modern notions of time. Of all historical periods, modernity, Terry Eagleton argues, is the only one to designate itself in terms of a dazzling, dismaying experience of time that is no longer located in history, habit, or custom but in their opposite. "The modern," he writes, "is that which reduces everything which happened up to half an hour ago to an oppressive traditionalism," an ironic self-representation given that nothing is more time-honored than efforts to break with the past.[49] Second, there is a vertiginous historicizing that reveals every thought, feeling, attribute, and event to be a historical construction with its own particular formation and trajectory. In this narrative nature, God, citizen, and self are presented in an assemblage of ideological symptoms and cultural practices that, precisely because they are invented by power, lose any political innocence they may have had.[50] As the previous discussions indicate, I have considerable sympathy for such skepticism and the genealogical analyses that often accompany it (though I do think Machiavelli escapes their strictures). But too often the critique of nostalgia is too impatient with the sense of loss that makes it attractive to many and compelling to a few. Though usually critics of Enlightenment thought, genealogists sometimes assign the same rhetorical function to "nostalgia" that their theoretical opponents assign to "unrealistic" or "irrational." Finally, the precipitous critique of nostalgia intimidates naming loss, thereby contributing to what might be called the nostalgia of the present. This is particularly so when present conditions of fragmentation are projected back onto all previous ages.

This impatience is more problematic when, as now, a sense of loss pervades or informs our public discourse. Consider the unrelenting pace and demands of globalization; the lamented end of what Henry Luce dubbed "the American Century"; Samuel Huntington's disappointment that the revolutionary hopes of 1989 have ended not in exultation or harmony but in delusion and bloody local conflicts; Robert Bellah's conviction that our spiritual life is utterly "impoverished"; Alisdair MacIntyre's complaint that not only is morality not what it once was but what once was morality has, for all intents and purposes, disappeared; and Robert Putnam's concern that we are bowling alone. In sum, modernization was a bill of goods with the price tag left off. Since America was the harbinger of the modernized future, such disillusionment affects us most of all. We are no longer a new world dedicated to spreading liberty everywhere. We are no longer innocents with a special mission and vision of the future. But if our motives are no purer than those of others, if we are not exceptional and a vision of the future, then we must renounce any special moral mission in the world. Such renunciation brings mortality to center stage. When revolutionary hopes are crushed and projects for reform are frustrated, erasure of pain and loss is less successful. Perhaps part of the cynicism, apathy, dystopianism, and commodification of religion adhered to dogmatically is the return of the repressed in the form of a tragic sensibility.

How might political theory deal with this sense of loss while resisting both an enervating nostalgia and a redemptive politics? To begin with, it might explore the distinctively political dimension of such loss. By this I mean three things: examine historically and comparatively those conditions that have called such responses forth; rearticulate a notion of politics as preeminently concerned with a public realm, as distinct from but not opposed to "the" private realm; and attend to the way inequalities of power and wealth must shape any analysis of or response to loss. Second, it might explore what may be a prototypical American way of dealing with loss—that is, not dealing with it at all. Whether we look to Tocqueville's discussion of how Americans are in constant motion, or the harsh lesson of equality of opportunity for those who lose the race, or our quarantining of signs of mortality by having the aged, diseased, infirm, senile, and dying put in special places run by professionals, this is not a nation that understands loss publicly. In this regard political theory might explore public forms of grieving, allowing "we the people" to confront, integrate, but also move on from loss as Sethe and Paul D seem to do in Toni Morrison's *Beloved*. Third, political theory might do the same with genealogy so that "real" loss, including the sort Butler discusses, can be acknowledged. This means talking again about the common good, public spiritedness, civic virtue, citizenship, public freedom, and power as part of what Simon Critchley calls an "austere messianism."[51]

Finally, political theories may need to reject the fetishism of the present as well as narratives of inevitability for Machiavellian reasons. That means generating critiques of the present drawn from the past and finding spaces for theoretical and civic agency no matter what the pace of change and how deep the crisis. That is what this and the other essays in this book hope to provide.

VI

The Polis, Globalization, and the Citizenship of Place

As my work proceeded, it acquired anunexpected and in ways
alarming dimension. I could not help being struck, again and
again, by an overpowering sense of déjà vu, far more than for
any other period of ancient history known to me: the distant
mirror that Barbara Tuchman held up from the fourteenth century
A.D. for our own troubled age is remote and pale compared to the ornate, indeed, rococoglass in which Alexandria,
Antioch and Pergamon reflect contemporary fads, failings and
aspirations. . . from the urban malaise to religious fundamentalism, from Veblenism to haute cuisine, from funded scholarship and mandarin literature to a flourishing dropout counter-
culture, from political impotence in the individual to
authoritarianism in government, from science perverted for
military ends to illusionism for the masses, from spiritual
solipsism . . . to the pursuit of the plutocratic dream. Contemporary cosmopological speculation seems to be taking us
straight back to the Stoic world view.
—Peter Green[1]

[T]he clock of transition runs at three different paces. "The
hour of the lawyer" is the shortest; legal changes may be
enacted in months. "The hour of the economist" is longer:
dismantling command economies and establishing functioning
markets must take years. But the longest is "the hour of the
citizen": transforming ingrained habits, mental attitudes,
cultural codes, value systems, pervasive discourses. This may
take decades and presents the greatest challenge.
—Ralf Dahrendorf[2]

THE QUESTION that frames this chapter is easily stated even if its answer is not. Is there an illuminating analogy to be drawn between the experience of political dislocation and the theoretical struggles to understand it that accompanied the eclipse of the classical polis, and our experience of globalization, as process and ideology, and our attempts to understand *it*? More particularly, do the various efforts to redefine citizenship in the face of the huge transformations of scale then provide an inspiration or object lesson for current efforts to redefine citizenship in globalized deterritorialized terms?

Most analysts of globalization insist that we must think as citizens of the world, and that this entails a nonspatial conception of citizenship. Something similar is present with the Stoic idea of *cosmopolis* and insistence that we think of ourselves as citizens of the world. One view of citizenship is that it not only confers rights and obligations, but entails acquiring an identity and becoming a member of a political community with a particular territory and history. But if Richard Falk and William Connolly are right that global citizenship operates temporally so that we must give up our fixation on particular place as *the* ground of citizenship—Connolly calls this the "optics of political nostalgia"—then we, like Hellenistic thinkers, find ourselves in a situation where political conditions no longer correspond to traditional categories of political thought.[3]

Yet it is not clear who the "we" are, since it seems that many people in the world remain rooted in a place and depend upon a particular culture and language for their identity and sense of well-being. Nor is it clear what it means to think globally. Now, as then, a global framework is difficult to theorize because it is not just an extension of preexisting forms (the polis and nation-state respectively).[4]

Nor, finally, can we avoid the Rousseau question about whether democracy can survive huge transformations of scale represented by the rise of Hellenistic monarchies and by globalization. This is not to assume that there is one "natural" form of democracy, to ignore the way the consolidation of the nation-state itself represented such a transformation (which was Rousseau's point), or to equate localism with democracy. It is to press the question of whether the internationalization of political, economic, social, and cultural life requires us to "redefine" democracy, or whether calls for such redefinitions indicate the extent to which democracy is becoming increasingly irrelevant as a form of experience and mode of thought despite its being what John Dunn, in *Western Political Theory in the Face of the Future*, calls "the moral esperanto of the nation-state system."

I admit that the globalizing of markets, communications, monetary exchanges, transportation, disease transmission, strategic planning, acid rain, the greenhouse effect, resource depletion, terrorist activity, drug trafficking, nuclear threats, and tourism make any recurrence to premodern politics and thought seem hopelessly anachronistic. Given a world economy that we are told is beyond the control of the nation-state, and the rapid growth of new forms of collective decision making and concentrations of unaccountable power, it is hard to disagree with John Thompson that the Greek model of "co-presence, specific locale, and the demand for dialogue" is inadequate "to the social and political conditions of the late twentieth century." We must, he continues, free ourselves from "the lure" that the image of direct democracy continues to exercise on the modern imagination, and from the "rather dim view of the quality of contemporary public life it encourages."[5] "Such democracy," Mary Beard adds, is "conveniently impractical and almost totally inimitable."[6] The polis, W. G. Runciman concludes, came to a "dead end, in the sense that its institutional development stopped while the political environment was changing. Its incapacity to adapt, i.e., its inability to retain economic, ideological, and coercive power relative to other political forms with which it was in competition," was due to the simple fact that "the *poleis* were all, without exception, far too democratic."[7]

If the lure leads us to regard the polis as some kind of blueprint or model to be applied in the present, then it certainly must be rejected. But suppose we think of the polis—not the city-state, in its physical location or specific historical configuration—in Arendtian terms as the organization of a people as it arises out of acting and speaking together. Then the space for democratic participation finds "its proper location in almost any time and anywhere."[8] In these terms, the polis is an ever-present possibility even under the most inhospitable conditions. It is this vision of the polis that seems to have inspired the idea of the "parallel polis" put forth by Václav Benda, Václav Havel, and Adam Michnik.

This essay has four sections. The first elaborates the idea of a democratic ethos broached in chapter 4, drawing mainly on classical Athens; section II considers the Cynic and Stoic effort to redefine citizenship and politics in the wake of the polis's decline. More particularly it examines their endorsement of world citizenship and community as a substitute for, recompense for, and critique of the polis as a set of institutions and as a moral idea. Section III considers Martha Nussbaum's rearticulation of Stoic cosmopolitanism as a way of moving from ancient to modern thought. Though I will be critical of her Stoics and neo-Stoicism, she has done much to bring their thought into contemporary debates about multiculturalism, education, nationalism, patriotism, and cosmopolitanism. The final section pieces together the beginning of a political cosmopolitanism in contrast to Nussbaum's, relying on the work of Richard Falk, William Connolly, Saskia Sassen, and Roger Sanjek, and on the idea of the parallel polis.

I should say at the outset that I regard globalization as an ideological and cognitive process as much as a material one. It is a material one in the sense that it involves the movement of capital, technology, goods, and labor to areas with high returns on investment without regard to the social and political impacts on communities or people to which it moves or on those it leaves behind. It is ideological in the sense that such movements are rationalized in the name of efficiency, competition, and profit. It is cognitive in the sense that globalization fosters social innovation and reorganization oblivious to the disruptions it causes in existing arrangements.[9]

II

As I suggested in chapter 4, a democratic ethos entails an egalitarian constitution of cultural and political life that encourages people to participate in defining their own troubles and possibilities, and to articulate those troubles in public and as citizens. It encourages the sharing of power and responsibility and insists that the sharing of it is a prerequisite for dignity as well as self- and mutual respect. A democratic ethos is suspicious of hierarchies and skeptical of claims to authority. Moreover, while democrats may treat political leaders with respect, they never forget that the people are the government and leaders are more advisers and competitors for public stature than august representatives of the state. A democratic ethos presumes that political knowledge is constituted discursively rather than deductively, in sometimes heated debates among people who may differ intensely about what they should do and who constitutes the "they." A democratic ethos can tolerate some economic inequality if it does not compromise political equality and is a social process through which conventions periodically confront their conventional status. Finally, a democratic ethos assumes that democracy is as much a politics of disturbance as a form of government.[10]

The ethos took shape with the democratization of power and responsibility that occurred from the sixth century B.C.E. on in virtually every Greek city-state. Even in the exclusive society of warrior-aristocrats power became the concern of all citizens rather than the property of one man or clan. Thus "political life became centered on communal spaces such as the agora, public hearth, and assembly of citizens." This democratization of power and responsibility meant the preeminence of speech defined not as inspired declarations received from a god by initiates who pronounced what justice was, but as debate and argument. The very existence of such debate implied an audience that could be expected to judge what it heard by voting for one of the parties or policies presented to it. No matter how limited that audience might be in an oligarchy, and however much *arche* (power, initiative, sovereignty, rule) remained in the hands of an elite, the polis was a place for speaking and judgment.

The emergent spaces were public in two related senses: they were (ideally) arenas for the expression of common as opposed to private concerns; and they involved open practices openly arrived at as opposed to secret procedures. The insistence on openness entailed the progressive appropriation by the community as a whole of the conduct, knowledge, and procedures that had been the exclusive prerogative of king or clan. The workings of power were visible; decisions were debated; conflicting positions were presented.[11]

Athenian democracy gave a radically egalitarian articulation of this aristocratic ethos of public life.[12] Until the Macedonian overthrow of the democracy in 322 all important political work was done in the open, in the popular Assembly and courts by all residents of the city who were culturally defined as citizens regardless of class, status, or property holdings. Such citizens thought of themselves not merely as the best judges of policies and leaders but as coequal actors, initiators as well as reactors to elite initiatives. The reforms of Cleisthenes, Josiah Ober has argued, were "not a gift from a benevolent elite to a passive *demos*, but . . . the product of collective decision, action, and self-definition on the part of the *demos* itself."[13]

It was the active sharing in and shaping of what Steven Lukes and John Gaventa define as the three dimensions of power—deciding after something has come before the public, deciding what comes before the public, and establishing the terms of public discourse by cocreating the legitimating language myths and symbols of the culture—that enabled Athenian men to maintain the conditions of equality, freedom, and dignity against elite challenge. It was "positive freedom," that is, the day-to-day political activities of ordinary men, that enabled citizens to remain free, guaranteed respect for persons, and ensured *political* equality.[14] For the Athenians combined political equality with socioeconomic inequality even within the group of male citizens. Though demands for redistribution of wealth were sporadic,[15] the rich had to constantly "prove" their patriotism by designated expenditures of money. This was so in part because wealth was not regarded as conferring any moral status, in part because every vote in the sovereign Assembly Council and courts counted the same and was exercised by a sophisticated, politically self-conscious citizenry.[16]

It was in democratic Athens that political and social reality was regarded as created and re-created through the continuous practice of public debate and communication. It was there, too, that the relationship between knowledge and action was based on common opinion built from the bottom up, and where the controlling phrase was *edoxe toi demoi*: it appeared right to the citizens that such and such was the situation or case.[17] In sum and in principle citizens had the right to an equal say in determining the context of their collective and individual lives and, by and large, exercised that right in practice.

Though the question of why the Athenians failed to extend political rights to women, slaves, and foreigners must always press against any idealizing of Athenian democracy, an equally pressing question is how it was that thousands of ordinary citizens with no specialized knowledge or education were able to share power and make generally intelligent decisions about complex political questions without an institutionalized elite or the assistance of professional experts.

Compared to other poleis the inclusiveness of Athenian citizenship was as remarkable as the inclusiveness of the polis generally when compared to the severe political hierarchies present in contemporary civilizations in Egypt, Anatolia, and western Asia, a contrast of which Greek aristocrats were ruefully aware.[18] Such inclusiveness brought the expected condemnation from conservative critics even when, as with the Old Oligarch, they recognized that democracy had a certain cultural logic.

Whether democratic or not, Greek poleis regarded the political/moral purposes of their cities as controlling the extent and nature of economic activities, though the Greeks had no conception of "the economy" as an independent system or subsystem, with its own laws of supply and demand, in which the production and distribution of material goods operated through a self-regulating system driven by the desire for gain and fear of hunger.[19]

Of course the Greeks engaged in economic activities. But these activities were regarded as discrete acts, guided and integrated only by the higher political purposes of the *oikos* and polis. One such purpose was to isolate citizens from any "economic" activity that might prove injurious to the friendship and reciprocity essential for maintaining a community of citizens. (In Thebes, anyone who had made a profit from a transaction with a fellow citizen was barred from political appointment for ten years.) Cities had little economic policy beyond ensuring the importation of essential goods such as corn, and even then it was primarily a political concern.

Given this, it is hardly surprising that thinkers such as Thucydides were relatively uninterested in economic matters except as preconditions for political power. Economic factors were dominant only when political ones were not, and their dominance, rather than being a sign of freedom, indicated the opposite. What mattered most to Thucydides and to the protagonists in his *History* was power and glory, which meant that the problem of scarcity was political, not economic, due to the competition for honor rather than the stinginess of nature or the burden of labor. Read in this light, Pericles' Funeral Oration is an attempt to solve the problem of political scarcity by urging the Athenians to think of themselves as collective heroes.

It is true that Aristotle had an idea of market exchange. But he regarded such exchange as increasing anxiety about life and livelihood beyond what is natural. In doing so, it destroyed the proper limits on acquisition as dictated by the ends of the *oikos* and polis, permitted (or even promoted) the escalation of "needs" beyond resources, and transformed virtues into means for the accumulation of wealth rather than the other way around. As this occurred, reason became mere calculation, and courage, which should rightly draw us away from the preoccupation with survival and wealth, became animal cunning in its service. While men certainly do need wealth to live, it is a category mistake to believe that the more wealth they have, the better they live.

Indeed, the overemphasis on material goods, whether at the level of subsistence or luxury, is the reason why an individual who was by nature a citizen—that is, a free adult male born into a polis—would choose to live a life that did not permit him to fulfill his nature. Where wealth took precedence over citizenship, there was no logical or practical reason why someone could not abandon the polis in which he held citizenship for one that provided him with superior opportunities for acquisition.[20]

It is the friendship citizenship presupposes that sets a necessary limit on and condition for exchange. The point of exchange is not to take advantage of another's vulnerability by bargaining hard and extracting the highest price, but to be most generous when one has the most advantage.

It follows that because foreign trade is impersonal, we cannot know the condition of those with whom we are dealing and so cannot know what reciprocity would entail. They are strangers rather than friends, distant from us both literally and metaphorically, and so seeking to profit from them is, if not admirable, at least not blameworthy.[21] It follows, second, that the right to property depends not on its mode of acquisition (any more than legitimacy of a regime depends upon consent) but on the use to which the property is put (as the legitimacy depends on the ends of the regime). The limit on its accumulation is not the negative criterion of whether it infringes the right of others to appropriate nature but the positive criterion of what sort of reciprocity is essential to sustaining the polis. Too little property would leave a citizen without sufficient resources for an active public life; too much emphasis on increasing property diverts his attention and capacities from it. Thus private property remains public even when it is private.

For Aristotle certainly, and Athenians possibly, people who participate in politics become morally and politically educated because of their participation. They learn to think and speak in public and as public beings, to make public claims and give reasons that appeal to a shared predicament and traditions. In acting politically, they confront those who are more diverse than members of their *oikos* or immediate neighborhood. Encountering difference in the context of deliberation, they are thereby able to develop the judgment and practical wisdom available only in the living of a public life. If the polis is indeed a "partnership in virtue," then representative democracy and empire make no sense. How could I delegate someone to be virtuous for me (any more than I could delegate someone to work out for me)? No one can act for me, not because he or she will misrepresent my interests, but because such delegation is a renunciation of what is distinctively human about me. It is like selling oneself into slavery or, less dramatically, like becoming a "citizen" of an empire.

But even for my purposes this is far too idealized a portrait of Athenian democracy and too much a progressivist narrative. In addition to the obvious social inequalities that existed along with an often imperfect political equality of male citizens, there is the fact that democratic Athens broke down the Panhellenic codes of international behavior in regard to the rules of war, which led to its increasing brutalization. Moreover, they developed an autonomous public realm that hardened the distinction between free and slave and male and female even as it protected male citizens from dependence and domination. And their belief in autochthonous nature promoted a sense of superiority and exclusivist citizenship laws.[22] It is only by acknowledging such deficiencies that we can avoid a narrative of simple decline, which does not of course preclude "normative" political judgments.

III

The rise of Macedon signaled the eclipse of the polis. There had of course been empires in the pre-Hellenistic world, but they had never dislodged the moral standing of the polis. Indeed, the Greeks took pride in their particularism, believing it to be the foundation of their freedom and power, which is one of the reasons they failed, as Runciman puts it, "to adapt." Men fought and lived bravely only where they were their own masters, not when ruled by fear of a king who demanded "oriental" reverence. Part of their contempt for barbarians lay in their belief that the latter were unable or unwilling to live in a polis.

Within fifty years, the Greeks had become like the barbarian "other" against whom they had measured their political power, freedom, and virtue. Thebes had been destroyed, and Athens had become subservient to Macedon. While the polis continued to exist as a political entity that, in certain respects, continued to hold its place as what Erich Gruen calls "a focus for loyalty and affection,"[23] it did so with diminished power and moral standing. Even seeming indicators of its autonomy, such as treaties that guaranteed an internal constitution, were tokens of political impotence, since the polis was allowed to function as the arbiter of morals and social habits as long as it pleased the king.[24] To have one's freedom depend upon the observation of rituals of obeisance was not only insulting; it rested on an identification of paternal and political authority that Aristotle had rejected as a misunderstanding about the nature of a *political* community.

The problem from the late third through the second century B.C.E. was twofold: what to make of the fact that the polis was not immortal; and how to comprehend a moral and political landscape in which Greeks were members of a heterogeneous empire encompassing unheard-of differences in culture and political sophistication, and where the locus of power and decision was remote from the everyday experience of the vast majority of people.[25] Heraclitus had urged citizens to fight for their walls as for their laws since together they defined a human space in which a distinctive political culture could be expressed and sustained, while Aristotle insisted that a polis should ideally be able to hear the voice of a single herald. But these sensual coordinates of sight and sound were irrelevant when public spaces ceased to be political except in an attenuated form.

Many commentators have noted the curiosity that the tutor of Alexander has no sustained discussion of empire in the *Politics*. One can conclude from this either that Aristotle did not see the lasting significance of this new political form or that he did not regard it as a political form at all.[26] If the latter, then Aristotle is suggesting that not all "political" forms are equally political. "How far," Sheldon Wolin asks, with an Aristotelian sensibility, "can the boundaries of political space . . . be extended, how much dilution by numbers could the notion of citizen-participants withstand, how minor need the 'public' aspect of decisions be before the political association ceased to be political?"[27]

The challenge during the Hellenistic period, then, was how theoretically to comprehend the transmogrifications of scale and sensibility that marked every aspect of public life. More specifically, the problem was finding new ways to talk about citizenship. For instead of citizens' instituting authority, they were expected to revere authorities whose physical distance from them was compounded by claims to divinity. Instead of participating in a polis that could then claim loyalty as a consequence of providing a space for speech and action, "citizens" were now expected to fight and die for powers they could not see or hear, and kings who monopolized what little public space remained. Citizenship had become formalized, at best a legal status that brought with it protection and some entitlements; at worst, a virtual fiction.

The reactions of the various philosophical schools to these changes were diverse and evolving (especially in the case of Stoicism), except for one constant: a reassessment of the status of "politics." For the Cynics[28] the controlling terms were a radicalized version of the sophistic opposition between nature and convention. From this perspective, politics and morality, freedom and virtue were not rooted in the purely conventional roles of the polis but could be truly found only in nature. The laws and walls of the city were insubstantial boundaries that artificially divided one place from another, one person from another, one culture from another. If we would only follow nature and acknowledge the cosmos as a city, we would both realize human social potential and recognize that individual freedom and self-sufficiency were within our grasp. In arguing that each of us dwells in two communities—a local one of our birth and a larger, more morally substantial community of the cosmos, where all humans are our fellow citizens, and true virtue, freedom, and justice can be found— Diogenes of Sinope managed, in one stroke, to undercut the polarities of Greek and barbarian, slave and free, men and women, and public and private that had legitimated the exclusivist citizenship of the polis. Insofar as the ideas of cosmopolis, natural law, the shared reason of men and gods, and justice require us to treat the interests of all humans impartially, the polis not only loses its moral authority but becomes an impediment to a moral life. If, pace Aristotle, women, barbarians, and slaves have as much reason as "free" Greek men, and political commitments are partial, parochial, and irrational, then no hierarchy is legitimate except the one distinguishing those who follow right reason from those who do not. If wealth and power, reputation and external goods weigh us down, if they distract us from a moral life, then the poor who lack them are the only ones who could possibly live a just life.

Diogenes himself chose "exile" from the exclusions and pretensions of polis life. Happiness was attained not through citizenship of place. Nor was freedom experienced in the sharing of power with equals who jointly shaped their collective purposes. Happiness, freedom, and power required escape from such constraints and satisfying whatever needs were natural whenever and wherever they needed satisfying. Nothing natural, whether it be poverty or defecation in public, was indecent. True citizens lived a self-sufficient ascetic life indifferent to shame and external rewards.

When the Cynic Crates (365–285 B.C.E.) refused to return to his native Thebes, he did so for two complementary reasons. The first is found in his declaration that "I have no one city . . . but the whole world to live in."[29] His city is the universe; his community, the community of humankind; his citizenship, a citizenship of the world. He is a *kosmopolites*. The second reason is suggested by his claim that his home was the backpack he carried from place to place. The counsel is obvious: travel lightly—and the implication clear: the ideal city consists of individuals of self-sufficient virtue. Citizenship has become exclusively a function of moral goodness, while consideration of political institutions and regimes is discarded.

The sense in which the ideal city was a city is indicated by Crates' claim that he was a "citizen" of Diogenes, that his "place" was not Thebes but the Cynic way of life that Diogenes initiated and exemplified. It was a life that could be lived any time and anywhere. Though there were some gestures toward concrete sociability and space in Cynic teachings, their use of words like *polis* and *politeia* was mostly metaphoric for the Cynic way of life.[30] Since the Cynic state was the state of adhering to the Cynic way of life, patriotism, honor, military valor, and fighting for one's country—all significant aspects of Greek civic ideology—were superfluous.

The Cynics claimed to be following Socrates, and in some respects, such as their concentration on "inner" virtue rather than external markers of success and a refusal to accept traditions because they were traditional, they were. What they lost was the Socratic tension between city as place and philosophy, which in their hands became a simple opposition.

Though evidence suggests that some Cynics wrote didactic works of moral instruction, most of those André Laks calls "hard Cynics" preferred diatribe, dialogue, and theatrical entertainment to systematic philosophical argument. In fact, one could regard the enactment of their theoretical claims as a kind of street theater, as when Diogenes set up a tub in the marketplace as his home or walked around in daylight with a lantern looking for an honest man. One could also regard their discussion of the need to choose a life and live it as playing a part in a self-generated script (even if that script was based on "nature" rather than convention).

Such theatricality made perfect sense given that their projected audience was not philosophers, along with evidence that they regarded systematic philosophy as a useless intellectual conceit. It was left to their Stoic students to provide such a political theory. This they did through the elaboration, systemization, and rearrangement of Cynic ideas, made easier by the purposely unrigorous character of Cynic doctrine.

It was Zeno of Citium (335–265 B.C.E.), the founder of Stoicism, and his student Chrysippus (280–207 B.C.E.) who first elaborated the idea of a cosmopolis or world state. According to Plutarch, Zeno argued that we must "cease thinking of ourselves as citizens of separate cities and peoples divided by opposed conceptions of justice, and regard all men as members of one city and people, having one life and order." For this to occur we must acknowledge the presence of a rational universe and cultivate that rational part of ourselves which enables us to become members of it. Once "we" morally good and wise do that, we come to constitute a city regardless of where in the world we are geographically located at the moment.[31]

Though there are moments when Chrysippus especially allows that a historically located polis can be a place worthy of attention and commitment, it is clear that, on the whole, Stoicism redefined citizenship in nonspatial moral terms. The more contingent aspects of citizenship were seen as obstacles to be overcome, the more membership in a community came to be defined as obedience to the injunctions of right reason and justice according to the law of nature. With this, Stoicism at once depoliticized and moralized "political" terms, activities, and status.[32]

Like the Cynics, Stoic thinkers dismissed the exclusivist principles of the polis as a parochialism that fails to acknowledge the fundamental dignity of all human beings grounded on shared reason. For Marcus Aurelius, as for earlier Stoics, nothing is better than reason. If men have reason in common, they also *must* have right reason. Those who have this in common also have law and justice in common. And those who share all these things must be held to belong to the same *civitas*.[33] As this indicates, Stoics had a substantive rather than instrumentalist view of reason. What all rational humans have in common is not just a skill of argument but an attachment to certain values prescribed by reason that direct both the universe as a whole and humans as part of it.[34]

Stoic philosophers regarded themselves as obliged to promote the good of humanity by championing reason over passion, harmony over discord, and healthy over diseased souls. Once purged of passion and partiality, men and women might be capable of becoming citizens in a universal community to which, in some sense, they already belonged. Though various Stoics articulated the basis of this community differently—Seneca emphasized universal sympathy, Epictetus that we are all sons (and presumably daughters) of god—all agreed that membership in a *cosmopolis* took moral precedence over lesser associations, such as family, neighborhood, and city. Here is Seneca:[35]

> Let us embrace with our minds two commonwealths [*res publicae*]: one great and truly common—in which gods and men are contained, in which we look not to this or that corner, but measure the bounds of our state with the sun; the other the one to which the particular circumstances of birth have assigned us . . . which pertains not to all men but to a particular group of them [*certos*]. . . . This greater commonwealth we are able to serve even in leisure, or rather perhaps better in leisure—so that we may inquire what virtue is, whether it is one or many, whether nature or art makes men good; whether this world which embraces seas and lands and things grafts on to sea and lands, is unique, or whether God has scattered many bodies of this sort.

For Seneca as for other leading Stoic authors of the early empire such as Epictetus and Marcus Aurelius, the true city is the cosmic city.

It is not just that the city into which we are born is unchosen and marks prerational commitments, but that the world of politics and power is itself a trap and a snare. For Seneca the world is pain and suffering, and the fate of those who seek fulfillment in it can only be disappointment and failure. To care too much about worldly affairs is to leave oneself dependent on and therefore vulnerable to others and to circumstances beyond one's control. It is to be tossed at sea, living restless unhappy lives in thrall to glory and avarice, confounding what is fleeting and superficial with what is not. "No good thing renders its possessor happy," Seneca counsels, "unless his mind is reconciled to the possibility of loss."[36] Only philosophers can escape the vicissitudes and seductions of the world, because they have access to knowledge of the sages that, like reason itself, is outside time and space. "What joy it is," Lucretius writes, "when out at sea the storm winds are lashing the waters, to gaze from the shore at the heavy stress some other man is enduring: Not that any one's afflictions are in themselves a source of delight; but to realize from what troubles you yourself are free of is a joy indeed."[37]

One way to think about the revolution in thought Stoicism represented is to contrast it with Aristotle. Though Aristotle regarded contemplative activity as the highest for men because it partakes of the divine, the highest human association is the polis. But the Stoics believed one could have an association of contemplative men, which meant that the instrumental *aspect* of the Aristotelian polis came to define it. Similarly, while Aristotle believed humans had a spark of the divine, he never envisaged, as the Stoics did, a community of gods and men. Second, the Stoic community, in contrast to the Aristotelian polis, is ruled by common reason, which directs people how to treat each other as social animals even if they never inhabit the same place or share a history. Third, several Stoics argued, in opposition to Aristotle, that it was the *oikos* that most completely realized the social impulses of human beings. Fourth, the Stoics rejected the idea that the authority of law rested on its being the voice of the city or community. Right reason, not a particular ethos, could create binding obligations. Similarly, while Aristotle (as well as Plato) regarded justice as a principle of distribution among citizens who inhabit a specific regime, Stoicism defined justice as a purely moral imperative governing our conduct toward all humans regardless of whether they were citizens in a conventional sense. These considerations, as well as the Stoic indifference to debating the merits of particular constitutions, suggest the transformation of political theory in which political and moral considerations vied with and complemented each other into moral philosophy and political moralism.

Fifth, unlike Aristotle, Stoics tended to endorse the desirability and possibility of self-mastery, presuming that the self could be unequivocally
transparent to reflection. To keep oneself out of the violent turmoil and
unpredictability afflicting public life, one had to take total charge of who
one was, where one's life was going, and indulging one's emotions and
appetites only to the extent one determined. Such a possibility and goal
transformed the Aristotelian understanding of freedom.[38]

It is true that, for various reasons, Aristotle never identified freedom
with membership in a polis. Yet citizenship remained for him a largely
political concept and freedom an experience of acting with others in the
public realm. He would not, as the Stoics did, regard freedom as the sovereignty of unencumbered individuals who had "freed" themselves of relationships and public affairs. Cities, not individuals, should aim at *autarky*.
But for Epictetus such *autarky* was a necessary condition for freedom
and happiness. Only the completely self-sufficient man could achieve that
inner freedom which provides the space into which he could escape from
external coercion. A free man limited his desires to what was in his power
and avoided reaching beyond himself into an alien world that existed not
as possibility but as hindrance and threat.

Of course it was also Aristotle who insisted that women and slaves
(which Epictetus was) were naturally inferior human beings, and the Stoics who insisted that they could be fully rational and thereby achieve full
membership in the *cosmopolis*. And this reminds us of the impressive
contributions Stoicism has made to the ideas of human dignity, moral
equality, and natural law. Its critique of parochialism and excessive partisanship to one's own, its rejection of derogatory constructions of "the
other," and its ideal of world citizenship have provided a ground for the
critique of slavery, ethnocentrism, and hierarchies of all kinds, critiques
that have hardly lost their salience. And it is they, rather than defenders
of the polis, who seem worthy interlocutors in contemporary debates over
citizenship, given political, economic, social, and ecological developments
and dependencies that are worldwide in scope and consequences.

This is especially so if we recognize the political commitments present
in early Stoicism and the extent to which the Middle Stoa of the second
and first centuries modified the antipolitical tendencies of Stoicism by ad-
justing them to Roman life. There are places where Zeno (as well as
Cleanthes and Chrysippus) argues that man's social nature entails an obligation to seek to strengthen the society in which one finds oneself by
marriage, procreation, and political activity, at least when the circumstances are right.

But they were never right, and there is little evidence that the early
Stoics ever analyzed present or possible political circumstances in ways
that would allow us to take their political commitments seriously. This

impression is strengthened by the fact that though Zeno, Cleanthes, and
Chrysippus all declared that a man should take part in the political life
of his city, none of them ever did anything of the kind in Athens; and by
how improbable a city of the virtuous wise would be if it was true that
good men (and presumably women) are as "rare as the Ethiopian
Sphinx."[39]

In the end, and despite its impressive contribution to the ideals of
human dignity and inclusive citizenship, Stoicism inscribed a new exclusiveness based on differential commitment to and practice of rationality.
In practice it often turned out that only a very few exceptional humans
could actually be full members in the human community of reason, since
most lacked the will (or perhaps even capacity) to be the morally just men
and women universal law prescribed. In this, Stoicism was something of
a mirror image of Athenian democracy. While the latter justified social
and cultural inequalities based on a political principle that could be extended to undermine such inequalities, Stoicism denied in practice the
radical political possibilities of its philosophical commitments. Even when
the Stoic ideal of virtuous and capable man was not primarily defined in
political terms, it proved, nonetheless, especially congenial to monarchical and personal rule. Its leveling potential remained abstract because (especially) early Stoics frequently refused to relate their thinking to the political and material conditions in which men lived their daily lives, and
because they accepted ("stoically") the existence of extensive social hierarchies as necessary facts.

Even the Middle Stoa, who were sometimes highly political beings, regarded participation in public life as a moral obligation, in contrast to
Aristotle and most Athenian democrats. An ethic of service they certainly
had; a view of politics as a realm of freedom, power, and justice they just
as certainly did not.[40]

The challenge, then, is to keep the critical moral edge of cosmopolitanism *and* the political focus of the polis in tension with the aim of intro-
ducing a generative political and theoretical voice in the sometimes presentist debate over citizenship and democracy in an era of globalization.

IV

The contemporary thinker who offers the most powerful rearticulation
of Stoicism is Martha Nussbaum.[41] She has brought her sympathetic reading of Stoic authors to bear on debates over nationalism and patriotism,
citizenship and community, and education and human rights in the conviction that "the values on which Americans may most justly pride themselves are, in a deep sense, Stoic values,"[42] and in a way that suggests (or

reminds us of) the expansive possibilities of Stoic philosophy and the limits of Stoic politics.

Nussbaum is critical of ethnocentrism, partisanship, parochialism, and localism, whether centered on family, neighborhood, nation, or ethnicity. In each instance such localism is a kind of faction that is easily manipulated by demagogues who intimidate critical scrutiny and reasoned debate.[43] Local allegiances can too easily justify brutal wars and ethnic cleansing, imperial ambitions and contempt for those who are different and other. Against these destructive forces she invokes Cicero's admonition that it is our duty to regard all humanity with respect, which means treating aliens in our society with honor and hospitality, refusing to engage in wars of aggression, behaving humanely to enemies when forced to fight, placing justice above expediency, and never forgetting that we are all members of a universal human community. No matter how insolent, obnoxious, or duplicitous a man may be, we must not, Marcus Aurelius warns, read him out of the human community.[44]

But Nussbaum and her Stoics are more than occasional critics of particular injustices; critique is their way of life. Like Socrates, their aim is to remove the false sense of naturalness and inevitability of existing practices that discourage men and women from living an examined life. Because such critics must be willing to doubt the goodness of accepted conventions, they are a threat to their compatriots. To consider oneself a citizen of the world rather than of a particular country, as we must, is to become "a philosophical exile" from one's own way of life. Being a cosmopolitan citizen is a lonely and heroic business: lonely because one becomes exiled from "the comforts of assured truths, from the warm nestling feeling of being surrounded by people who share one's convictions and passions"; heroic because the task, lessening the appalling ignorance Americans have of the rest of the world and so of themselves, is so difficult and so urgent.[45]

It is not that Nussbaum and her Stoics ignore the pull of local attachments entirely. We do need "to take our stand where life has placed us and devote special attention and affection to immediate surroundings."[46] But accidents of birth and obligations that arise from them are the necessary rather than chosen conditions of our lives, and the ultimately arbitrary principles that convert these accidents into natural and desirable norms are morally inferior to rationally chosen, rationally justified affiliations. In this light, divisions of nationality, class, or ethnicity are epiphenomenal barriers between us and our fellow human beings. Our "fundamental" obligations come from what is fundamental about us, and what is fundamental about us is reason. "In this sense we should view ourselves as citizens of a world wide community of rational beings, members of a community because of our participation in reason." Our first loyalty must be to the whole. Our loyalty to the political community "in which we are placed" is "secondary and artificial."[47]

This argument is Platonic rather than Aristotelian in the sense that the value of what is local derives from its participation in some larger reality that gives it ontological and moral dignity. Thus Nussbaum urges us to use local affiliations to discover and respect the dignity of all mankind. It is a rejection of Aristotle in the sense that what he regarded as a realm of freedom, justice, and virtue becomes a realm of necessity. The *cosmopolis* is to the polis as Aristotle's polis was to the household.

Though politics is exclusively instrumental, Nussbaum does have three political concerns. The first is to prepare U.S. citizens to play their global role so that "our business efforts [can] be successful," and international debates about human rights, medical and agricultural problems, and gender relations can "make progress." The second is to create "a more reasonable style of political deliberation and problem solving," which is possible once we recognize the moral/rational community as fundamental. Third is an educational agenda focused on teaching students "what it is like to see the world through the perspective of another language, an experience that quickly shows that human complexity and rationality are not the monopoly of a single linguistic community."[48]

These are all admirable goals, and Nussbaum defends them with an equally admirable combination of forthrightness, urgency, and lucidity. Who can object to the desire to enhance the outlook for justice, rights, reason, and morality in the world? Who could disagree that we share the planet or reject calls to alleviate hunger, poverty, economic inequality, and the threat of ecological disaster? The very meaning of cosmopolitanism— unprovincial, nonpartisan, worldly, sophisticated, urbane—suggests a generosity of spirit and catholicity of commitment that are "morally" compelling.[49]

Yet there is something parochial about this cosmopolitanism. In the broadest terms what is missing is politics, including any political analysis about the nature of her moral critique. In part, this is a matter of principle rather than of inadvertence. While Greek Stoics proposed an ideal city, and Roman Stoics tried to put ideas of world citizenship into practice in the government of empire, the Stoics' "basic point was more radical": that "we should give first allegiance to *no mere* form of government, no temporal power, but to the moral community made up by the humanity of all human beings."[50] But the problem with ignoring such analysis is not only an absent dimension of self-critique, but a partial misreading of the issues she considers and the ultimate danger of imitating Stoic accommodation to reigning structures of power.

"Most important," Nussbaum asks, "should they [i.e., young people] be taught that they are, above all, citizens of the United States, or should they instead be taught that they are, above all, citizens of the world of human beings?" And the answer is clearly the latter. But there is good evidence that young people do not see themselves as citizens at all, that citizenship is not, for them, a significant status or category or activity. If it is not, then it is hard to see what world "citizenship" could mean.

It is hard for another reason. "I am not a citizen of the world," Michael Walzer writes. "I am not even aware that there is a world such that one could be a citizen of it. No one has ever offered me citizenship, or described the naturalization process, or enlisted me in the world's institutional structures, or given me an account of its decision procedures . . . or provided me with a list of benefits and obligations of citizenship, or shown me the world's calendar and the common celebrations and commemorations of its citizens."[51] In those terms, extending one's allegiance to the cosmos as if it were a society may be an act of wisdom, but it is hardly an act of citizenship.[52]

While I do not accept the argument that since this is the way we define citizenship, that is what it must be—both because I think the definition of citizenship more fluid and evolving and because I think the argument in general can become uninterestingly circular—Walzer is right that we need some content and concrete indication of what world citizenship entails even if only in anticipation. This is especially so if, as Bruce Robbins argues, larger loyalties must be built up out of particular "imperfect historical materials, churches and mosques, commercial interests and immigrant diasporas, sentimental commitments to hungry children and capitalist technoculture."[53]

Too much of our politics is pervaded by an often justified yet politically disabling cynicism, passivity, and resentment. Many of the students I teach have an ironical stance toward their own commitments and involvements. They know themselves to be part of a consumer culture toward which they are deeply ambivalent. If I am right, then "the greatest barrier to rational deliberation in politics" may not be "the unexamined feeling that one's own preferences and ways are neutral and natural,"[54] as Nussbaum believes, but something close to the obverse. In these terms the problem is that nothing is seen as neutral and natural, that deeply held preferences are rare, and that only the immediately satisfied, self-regarding ones are deemed worth embracing in a system hostile to larger democratic initiatives. Under these circumstances Nussbaum's cosmopolitan universalism may make things worse by promoting a dialectic between increasing withdrawal and self-righteous interventions.

An extended analysis of power, whether political, economic, cultural, or social power, whether inspired by Hobbes, Marx, Foucault, Weber, Arendt, or Dahl, is also missing. Thus there is no consideration of how people come to have the preferences they do, or of the sense in which such preferences are "theirs." Absent, too, is any discussion of what happens to those aspects of a self that have to be hidden, discarded, or disowned as a precondition for incorporation in the dominant global structures of awareness and power,[55] or of the ways in which liberalism (her unproblematized politics) can operate as a kind of moral fundamentalism.

Nor does Nussbaum have much to say about democracy,[56] which is to be expected given her assertion that our primary commitments must be to moral principles rather than any form of politics. Yet here, as in the case of power, the absence of any consideration of the democratic and antidemocratic developments present in globalization, philosophical universalism becomes an abstract moralism susceptible to a Stoic-like compromise, where potentially democratizing commitments are aborted by an accommodation with centralized power and existing social hierarchies. In her neo-Stoic mood it is not clear that Nussbaum understands the argument for politics, except in a quasi-Aristotelian sense that becomes in these works a touchstone against which to praise the superiority of Stoicism. There is no engagement with political thinkers such as Machiavelli and Arendt, and Jefferson's idea of public happiness or the anguish of Weber's political leader is unintelligible in her world.

Without some attention to how power operates to enhance democracy, one cannot have a realistic sense of the possible forms globalization is taking or could take, how its terms of discourse will be established, or whose conception of "genuine needs and aspirations" will prevail. Marx predicted that capitalism would sweep all particular cultural, political, and social forms and values away like an all-conquering army. More and more states and more and more of life within each state would be subject to commodification. He pushes us to ask the questions necessary to fill out any argument for cosmopolitanism, even if his own answers are part of the problem. Have cultures and nations ceded so much to the modern economy, the modern state, and liberalism's emancipatory aspirations that substantive differences of meaning and practice are shrinking? And to what degree is globalization in fact American capitalism and culture writ large, especially if, as seems to be the case, the hidden premise of global unity is American popular culture?

More generally, haven't we learned how purportedly universalistic traditions that promise emancipation from tradition *and* politics—Christianity, liberalism, and Marxism—have in fact elevated the transitory and local into universalistic ideologies? This is not to claim that cosmopolitanism is necessarily ethnocentric, but to caution against the unobtrusive ways in which dominant particulars represent themselves as the universal and actually become so in the sense of being the point of reference in relation to which others recognize themselves as particular.[57] It is also to suggest the significance of sustaining particular ways of life against those globalizing forces (often presented as necessities) that threaten to consume diversity even as they celebrate differences.[58]

Nor is there any critical distance from the celebration of reason and reasonableness. Indeed, those terms are repeated so often that they become an incantation and article of faith against which only heretics and schismatics would speak. There is no discussion of conflicting conceptions of reason, or the tyranny of reason, or reason's parochialism. All this is from one of the most original interpreters we have of Greek tragedy in general and *Antigone* in particular. And *Antigone* is a play in which the principal characters assert their reasonableness as a bludgeon against their political opponents, who are said to be without sense, irrational, and mad.

It turns out that cosmopolitanism is possible and useful only among "reasonable" people. "We can see ourselves more clearly," Nussbaum writes, "when we see our ways in relation to those of other *reasonable* people"[59] (my emphasis). And who are these reasonable people, or, more pointedly, who aren't they? They are people like us: Western academics who define what counts as reasonable. When Jürgen Habermas argues that "to gain distance from one's own tradition and broaden limited perspectives is the advantage of Occidental rationalism,"[60] it is assumed that those outside the Occident lack the reflective awareness that would protect them from being possessed by their mythical worldviews.

But there are good reasons to question the assumption that Occidental rationalism has a monopoly on self-doubt, even if it is extensively institutionalized in the West. On the contrary, if critical self-examination is born out of contest, there is reason to believe that the encounter with the hegemonic West has intensified already existent self-reflection in formerly colonized societies, including reflection on the ambiguities of modernity. One could go further and argue that the condition of being on the "periphery" is often, though not inevitably, a condition of constant mediation, between past and present, "Occident" and "vernacular." Those living at such crossroads are arguably far more cosmopolitan (and multiculturalist) than Western intellectuals, who usually do not have to negotiate contradictory demands and incommensurate outlooks in the context of everyday life.[61] Of course this is a different kind of cosmopolitanism, including different kinds of people, from that praised by the Stoics and Nussbaum, for it does not claim universality by virtue of its detachment from the bonds, commitments, and affiliations of everyday life, and it extends to particular transnational experiences that are unprivileged and often coerced. In these terms cosmopolitanism is an "ethic of macro-interdependencies and particularities of places, characters, historical trajectories, and fates."[62]

Nussbaum's neo-Stoicism seems a far cry from her *Fragility of Good-ness* and her writings on Aristotle.[63] The complexity present there seems to have yielded to a less phenomenologically rich appreciation of moral and political life. Perhaps she has changed her mind. Or perhaps, given her other writings with Amartya Sen, she views her project and audience in *Cultivating Humanity* and *For Love of Country* as simply different. But perhaps she regards herself *as* a citizen of the world community in which the values of the university are universalized. Then cosmopoli-tanism becomes an intellectual ideal dependent on the mobility that ac-crues from social, economic, and cultural privilege.[64]

Though Stoic values are also American ones, Nussbaum's philosopher is, we recall, a "lonely exile" from her people, an outsider in her own land, removed from "the comfort of assured truths, from the warm nest-ling feelings of being surrounded by people who share one's convictions and passions." But Nussbaum is perfectly at home in the globalized aca-demic community, which has its own assured truths (about reason) and shared convictions and passions. It is a community that, from one point of view, is as local as and perhaps more parochial than my neighborhood in Santa Cruz. Richard Falk tells the story of having a conversation on a plane with a Danish business leader who claimed to be a global citizen, by which he meant that his friends, social network, and travels were all global. He slept in the same hotels whether in Tokyo, London, or New York, spoke English everywhere, and was, in general, part of a global culture of experience, symbols, infrastructure, goods, and music that con-stituted a way of life.[65]

If Nussbaum's neo-Stoicism is as politically inadequate for elucidating globalization as Stoicism was for politically elucidating the collapse of the polis, what are the alternatives? How is one to combine moral critique without moralism with a Greek sense of politics without polis envy? If one is primarily concerned with enhancing democratic citizenship in a world that seems increasingly hostile to it, how is one to think about the threats and opportunities globalization presents?

In the final section I want to use five thinkers—Richard Falk, William Connolly, Saskia Sassen, Roger Sanjek, and Václav Benda—to set out the parameters for such thought. What I offer is less an answer to my ques-tions than a prolegomena to an answer.

V

"The reality of global citizenship is unavoidable," Richard Falk writes, "but its form remains contested." For him the question is whether the citizens of the future will be global elites in charge of international finance and the integration of capital, or whether it is possible to encourage the growth of "human solidarity from an extension of democratic principles as a result of the extension of peoples and their voluntary associations" (46). He knows well enough that citizenship has always meant different things for different peoples throughout the world and within particular states, including liberal democracies where formal rights and powers are compromised by informal hierarchies based on race, religion, class, region, ethnicity, and gender. But he fears that these will become exacerbated by globalization.

In these terms there are two kinds of globalizing imperatives: globalization from above, reflecting the collaboration between leading states and the main agents of capital formation; and globalization from below, consisting of an array of "transnational social forces animated by environmental concerns, human rights, hostility to patriarchy, and a vision of human community based on the unity of diverse cultures seeking an end to poverty, oppression, humiliation and collective violence" (39–40). Where globalization from above disseminates a consumerist ethos and propagates a New World Order as a geopolitical project of the U.S. government, and/or as a technological and marketing project of large-scale capital (epitomized by Disney theme parks, McDonald's, Hilton Hotels, etc.), globalization from below "inclines" toward a world community premised on what Falk calls "a politics of aspiration and desire" found in the "institutional forces and activities associated with global civil society." This globalization from below is an expression of "democracy without frontiers" as against the homogenizing tendencies of globalization from above (40–41). It seeks, at a minimum, to extend the order of moral, legal, and environmental accountability to those now acting on behalf of the state, market, and media. Where the former provides a framework for a functional utopia, the latter accepts social hierarchies, growing economic disparities, and the depoliticizing of "public" life as inevitable.

Falk identifies four forms or varieties of global engagement and five types of global citizenship that result from various amalgams of them (41–45). The first variety of engagement is "aspirational" and normative in its commitment to the ultimate unity of human experience and planetary peace and justice. The second variety accepts and accommodates to the global integration and consolidation of financial markets, the concentration of capital formation, and the emergence of a new world system defined by the G-7. The third, what Falk calls "a politics of impossibility," insists that human survival demands global citizens to redesign political choices on the basis of ecological variables. Finally, implicit in this ecological imperative is a politics of mobilization as represented by transnational militancy.

Interaction of these levels of engagement yields images of the global citizen: as a reformer who relies on political centralization in the form of a stronger UN or world state; as an international businessman (almost never a businesswoman); as environmental manager; as regionalist (he is thinking mostly of the European Union); and as transnational activist (Amnesty International and Greenpeace would be examples). For Falk it is this activist citizenry that provides hope for generating a democratic alternative to elitist globalization.

This democratic alternative based on institutional arenas of action, participation, and allegiance in global civil society requires a redefinition of citizenship, most dramatically so in the separation of citizenship from a sense of place, most notably from the territorial state. While "traditional citizenship" operates spatially, global citizenship operates temporally, "reaching out to a future to-be-created, and making a person a 'citizen-pilgrim' " (48). Falk is unembarrassed by the religious connotation of that phrase, for he regards global citizenship as a religious as well as a political project. The possibility of a future political community of global or species scope (in which time partially displaces space) means that citizenship becomes "an essentially religious and normative undertaking based on faith in the unseen, salvation in a world to come" (51).

There is much to be said for Falk's argument. He makes the issue of power central and offers astute observations about the convergence of imperial visions and global reform, proposals that just happen to produce ascendancy for the state, religion, or region of the proponent. Moreover, he is generally and rightly suspicious of all rationalist strategies, whether endorsed by global, capital, or state critics of capitalism, recognizing how they marginalize democratic politics. Similarly, he warns against environmental managerialism, which legitimates massive technical efforts coordinated at the global level by the concerted action of states and international institutions. Penultimately, he distinguishes global citizenship as a sentimental ideal mechanically imposed on existing reality from global citizenship as a process in the making. Finally, he recognizes the need for some vision of the future other than the theology of neoliberalism, which leaves the market without the moral and political limits Aristotle thought essential for politics.

Despite these virtues, we know too little about the ways in which the new community will be political, and the extent to which it will be a "community." These are serious omissions, given the history of idealistic ventures whose redemptive promise turns out to have too little of the former and too much of the latter. I am not insisting that Falk fill in details in a way that would make him the rationalist he warns us against—only that without more historical detail globalization appears as a natural force confronted by an amorphous idealism.

Like Falk, William Connolly[66] is concerned with the limits of state sovereignty and statism, the prospects for democratic citizenship amid globalization, the dangers of rationalist projects, and the need to think about politics in deterritorialized terms. In these respects, Connolly offers an elaboration and extension of Falk's analysis. But in other respects he provides a corrective to Falk's global vision.

A "revivification of the democratic imagination," Connolly writes, "requires a compromise of sovereignty in both its 'internal' and 'external' manifestations" (250). Without this the simultaneous presence of the globalization of life and the confinement of democracy to the territorial state is likely to encourage "state chauvinism abroad and the suppression of fundamental issues internally." In this way "being" a democracy justifies the exercise of hegemony while deflecting criticism of the undemocratic aspects of "democratic" states. To prevent this, we must challenge "American nostalgia for a 'politics of place' in which territoriality, sovereignty, foreign relations, electoral accountability and belonging correspond to each other in one political place" (250).

Notice that Connolly is not arguing that we should ignore a sense of place, belonging, or the territorial state, but that the superimposition of these in a particular space "imprisons" democracy. "But if the practice of modern democracy involves shared understandings, formal institutions of electoral accountability, and the capacity to act in concert within a sovereign state, does it not," he asks, "therefore require state territorialization to be?" His answer is yes and no: yes because "institutions of electoral accountability are a critical component of democracy and the modern state is the place where it is institutionalized"; no because "there is more to a democratic ethos than electoral accountability" (264). What more is there?

Connolly, like Falk, provides a number of examples of social movements that extend aspects of the democratic ethos beyond the confines of the state. However distinct their agendas they all "contest the cultural assumption of alignment between a citizen's commitment to democracy and her commitments to the priorities of a particular state, thereby attenuating those nationalist sentiments flowing from the state as the only legitimate site of democratic action" (268). This means that a democrat must sometimes be disloyal to the state that "seeks to own her morally or politically," including, presumably, the state that helped educate her to appreciate the virtues of democracy.

Clearly Connolly's notion of democracy requires a reconceptualization of citizenship, or, rather, a recognition of a reconceptualization already underway. Existing pluralism *within* the state means that loyalties already move from one place to another as issues and concerns shift. Indeed, in a multidimensional pluralist world every particular allegiance is contingent because "the occasion might occur when it collides with another one you have found to be even more fundamental at this time" (268–69).

Connolly resists the temptation to posit another place that could compete for loyalty with the state and thus break the latter's hold on our political allegiance for the simple reason that "there is no such 'place,' " if place is defined by "the optics of political nostalgia" (269). He calls instead for an extension of political identifications to a "distinctive global time" that impinges on us even if it is not organized into a political place. It is a notion of time responsive to the distinctive rhythm of modernity, "where globalization has become more intense, extended and interlocking, more tightly wound at speeds that make the world smaller and tighter, closer and faster than it has ever been before" (269).

I think Connolly right in his warnings about democratic chauvinism, the imprisonment of the "democratic ethos," and I agree with his characterization of that ethos. He is also right to regard deterritorialization as part of a decisive shift in an internationalization and transnationalization of politics that challenge political and social theorists to rethink their categories and terms. And I am sympathetic to his rejection of nostalgia, as the previous chapter indicates. Nonetheless, I am uneasy about his relative silence concerning what is lost with deterritorialization, and his pathologizing of nostalgia.

My uncertainty about loss involves the degree to which displacements disorient and intimidate people and peoples, deterring them from action, and, conversely, the degree to which particular places, histories, cultural formations, and traditions can be empowering. Under what circumstances does a sense of place provide sustenance, courage, and inspiration for larger commitments and pluralistic understandings? I do not dispute Connolly's characterization of modernity as a story of continuous displacement. The lesson, differently presented, is there in Marx, Weber, Durkheim, and Tonnies, in Peter Laslett's *The World We Have Lost*, and in Robert Wiebe's portrait of "the distended society" in his *The Search for Order*. Each maps the radical transformations of scale and time as well as the reactionary idealizations of community such transformations engender. What I think worries Connolly are precisely these idealizations. While I share that concern, as is evident in the previous chapter, I wonder whether strongly integrated identities are not a prerequisite for the contingency and pluralization Connolly finds necessary and admirable.

My unease about nostalgia is parallel. As Marx recognized when he distinguished between those instances when recurrence to the past inspired revolutionary movements and those instances when such recurrence meant a distraction from analysis of the present, there is nostalgia and there is nostalgia. In the same way, Machiavelli was relentlessly hostile to nostalgia even as his celebration of Rome was a form of it. The

question for him was about using the past to create a volatile yet energizing collaboration between prince and people, thus generating *political*
power against the power of fortune.

While criticizing what he regards as Michael Walzer's false opposition
between an inside of shared understandings and an outside that can only
be the anarchy of the market or the dominance of a world state, Connolly
points to the sense in which there is a third world inside every city that
closely corresponds to the third world outside the state. That is central to
Saskia Sassen's argument about the increasing centrality of place to the
circuits through which economic globalization is being constituted.[67]
With great vigor and in great detail she has insisted that global cities such
as New York, London, São Paulo, Bombay, and Hong Kong have become
sites of contestation between global capital and equally internationalized
sectors of the urban population upon which that capital depends. This
denationalizing of urban space and the formation of new claims by transnational actors raise the question "Whose city is it?" (xx). Thus global
elements, including labor and diverse cultural identities, have become de-
and reterritorialized in locales that are also linked to global networks of
communication. Like Connolly, Sassen notes the "unmooring" of identities from traditional sources, though, like Falk, she emphasizes how this
is engendering new notions of community, membership, and entitlement
(xxxii). This space, constituted by the "grid of global cities," is place-
centered in the sense of being embedded in particular locations but is
transterritorial in its connecting sites that are not geographically proxi-
mate, even if intensely connected to each other. Sassen reminds us that
even the most advanced information industries have a place-bound work
process, and that cities are production sites for the leading service industries, which means that studying the infrastructure of activities, firms, and
jobs necessary for the advanced corporate economy reveals the practice
of global control (xxiii).

Sassen's analysis of the disparities of wealth and power present in the
process of globalization could be taken as confirmation of Runciman's
conclusion that increases in scale necessitate a diminishing of democracy,
especially its participatory dimensions, which become, under such circumstances, dangerously mythic. But it can also be interpreted in the opposite
way: her emphasis on place provides the challenge but also the opportunity
for face-to-face politics that must now include issues of race, class, gender,
religion, and region too quickly dismissed by democrats who think citizenship must be constituted wholly independent of such identities.

"The global city," she writes, is a "strategic site for disempowered
actors because it enables them to gain presence, to emerge as subjects,
even when they [immigrants, women, African Americans, peoples of color
generally] do not gain direct power" (xxi). Such people exist as potential

or putative citizens who can make claims for power based on a democratic ideology in the same sense as and similarly to the way poor Athenian males could and did in fifth-century B.C.E. Athens.

For all its power, subtlety, and originality, Sassen's analysis is too econo-mistic. It largely ignores the sort of democratic potential of neighborhood politics considered by Roger Sanjek in *The Future of Us All: Face and Neighborhood Politics in New York City*.[68] Sanjek describes how every-day interactions around block and tenant associations, houses of worship, coalitions of small business people, civic rituals, the working through of incidents of racial and ethnic tension, struggles against overdevelopment and for more schools and youth programs have built up a rich pattern of associational life such as Tocqueville admired and Putnam says no longer exists. These networks of affiliation overcome racial stereotypes and bridge ethnic and national borders while sustaining such occasions as In-ternational Nights and the Parade of Nations that symbolize multiethnic, multiracial communities. As neighbors come to realize they share a com-mon fate at the hands of city planners, realtors, and political leaders, they generate a vibrant neighborhood politics. It is a politics that resists the imperatives of neoliberalism by fighting against government while making demands of it, both of which help constitute informal centers of power and resistance independent of that government, which is not a bad de-scription of a parallel polis.

"Parallel polis"[69] was a way of naming the places within civil society where participatory opportunities, those denied citizens in larger forums monopolized by mendacious regimes that, in Havel's phrase, "pretended to pretend nothing," presented themselves. Looking to the state or hoping to seize power from it by violent means was not only dangerously unreal-istic; it was also insufficiently radical (since such violence merely mirrored state politics) and ignored the linked possibility of multiplying what Arendt calls "the space of appearance" while recapturing utopian mo-ments without replicating the evils of a utopian project.

More specifically, a parallel polis meant the cultivation of democratized practices and institutions that would shadow and parallel those of the state: parallel information networks, forms of education, trade unions, foreign contacts, and economy. It was in and through these anti-institu-tional institutions that people could combat the dialectic of cynicism and self-righteousness that accompanies the reality of powerlessness.

The notion of the parallel polis was generated by the specific circum-stances of what Havel called "post-totalitarian" politics, or rather antipoli-tics. Yet Havel also argued that the situation it was meant to combat—passivity, indifference, petty preoccupations, narrow self-interest—was present in the Western democracies as well. And so the impulse behind the parallel polis to have citizens rather than subjects, participants rather than spectators, agents rather than cogs in the machine, applied to the industrial now-globalizing world as well. In this regard it is no accident that they used the word "polis" with its ideal of "co-presence, specific locale, and the demand for dialogue" that we are assured is irrelevant "to the social and political conditions of the twentieth century." My own view is that the parallel polis, with its Greek resonance, is a necessary, though hardly sufficient, condition for the revival and extension of democratic politics.

It is a necessary condition providing we think of the polis as a way of doing politics and being political. Themistocles (in Thucydides' *History*) tells the Athenians that they did not cease to be Athenians when they abandoned the land, public spaces, and shrines of their ancestors, because a city exists wherever citizens meet to speak and act together. Though Athenian conservatives were no doubt shocked by the baldness of his claim, they, like other Greeks, would not have equated the city with its territory. For them, too, the polis was its people, which is why the Peloponnesian War was a war not between Athens and Sparta, but between the Athenians and the Lakedaimoneans. Of course the Athenians were concerned with territory. Frontiers between cities were crucial, as my earlier references to Heraclitus and Aristotle suggest, and we know that exile consisted precisely in the right of anyone to kill the outlaw if he were found within the territorial bounds of the city. But territory was not nearly as important for them as for us, which suggests a connection with and pedigree for Falk's and Connolly's exploration of democracy and deterritorialization, as well as Benda's, Havel's, and Michnik's exploration of decentralized power and freedom within the state.

The parallel polis is a necessary condition only if we do not, as Nancy Rosenblum said about "civil society," turn it into "the chicken soup of political analysis" (e.g., by ignoring the fact that evangelicals and militias are also part of civil society) or turn our backs on the state as if that would make it go away. At the very least one should be suspicious about the politics of antistatists while acknowledging the antidemocratic logic of what Sheldon Wolin calls the "megastate."[70] However remote, abstract, and technical megastate politics may be, citizens need to participate in it, if only to force the debate to remain more open and prevent the depoliticizing of significant political matters (such as education and criminality). Critique of the undemocratic aspects of the state in the name of an idealized form of democracy is one thing; ignoring the state in the name of that ideal imitates Stoic moralism.

This means that a citizen of the modern state must be, in Wolin's phrase, "a multiple civic self," engaging in politics in the sorts of diverse settings Falk, Connolly, Sassen, Sanjek, and Benda analyze.[71] That requires not only participating in multiple venues—state, neighborhood, nation, civil society, social movements, voluntary associations—but participating in different ways: directly, through representatives, or in more complexly mediated ways.

The parallel polis is a necessary condition because it provides moments and places to recuperate the life of active citizenship, freedom, and sense of agency against the prevailing mood of powerlessness and cynicism. It is necessary because direct political experience is a fundamental form of political education and a way of developing a sense of political judgment that can be exercised in other contexts. And it is necessary because of the opportunities for face-to-face politics it provides, though the faces now have many more colors and shapes than they ever did in the polis.

VII

Platonic Noise

When it is evening, ye say, it will be fair weather: for the sky is red.
And in the morning, it will be foul weather today: for the sky is red and
lowering. O ye hypocrites, ye can discern the face of the sky: but can
ye not discern the sign of the times?
—Matt. 16:1–3

If he's so fucking smart how come he's so fucking dead?
—Jack Nicholson in *Prizzi's Honor*

In this concluding chapter, I offer
some reflections on the interrelationship of mortality, politics, and political theory at the beginning of the new millennium. In some respects such
reflections have been anticipated in chapters 3 and 5. Hannah Arendt is
not only one of the few contemporary political thinkers to take the polis
as a point of reference; she is also one of the few who regard mortality as
a political problematic, and the connection between those preoccupations
is hardly coincidental. "Hannah Arendt at Colonus" considered the death
of Oedipus as enigma, gift, and loss, the idea of politics as a redemptive
moment against the Wisdom of Silenus, and the way death provides both
authority for the storyteller and solace for his or her listeners. One could
extend what Arendt says about stories to the one she tells about Athens
and politics, and to the ones being told about her.

Considerations of loss and mortality were also present in chapter 5.
That chapter began with the death of Michael Eugene Mullen and the
story his mother came to construct about him. That prefaced my own
story about political theory, a story that suggested how a sense of loss
drives men and women to theorize, how such theories never quite erase
the presence of loss, and which temptations invite us to master or evade
that presence. But in other respects, the reflections in this chapter represent a shift in focus, theme, and referents.

To study the interrelationship of politics, political theory, and mortality is daunting in the extreme. This is due not only to the stature of those who have engaged, if not anguished over, the subject, or to the fact that one can trace the beginnings of "Western" literature and philosophy to Achilles and Socrates. It is due to the simple fact that I am a man in the last years of his life. Whatever the academic conventions that govern my story, the stakes in it are not only academic. Perhaps they never are.[1]

These conventions encourage a certain detachment, the assumption of an analytic or ironic mediation that allows death to become an idea at once manipulable and mastered in argument as it cannot be outside it. This constitutes a kind of forgetting in the heart of remembrance like the one proposed by Nietzsche in chapter 2 and illustrates this volume's epigraph from Proust. What this means, I suppose, is that I am, for better or worse, enacting the dilemmas I analyze, and that I participate in the fears and evasions present in Plato's *Phaedo* and Don DeLillo's *White Noise*. It also means that this chapter is itself grist for DeLillo's satirizing of the American academy.

I have another aim in this chapter, though it is less argued for than assumed, at least at the outset. It has to do with making a case for the generative relationship between literature and political theory. This is hardly a new or original claim. Political theorists have been "literary" from the beginning (which may help explain why they are regarded as "softheaded" by other social scientists). Socrates tried his hand at poetry, and Plato's critique of the poets was something of an in-house affair. Contemporary philosophers such as Bernard Williams, Martha Nussbaum, and Stanley Cavell engage works of literature as a way of thinking about traditional philosophical problems while at the same time challenging the view of the subject as defined by Anglo-American analytic philosophers. The American Political Science Association includes a subgroup called Literature and Politics, which puts on its own panels and has a newsletter. Finally, professors of law increasingly turn to "great" literature as a way of exploring legal issues in novel ways.

My assumption cum argument is narrower and more grandiose. It is that the dialectic between two works of "literature," namely, Plato's *Phaedo* and Don DeLillo's *White Noise*, can, for all their obvious differences, help us think about mortality and its relationship to politics and political theory. Though the "proof" of such a claim lies in the pudding, let me offer a few of the recipe's ingredients. They are already present in chapter 1 on Roth's *Human Stain*, and in chapter 3, where Arendt praised Lessing for a love of the world that enabled him to sacrifice the axiom of noncontradiction and the claim to self-consistency, and in her endorsement of Isak Dinesen's statement that "all sorrows can be borne if you put them into a story or tell a story about them."[2]

The *Phaedo* raises the question of what constitutes a "good" argument. Should such an argument be conclusive in a way that removes the likelihood or the possibility of doubt and ambiguity? Are rigor and consistency invariant signs of a good argument, or do the value and nature of such qualities depend upon what is being argued about, as Aristotle suggests when he insists that a well-educated man will bring no more precision to a subject matter than the subject matter warrants? Socrates makes it clear that the stakes in their consideration of the question are high, since offering the wrong kind of argument encourages misology, which in turn promotes misanthropy. The dialogue raises the stakes higher still, since it implies that a good argument has to do with living a good life. and that living such a life is itself a kind of argument.

But what, then, is a good or appropriate argument when one is discussing death, which is, after all, the subject of the dialogue? What sort of precision does the nature of this subject matter warrant (if indeed it has "a" nature)?

Gotthold Lessing has an answer.[3] It is not the "force" of the argument or the "power" of the conclusions that matters, but something else entirely. "I am not duty bound," he writes, "to resolve the difficulties I create. May my ideas always be somewhat disjunct, or even appear to contradict each other, if only they are ideas in which readers will find material that stirs them to think for themselves [*selbstdenken*]." Lessing wanted no more to coerce others than to be coerced himself, whether such coercion came from force or proofs. Indeed, he regarded the tyranny of those who attempt to dominate thinking by reason and by making "compelling" argumentation as more dangerous to freedom than orthodoxy is. Instead of fixing himself in history with a perfectly consistent system, he "scattered" the world with provocations. For Lessing, to *think* about death requires what I would call polyvocality, by which I mean the interruption of coherence, dislodging the compelling force of reason and argument. The arrival of Truth or discovery of Reality both silences such provocations and is an ultimately futile attempt to triumph over the finitude of human life. But polyvocality in the *Phaedo* is more than a plurality of voices. What is distinctive, if not unique, about the *Phaedo* is the cumulative impact of unredeemed promises and problematic certainties, its unstable amalgam of consolation, argument and myth, the doubts Socrates expresses about the philosophical life he has led, the unsettled mood of the dialogue's final scene, and the unexpected content of Socrates' last words.

But what about thinking about *death*? Here, Dinesen provides the beginnings of an answer. Glossing Dinesen, Arendt says (in her Benjamin-inflected voice) that "storytelling reveals meaning without committing the error of defining it."[4] Elsewhere she claims that death "not merely ends life but bestows upon it a silent completeness against the flux to which all human beings are subject."[5]

I agree that a story can give shape to a life, providing aesthetic completeness even when that life is wracked by suffering, hardship, and doubt. I also agree with her and Benjamin that stories reveal previously unrecognized depths of meaning with each retelling, and that such stories do not expend themselves but preserve and concentrate their strength so that events are not consumed by the moment. This is certainly true of the story of Socrates. No doubt the *Phaedo* helped establish the interpretive frame for subsequent narratives of Socrates' life and death. But the "event" and "Socrates" live on in the dialogues about it and him. In these terms, a definitive interpretation that filled the frame and stilled the controversy would kill Socrates in a way that Athenians could not. "The Storyteller," Benjamin claims, "borrows his authority from death."[6] That is as true of DeLillo as it is of Plato. But both, I will argue, return that authority to the reader, guiding him or her to fashion along with others a narrative in which life assumes dignity and purpose.

I have one final aim in this chapter. Announced first in chapter 1, it animates every subsequent chapter, as it has my previous work. It is to suggest the "usefulness" of thinking about contemporary politics and political theory with "the Greeks," more particularly with Athenian political thought. But the juxtaposition of DeLillo in *White Noise* and Plato in the *Phaedo* strains credibility, given that the one is thought to be a founding text of Western metaphysics, while the other is said to be the quintessential postmodern novel. Moreover, the *Phaedo* has as little to say about politics as *White Noise* does, and DeLillo has explicitly said, "I don't have a political theory."[7] And why choose these texts to think with rather than *Leviathan*, *The Human Condition*, *Being and Time*, or *Endgame*?

In some respects, critics are right to regard DeLillo as "the poster boy for post-modernism" and *White Noise* as the quintessential postmodern novel.[8] In his postmodern voice, DeLillo is the wised-up child of randomness and incongruity, the master of bricolage and conspiracy theories of corporate power and government secrecy.[9] In it, he rejects conventional notions of Truth and Reality and forms of storytelling, while portraying fragmented identities moving dazedly through an intellectual landscape disrupted by non sequiturs, and mediated by a vast number of sound bites that may or may not be connected to worldly causes and consequences. Finally, this novel is not only about codes imperfectly deciphered by sometimes cartoonish characters who are both objects of parody and ciphers for deadly serious reflections on mortality; it is one itself.

Such codes are constituted by recursive language games and pyramids of meaning saturated with references whose ironic content is only partly understood by characters who are relentlessly self-aware and who have more in common with Narcissus and Sisyphus than with Horatio Alger. (Sisyphus was the legendary founder of Corinth who cunningly outwitted death only to be condemned by Zeus to the perpetually futile task of pushing a boulder up a hill, always to fail at the last moment.) *White Noise* presents us as having fallen in love with our own technological ingenuity, which we cannot fully or finally master. We have overcome all natural obstacles to life but one, the Chorus in *Antigone* sings, and that one is death.

But the novel has two other voices that move against as well as with this first one. In the second voice the dread is real as politics and history drift deathwards. In it, nostalgia is a symptom of a real disease; the arbitrary notoriety of the most photographed barn in America is an erasure of the past contributing to the tyranny of the present, and the wailing of Jack's son Wilder is a cry of despair. "[D]eeper down than bomb shelters, commodity pits, and radioactive waste, than the denial, repression, and fossil fuels of memory," John Leonard has written of the bottom circle of DeLillo's *Underworld*, "there is a village of deformed children not on any map of Kazakhstan."[10]

In the third and final voice, DeLillo is a holy man seeking signs of transcendence and light, grasping the tendrils of redemption. In it, *White Noise* becomes a theodicy, and the non sequiturs that disturb the narrative, though they could represent consumer culture's corporate takeover of our souls, might be intimations of still living gods whose elusive presence is everywhere.

All this means that the novel is polyphonic and dramatizes the condition of postmodernity without endorsing, let alone celebrating, it. In the end, *White Noise* leaves it up to us to interpret and judge, thus exemplifying what Benjamin called the "amplitude" of a story that distinguishes it from information. For example, possibilities for cultural regeneration may reside in everything from TV ads and tabloids to car crash movies and Elvis, but the very belief that they do may be a symptom of our desperation for meanings denied when all that is solid melts into air. Similarly, the barely discernible voices that disturb the narrative and lives of the characters may be an alternative to rational discourse, Nietzsche's thoughts behind thoughts and thoughts behind those thoughts, concealed gardens and paintings below the threshold of reflective surveillance, or simply baby talk, nonsense, and media babble.[11] Yet again, truth, reality, and redemption may represent a "post-metaphysical hangover"[12] or something novels must take seriously and help provide. Finally, there is the epistemology of the most photographed barn in America. For Plato as he is usually read, a simulacrum is a copy of a copy, its untruth defined by its distance from the original, its danger being that as an imitation it will be taken as reality. Gilles Deleuze denies the priority of the original

over the copy and rejects the sense of loss and epistemological insufficiency such ruptures are thought to portend. Indeed, cutting representations off from their original (which is anyway already a copy) frees us
from a Platonic ontology. Confronting the issue and the barn, Jack Gladney, the principal character of *White Noise*, is silent.

I shall argue that a comparable polyphony exists in the *Phaedo*, and
that DeLillo's three voices find an anticipation there. But the dialogue's
polyphony is more than the explicit exchanges among the interlocutors.
The dialogue as a whole speaks against as well as about its own metaphysical aspirations, just as *White Noise* does about its antimetaphysical ones.
And though the *Phaedo* lacks the non sequiturs of *White Noise*, its rapid
changes of mood and subject sometimes function as such, and it does have
at least one and it is a beauty: Socrates' last words to Crito.

The polyphonic quality of each text makes the generative potential of
a conversation between them more promising. Nonetheless, the radical
decontextualization such a conversation presupposes is even more extreme than the juxtaposition of Old Comedy and TV sitcoms framed in
chapter 4. Think of how bizarre a script would be if Jack Gladney or Don
DeLillo were a presence in the *Phaedo* and Socrates or Plato were an
interlocutor in *White Noise*.

Yet Socrates, Plato, and the arguments of the *Phaedo* do have a presence
in *White Noise*. To begin with, the dialogue's view of the soul's relation
to the body and of philosophy as a preparation for death is present in
White Noise in a discussion of Tibetan religion. Though it represents an
alternative understanding of death, it is quickly shoved aside with an
ironic push. One of Jack's ex-wives, now called Mother Devi, handles an
ashram's investments, real estate, and tax shelters. "It's what she always
wanted: peace of mind in a profitable context" (87). Second, there is the
story of Atlantis. In Greek legend, Atlantis was a magnificent civilization
that flourished on an island until destroyed by an earthquake. It may well
have been the model for *The Republic* and figures prominently in the
Timaeus and *Critias*. Here is what happens to this utopian vision in *White
Noise*. Jack's wife Babette is reading from the tabloids to a gathering of
blind people at the shelter where they have gathered to avoid the Airborne
Toxic Event (ATE), a chemical spill that has enveloped their community.
(In Greek, *ate* is the kind of madness that blinds men to the distinctions
between right and wrong, advantageous and ruinous conduct.) The story
is about a physicist/fitness guru who used regression on two apparently
unrelated women only to discover "that they had been twin sisters in the
lost city of Atlantis fifty thousand years ago." Both women describe the
city "as a clean and well run municipality where you could walk safely
almost any time of day or night. Today they are food stylists for NASA"
(143).

Third, there is the parody of a Socratic dialogue when Jack's son Heinrich plays the sophist to his father's Plato. The subject is rain, and the issue is how one can be absolutely sure it is raining. There is no truth, Heinrich insists, only my truth and your truth, no such thing as the here and now, since the here and now is always becoming something else by the time you say it. What is rain anyhow, and how can one be certain that what appears on the windshield of a car is it? "There is," he says, "no past, present, or future outside our own mind" (24). Yet this "hairsplitter and sophist," as Jack calls him, has a point. It isn't just rain, since it contains all sorts of deadly impurities. And if he is right about this, he may be right about other things as well.

Fourth and finally, one can view Jack Gladney as the latest incarnation of an intellectual tradition Socrates helped constitute, a tradition defined by the *Apology* and consecrated (I will argue) by the *Phaedo*.

In his own way Jack, like Socrates, engages in a search for meaning and truth. But something has gone terribly wrong with the Socratic vocation, as indicated by Jack's being a professor of Hitler Studies. Describing Adolph Eichmann, Arendt says that "he was not Iago and not Macbeth, and nothing would be farther from his mind than to determine with Richard III to prove a villain." Except for a preoccupation with his own advancement, Arendt continues, "He had no motives at all. . . . He merely, to put the matter colloquially, never realized what he was doing."[13] Arendt's foil for Eichmann is Socrates, and in her later Socratic reflection on the trial she wonders whether thinking itself might inhibit evil deeds.[14]

Jack Gladney is no Eichmann, and nothing would have been further from his mind than participating in bureaucratic murders or entering the marching columns of the Third Reich. He is obsessively self-aware. At times his relentless questioning seems a parody of Socrates as his preoccupation with mortality is of Socrates' view that philosophy is a preparation for death.

What neither Socrates nor Plato could possibly anticipate is that the terms in which their thought would survive, the opposition between metaphysics and skepticism, reality and appearance, fact and fiction, has been dissolved as intelligence has become commodified. Not only is there Jack's creation of Hitler Studies as a form of academic self-promotion, with its implication that universities mimic the consumer culture they purportedly stand against, but there is the existence of his ex-wives, who are intelligence operatives doing work the novel suggests is suspect, if not death-dealing. Finally, there are rationalistic models of life and death that treat real disasters as simulations and simulations as the "real" thing.

But for all this, my case for juxtaposing these two texts as a way of thinking about the interrelationship of politics, political theory, and mortality rests on performance, not promise. Section I of this chapter sets the scene by offering reflections on death and mortality in contemporary America. It is followed by a highly truncated presentation of the often intricate and difficult exchanges between Socrates and his interlocutors in Plato's *Phaedo*. Section III focuses, as do most commentators, on Socrates' last words and what I regard as a turn toward Athens and the politics it represents. Section IV turns to DeLillo's novel, *White Noise*. It is a story about a middle-class, middle-aged white male academic who basks in the achievement of having created a department of Hitler Studies and lives with his current wife and an assortment of children from previous marriages. Already preoccupied with death, he becomes even more so after being exposed to a chemical spill. Now utterly desperate, he turns to everything and anything—drugs, violence, domesticity, commodities, television, the disasters of others, Hitler—that might distract him from or alleviate the dread that has come to define his life. This section explores where that dread comes from, and the failed strategies he seizes upon to escape it. Section V focuses on the place of politics in *White Noise*'s America and why that place is what it is. The concluding section returns to the uncertainties about death broached in Section I and how those uncertainties look in light of the juxtaposition of the *Phaedo* and *White Noise* and Socrates' questioning about living a worthy life.

I have and shall continue to use an unproblematic "we" and "us" in this chapter. But I am aware that different cultures have different grammars of death, that as Philippe Ariès has argued, death is a socially constructed phenomenon to be understood in relation to the various cultural practices that surround it. For instance, Jainism includes the practice of sallekhana, a fast unto death that some monks are allowed to undertake in the final stages of their lives.[15] The fast can only be understood as part of a vision of life that sees no finality in death, a position in some ways consonant with that Socrates puts forth in the *Phaedo*.[16]

As this implies, even in the West there are radically different conceptions of death. For most (but not all) ancient Greeks the ultimate quality of a person's, or rather man's, life cannot be known until the moment of his death. This is so because, as Solon said to King Croesus, no one can be counted truly happy until death, since fortune could at any moment snatch the prizes one had won up to then, and because death was the supreme moral test that revealed a person's essential character. The day of death, as Montaigne declared, was "the Master-day, the day which judges all others." It was the climax and summation of all that had gone before.[17]

For most of "us," including Don DeLillo and Jack Gladney, the idea of judging an entire life on the basis of a single day's conduct or misfortune is cruel, if not bizarre. Why on earth make a dying man, probably suffering pain and forgetfulness, among other acute forms of mental and physical distress, accountable for a complete life? Why demand a definitive performance from people who may be "less themselves" than they have ever been before?

The reflections that follow, though aware of such differences, will not make much of them. And, as will become clear, such reflections come from someone who, to use Weber's phrase, is "religiously unmusical."

I

Death may be a historical constant, but the act of dying has become as uncertain as the rest of our lives. For one thing, it is no longer clear what it means to die, or how to locate death in life. For example, the question of where the dead live seems oxymoronic to us. But our forebears understood the question and had an answer for it: the dead live under the earth, which was why the living offered them food and libations of water, milk, and wine. That earth was where people lived, where their ancestors lay buried, and where their children and children's children would be as well. But now most of us do not know where we will be buried, and find the question of little import. When asked where we are from, we are more likely to answer by specifying our place of birth than the place where our ancestors are buried. With this, we seem to have freed ourselves from our attachments to the dead. And who can blame us for throwing off the burden of unspeakable hardships and indignities our obligations to the dead have entailed?[18] The dead weight of past generations, Marx famously proclaimed, weighs like a nightmare on the brain of the living. At last, we have awakened and claimed our own lives. One man, a doctor as it happens, in Bill Moyers's PBS series *On Our Own Terms*, wanted to be the master of ceremonies of his own death rather than allowing it or other people to write the script of his life. It is a desire that was shared by Achilles and Socrates, both of whom chose the conditions of their death.

In part, this uncertainty derives from our increasing capacity to prolong life, which makes the question of what it means to live all the more pressing and begs the question of when the prolongation of "life" becomes a misnomer. Many of us have watched in disquiet as the quality of life becomes compromised, when friends and loved ones lose their memory and feel their adulthood succumbing to an incontinence we associate with infancy. Embarrassed and depressed by these daily reminders of mortality, they increasingly consume the care, energy, and resources of their families, often with great reluctance. The Sphinx's riddle Oedipus solved asked what creature is four-footed, two-footed, and three-footed all in a single day. The answer was "man," who as a child crawls on all fours, walks upright as an adult, and uses a cane in old age. But where does the old person as child or those who persist on machines and tubes fit in the riddle or the answer? More pointedly, given the themes of self-knowledge and self-discovery in the play, where in the story are those forced to choose between clarity of mind and morphine?

A recent conference in southern California proclaimed the wondrous news that the lifespan of humans may be doubled in the next century.[19] This is something like the budget deficit. I know what it means to owe thousands, but not trillions. Similarly, I have a decent sense of what living to ninety would involve, but two hundred is as alien a number as a trillion. Is two hundred just a matter of added years? Or is there some qualitative shift in our sense of time and history when the number gets so large, some deep alteration of generational obligation or erosion of the boundary between life and death? Will such prolongation encourage integration of the old into "normal" life or further isolate the aged, infirm, diseased, and mentally fragile, making the acknowledgment of death even more unlikely among the young? Will adding years make the inevitability of death ever harsher, add to our resentment, and drive us to consume more of society's resources for lengthening our lives until we have eaten of that other tree which God anticipated when he banished us from Paradise for tasting the fruit of the first? Or is Herbert Marcuse right that we can, by reducing death to a biological fact, rob it of its horror, incalculable power, and "transcendent sanctity while stimulating efforts to extend the limits of life and eliminate decrepitude and suffering"?[20] Could one ever reduce death to a *biological fact*, or is the very idea of death, insofar as it indicates finitude and uncertainty, the spur for stories of transcendence?

These questions and the uncertainty they elaborate about what it means to die constitute the most anxious aspect of a more encompassing consciousness. Most of "us," Slavoj Žižek writes, no longer live our lives "in compliance with Nature or Tradition. There is no symbolic order or code of accepted fictions to guide us in our social life."[21] Things that once seemed self-evident—whether to have children and how to feed and educate them, how to relax and amuse ourselves, how to proceed with sexual seduction, how and what to eat—have become colonized by reflexivity and are experienced as something to be learned and decided upon instead of just lived. Babette, the wife of the protagonist in *White Noise*, teaches the elderly how to stand, sit, and eat.

One reaction to this relentless historicizing that Nietzsche warned about is rage at our finitude. Technophiles (and here I include Marcuse) regard the world as a series of problems to be solved, challenges to human ingenuity, hurdles to leap over. Death just happens to be the final hurdle, the last antiquated remnant of nature's resistance. But leaping that hurdle is no more possible than jumping on one's own shadow. Frustrated and overwhelmed by the dread of death that his obsessive (if selective) self-awareness generates, Jack turns to violence. The gun he fires at a man named both Gray and Mink is an explosion of rage against the final obstacle to mastery and self-mastery, death. Here he represents the furious drive to manipulate and alter (think of gene-splicing) or re-create (cloning) our own nature. Like the madness of Creon in *Antigone*, his is a fury against the stubborn fact of mortality. With only some exaggeration one could say, as I will suggest in detail, that Jack was trying to kill death.

Jack's preoccupation with death signals the porousness of those narratives of progress that had deflected attention away from morality and death, those secular theologies that provided a rationale, if not meaning, compensation, and solace, for our finitude. "My life is bounded to a limited time," Ludwig Feuerbach wrote, "not so the life of humanity."

> This history of mankind consists in nothing else than a continuous and progressive conquest of limits, which at a given time pass for the limits of humanity, and therefore for absolute insurmountable limits. But the future always unveils the fact that the alleged limits of the species were only limits of individuals.[22]

Change led not to death or decline, but to renewal and liberation. The death of the individual was redeemed by the deathlessness of the species, as Marx's notion of species being implies.

Though such redemption might be spiritual, its manifestation, as Weber saw, would be material. But for all the commodity fetishism in contemporary America, there is also a loss of faith in the consoling power of commodities and the culture of plenty. When a colleague catches Jack without his dark glasses and academic gown and remarks on his ordinariness without these items of authority, Jack goes on a shopping spree as if to rebuild his diminished bulk and power. After being exposed to the Airborne Toxic Event and the medical pronouncement that he will die, he gives things away. This loss of confidence in narratives of progress and the solace of material success has included a sometimes profound disillusionment with the romance of American nationhood. Andrew Deblanco's and Richard Rorty's call for a revival of faith and hope in the promise of national self-realization is a testament to its erosion.[23]

It is this loss of faith that impels us to rethink politics, mortality, and history outside any all-embracing narrative, let alone one defined by progress, divine providence, or ontology. Against the conventional (but by no means unanimous) reading of the *Phaedo*, and recognizing the anachronism of my categories, I want to suggest nonetheless that aspects of this problematic are explored in Plato's dialogue.

II

Death, more precisely the death of Socrates, is a presence throughout the Platonic corpus, so much so that we could say that Plato invented philosophy as an act of mourning.[24] Indeed, the word "philosophy" implies a longing for a lost object, a love of wisdom as yet unattained and perhaps unattainable, the exemplary life embodied in a teacher one cannot hope to become and perhaps should not try to if one wants to be a student rather than a disciple. We are informed that Plato is absent from the moment of Socrates' death because of illness. But metaphorically that absence can be read as a symbol of the distance one needs to have to be like rather than to mimic Socrates.

Socrates' death provides urgency to any dialogue in which he appears, even when there is no mention of his impending fate. Then there are those dialogues, such as the *Gorgias* and *The Republic*, where that fate is central to the text's drama as well as its argument. Finally, there is the *Seventh Letter*, where, as we saw in chapter 5, Plato tells us that his turn toward philosophy and away from the political career that first beckoned him was a direct result of the treatment accorded Socrates. This suggests that Socrates' reflection on his death in the *Phaedo* is also Plato's reflection on a life shaped by that death.

The *Phaedo* is not just about the immediate circumstances of Socrates' death but about the choices, actions, and vocation that have led to it. Socrates calls attention to these choices and acts by recalling the *Apology*, as when he expresses the hope that his present defense of philosophy against the sympathetic questioning by his (mostly foreign) philosophical accusers will be more successful than his defense against the more hostile Athenian accusers in his previous trial. Though Socrates' references to his earlier trial make perfect dramatic sense, they are, nonetheless, a bit curious. On the one hand, what he says in this later dialogue is a more extreme version of what perplexed and angered the Athenian jury in his first trial. Here again, he rejects the views of the many as authoritative—though the idea that philosophy is a kind of death originates in their "commonsense" belief that disappearance from the affairs of men is a kind of nonexistence—and again focuses on the soul, though in a more esoteric and elaborate way than before. But on the other hand, his views about death in the *Apology* are not only different from those he defends in the *Phaedo*, but inconsistent with them.

Though the Socrates of both dialogues insists that our fear of death is unwarranted, his argument in the *Apology* is that death cannot be an evil because his daimon would have prevented him from doing and saying anything that would jeopardize his interests or lead him to injustice. Its silence speaks in favor of death's being good. But the *Phaedo* says nothing about a daimon. And insofar as the kind of human wisdom he acknowledges having in the *Apology* precludes any certain knowledge of death, his claim to know what and how valuable death is in the *Phaedo* is pretentious. Similarly, while the metaphor of death as a journey to another place without the injustices that plague this one appears in both dialogues, Socrates' elaboration of that journey and, more generally, the relationship between death and philosophy are, once again, very different. Death, he says in the *Apology*, is either a journey to Hades where he will encounter real rather than ersatz judges and be able to converse with the great poets of Hellas, or the soundest sleep we have ever experienced. (Of course the reason we value untroubled sleep is that we feel refreshed and rested upon wakening.) No such option is mentioned in the *Phaedo*.

The option is odd even in the *Apology*, given Socrates' likening himself to a gadfly who stings his fellow citizens, who would, without his prodding, "sleep undisturbed for the rest of their lives" (376). And why should he carry on his questioning despite past threats and his present predicament, and even though life is very dear to him? Out of piety and patriotism, for the sake of Apollo, and to make his compatriots think and examine their lives so that they might fully live them. Fear of death does not deter him from refusing to arrest Leon of Salamis, from carrying out an illegal verdict against admirals unable to save their men, or from ceasing to do philosophy. He will, like (his) Achilles, remain at his post no matter what the danger. Neither death nor anything else will make him act shamefully. Here, he is a citizen among citizens; in the *Phaedo* he is among mostly foreign intimates at a place as distant from public life as possible, though the terms of his death have been set by an Athenian court. His care for his compatriots and for the world in the *Apology* contrasts sharply with the hermetic atmosphere of the *Phaedo*.

Of course it seems hermetic only from the vantage of the *Apology*'s Socrates. Seen from the perspective of the *Phaedo*'s Socrates, philosophy is an opening up (in both senses) and turning away from the confines and uncertainties of discursive knowledge associated with politics, toward a larger, ontologically grounded vision of eternity. Within this vision, politics seems to disappear, as does political philosophy as enacted and described in the *Apology*. In these terms, the *Phaedo* is indeed a founding text of Western metaphysics, and it achieves its success, in something like an act of revenge, by sentencing politics to death. The question, of course, is whether these are the only terms.

The *Phaedo* is a report, long after the event, by the title character in response to a request by one Echecrates for a detailed account of the last words and deeds of Socrates. There is a certain anxiety attached to the request, since it is unclear whether an event that happened so long ago and so far away can be accurately recounted, or whether the mythologizing by his disciples has already begun. There is a second cause for anxiety: the exceptional lapse of time between Socrates' conviction and his death. Did the long wait make him more resentful about his fate and lead to some change of demeanor or argument? Or was he the same as always, consistent even to the end?

Socrates, we are told, was sanguine before death, since he had every expectation of joining good men and wise gods and was certain that his divine masters in Hades would be far more worthy than his earthly ones. This expectation comes from his devotion to philosophy that has led him to these conclusions and to the way of life he has lived. Philosophy, it turns out, is "nothing but dying and being dead," and philosophers, if they are genuinely philosophic, are always "verging on death." Thus death is not the final stage of life but a form of life, and those who seem half dead because they have disappeared from public life or care for what others do not are the only ones who are truly alive in this world and the one beyond.

Death is the separation of the soul from the body. *If* no such separation occurs or is possible, then there could be no such thing as knowledge and truth. If there is no such thing as knowledge and truth, humans would be condemned to wander in confusion, imprisoned by earthly entanglements, subject to every possible fear and lust, living with war, distrust, and faction, all of which come from the tyranny of the body and conspire to disrupt thinking. Clearly, philosophers must do all they can do to escape enslavement. Once liberated from the distorting influences of the senses, they will be able to see, not with the eyes but with the mind's eye; not to see things for the first time but to recognize and recollect them in their ultimate Form or Idea, undisturbed by the deceptions and delusions that mark the human condition.

> Now philosophy discerns the cunning of the prison, sees how it is effected through desire, so that the prisoner himself may cooperate most of all in his imprisonment. . . . [T]hen lovers of knowledge recognize that their soul is in that state when philosophy takes it in hand, gently reassures it and tries to release it, by showing that inquiry through the eyes [as well as the other senses] is full of deceit . . . and by persuading it to withdraw from these . . . and by urging it to collect and gather itself together, and to trust none other but itself, whenever it thinks of any of the things that are alone by itself. (83a–b)

Since the soul is immortal, it is homologous to and has an affinity with truth and being. Thus care for the soul means care for the truth, just as a commitment to truth and reason is unintelligible without the philosophic education of the soul.

There is something unsatisfying about the *Phaedo*'s "arguments." They seem to presuppose each other in a particularly incestuous way and to be convincing only to those initiates who already hold them. Given Socrates' theory of recollection and the Orphic and Pythagorean commitments of his interlocutors, this may be part of his point. Or it may be a necessary consequence of the philosopher's distancing himself from "real"-world multiplicities. But I think something more is at stake: misology. The issue arises at a moment in the text when Socrates seems to have gone back on an argument his interlocutors have found thoroughly convincing. Just as they had achieved a sense of calm and certainty, just as the argument seemed to be making progress and they had become confident they knew what Socrates believed and what is true (which they equate), Socrates pulled the rug out from under them.

The removal of certainty threatens to make them skeptical not merely of this particular argument but of arguments in general, and about themselves as able to make good as opposed to bad arguments, or at least able to discriminate between them. The point receives special emphasis because it is repeated by Echecrates in one of his few interruptions. "What argument shall we ever trust," he asks, "now that the argument of Socrates has fallen into discredit?" (88c–d).

In the *Apology*, Socrates was accused by his enemies of making the worse argument appear the better. Now he is accused by his friends of making all arguments doubtful and turning philosophy into eristic, an accusation whose seriousness is indicated by Socrates' explicit connection of misology to misanthropy. Both come from the violation of unconditional trust. If it happens enough, men become cynical and manipulative. Moreover, distrust was supposed to characterize those souls and men who remain attached to the body and the world. Perhaps philosophy cannot rest on the absolute trust discipleship demands, both because such trust is bound to be disappointed and because disciples love Socrates more than they do philosophy. Doing so, they mimic him and seek his approval rather than seek wisdom and truth, as Socrates himself says when he advises Simmias and Cebes to "care little for Socrates but much more for the truth" (91c). Philosophy may be a way of life and Socrates a model for it, but imitation, as I suggested earlier, cannot be slavish or it will not be an imitation of Socrates. Indeed, imitating Socrates may require a distance from him his disciples are unable to observe precisely because they are disciples.

So we are left with the question of what counts as a "good" argument. Must it be conclusive in a way that leaves little or no possibility of doubt? Or, as Socrates seems to indicate in the *Apology*, are all arguments subject to future refutations and in need of constant reconsideration? But the situation in the *Phaedo* is unique. Cebes, Simmias, and Phaedo may reconsider *their* arguments tomorrow but Socrates cannot. These are his last words, which is what gives them special authority, even if ironically enough his last words are not his final ones.

Socrates responds to the distress he created with what Phaedo regards as remarkable psychological as well as intellectual acuity (89a). Yet he does not give his interlocutors what they seem to want and need. He offers conditional, not conclusive, arguments that are more strategic than epistemological or ontological. *If* there were some "true and secure" arguments that were dismissed or overlooked because men had become skeptical about argument in general, *then* we would all be pitiable in having "to finish the days of our lives hating and abusing arguments and being deprived of the truth and knowledge of things that are" (90d). Far better (and truer?) it would be to blame not argument or reason or truth or philosophy, but their own intellectual lapses. Indeed, not theirs but his, since Socrates shoulders all the blame, thereby relieving them of their doubt and resentment and confusion. He admits that he might have been seeking victory, indulging in a moment of self-importance, allowing himself to be led by something other than the logic of the argument, and remaining too attached to the body.

But in something like a Pascalian wager Socrates claims that even if what he says is not true and there really is "nothing left for a dead man," it is better, safer, and more comforting to believe there is. This strategic consideration is also present in his last philosophical words, where he concludes that to insist that his arguments are true would not be fitting for a man of intelligence. What would be fitting is to believe that something *like* what he said is true about our souls, and that this belief should be repeated like a spell. It was for this reason and not for the sake of argument that he prolonged his story. Here is what is reasonable to believe and make into that spell.

> [A]ny man should have confidence for his own soul, who during his life has rejected the pleasures of the body and its adornments as alien . . . [but] has devoted himself to the pleasures of learning, and has decked out his soul . . . [with] temperance and justice, bravery, liberality and truth, thus awaiting the journey he will make to Hades, whenever destiny shall summon him. (114d–115a)

It has summoned him now, so he ends their discussion to bathe before drinking the poison. Lest this care for the body be taken to signify a shift of focus, he does it to save the women from having to wash a corpse.

As this makes clear, the *Phaedo* is, and is understood by its interlocutors to be, a narrative of hope and consolation. Halfway through the dialogue Cebes asks Socrates to reassure them and purge the child inside them that remains terrified of death. When Socrates suggests that they sing spells to this child every day until they have eliminated the fear, Cebes asks where they can possibly find a charmer to lead the chants now that he is leaving them (77e–78a). The tone here is jocular and bantering, even self-mocking. But it is also deadly serious and reminds us that their discussion is intended to build up their confidence and courage, relieve their flagging spirits, and enable them to console each other (89a, 115e).

III

Of course the vast majority of people who read the *Phaedo* care little about Socrates' arguments about the soul, the Forms, the idea of philosophy as a preparation for death, or the relationship between it and the *Apology*. They read the dialogue, or rather its last few pages, because they dramatize the final hours and words of Socrates. It is a moving scene, with Plato's dramatic skills on full display.

As the mortal chill moves up Socrates' body, the language itself becomes chastened, almost clinical and matter-of-fact, third-person nouns and verbs largely replacing personal ones.[25] We are told in the dialogue that Plato was ill and absent in these final moments. But these moments exist as they do because of Plato, which means he is everywhere.

But why are Socrates' final words, "Crito, we owe a cock to Asclepius. Pay it and do not forget it" (118b), rather than some elevated philosophical idea? What did Socrates mean by what he said, and what did Plato mean by having him say it?[26] What does sacrificing a rooster to a god of healing have to do with the preceding dialogue, or with Socrates' life as a whole, that it should not appear now in his final moment?

Nietzsche thought he knew. He regarded Socrates' last words—which he mistranslated by making a plural "we" into a singular "I"—as revealing the true purpose of Socrates' philosophizing. In Nietzsche's hands, the rooster is transformed into a "raven" devouring what is left of life. The purported physician is the disease; his bright, cold, overly conscious life, "without instinct and in opposition to all instincts," is turned against the world with resentment and revenge. "Did he himself know," Nietzsche asks, "did he in the end say softly to himself 'here death alone is the physician'?"[27] Socrates was sick a long, long time, "suffering life."[28]

Nietzsche has a point. Certainly part of the dialogue's argument as well as its mood confirms his diagnosis. But for my purpose this is too literalist a reading of the *Phaedo*, ignoring the fact Nietzsche helped bring about, that the dialogue's last words have been anything but final.

Indeed, there is a certain irony in the fact that the last words of a founding text of Western metaphysics should have engendered such controversy, and that the interpretations of the passage and so the dialogue as a whole should be discursive. The narrative of Socrates' life belongs to the various interpretive communities that vie with each other to define the meaning of those words and bring closure to his life and the dialogue.

As I mentioned earlier, it is the polyvocality of the *Phaedo* that provokes such controversy: the unfulfilled promises, certainties made problematic, the sometimes abrupt movements between consolation, argument, and myth, the unsettled mood of the dialogue, the peculiar injunction to Crito, and Socrates' explicit doubt about the philosophical life he has led.

Such doubts surface when Socrates recounts a recurrent dream in which he is told to make music and practice it. He had assumed that this meant doing philosophy. But he is no longer sure, and so he decides to write poetry, most notably a hymn to Apollo. Given what Socrates says about writing, about poetry as an inferior form of discourse, and about poets, whom he condemns for being unable to give an account of what they say or why they say it, the turn toward the writing of poetry is extraordinary.

Socrates' doubts about philosophy and his turn to poetry here may represent a recognition of the compatibility or even similarity between the two and suggest that he was too harsh in his condemnation of poetry and too confident in believing that philosophy could do what the poets could not—provide a full account of what they were saying. But such doubts must extend to Apollo, or at least to Socrates' reading of the god's answer to Chaerephon's question, that Socrates was the wisest man of all, which instigated (if it did not mandate) the philosophical life he has led and the death he must now face because of it. If he has misread the god or been tempted in these last moments to blame him, then the sacrifice of a cock to Apollo's son Asclepius may be a gesture of reconciliation not only with the god but with the life Socrates has led and about which he now has second thoughts.

But why a cock? Why, given the solemnity of the occasion, sacrifice something as lowly as a rooster and apply words connected with the care of the soul to it? Scholars disagree about whether the sacrifice was a traditional religious offering intended to rebut those who believed Socrates impious, or whether there is something sufficiently self-mocking and deflationary about it to confirm his impiety. Of course it is true that the crowing of a rooster signals the rising sun, and that *The Republic* connects the sun with the good (allusions to which appear at 99c). But that is considerable ontological baggage for a chicken.

But most of all, why are the last words addressed to Crito? Why is the sacrifice a joint endeavor with the least philosophic man in the dialogue, if not in the entire Platonic corpus? No doubt there is a special intimacy between these two old friends from the same deme and of approximately the same age. Only Crito is allowed to join Socrates' conversation with his wife and sons.[29] It is Crito who looks after the worldly affairs that allow Socrates to do what he does, and it is Crito who, in the *Apology*, stands surety that Socrates will remain in Athens. And no one has been present at more philosophical conversations than this old comrade. But Crito doesn't get it. He never gets it. True, it is not clear what "it" is. True, other interlocutors in the *Phaedo* and elsewhere say or react in ways the argument stipulates as inappropriate, worrying about things they have agreed are beneath worry and doing it often enough to make us wonder whether they (and we) can live by what Socrates convinces us is true. But Crito's incomprehension is of another order. He is the one who suggests Socrates do anything he can to postpone his death; he asks what Socrates wants him to do about his children, and how in general he can be of service, even though Socrates has told him (and now tells us) that he has answered these questions many times. And it is to Crito that Socrates says, "with a quiet laugh, 'I can't persuade Crito that I am Socrates here, the one who is now conversing and arranging these things being discussed; but he imagines I'm that dead body he'll see in a little while so he goes and asks how he's to bury me' " (115d). It is hard to imagine anyone more deaf to what seems the sort of arguments present in the dialogue.

What, then, do we make of the non sequitur that is Socrates' last words directed to Crito? And how does each reading of it alter the meaning of the dialogue as a whole and its connection with *White Noise*?

In one reading the sacrifice is a ritual giving thanks to the god for releasing Socrates from the illness of life, liberating him from those attachments to bodily desire that have been obstacles to the purification of his soul and his grasp of truth. The intimations of transcendent meaning partially available in a life tied to the body and history are redeemed by a revelation of permanent form grasped or recollected by a soul now freed from the distracting half-truths of the senses. In these terms, the sacrifice is a fitting end to the narrative of Socrates' life, rounding it out by giving it dramatic shape and point. But from a second point of view, the sacrifice of a chicken is a parody, a joke that deflates the pretentiousness of the first. Here, it is a reminder that Socrates is a man among men, subject, like them, to the mortality that marks off a human condition. From a third perspective, it is the collective nature of the sacrifice that matters, insofar as it unites Socrates with Crito, a fellow Athenian concerned with the materiality of Socrates' life and death. More than that it reminds us that it is the view of the many concerning philosophy that those who do it appear to pursue death. It is this belief that has set the terms for the philosophical debate we have just read.

In this, the final moment of his life, Socrates becomes again a citizen among citizens, a man with a body, attached to family, friends, and the city he has always refused to leave. In these terms, he heals the rift between philosophy as he had practiced it and as he had described it in the *Apol-*

ogy. But healing does not mean that the tension between philosophy and politics is erased. How could it be, given the circumstances? What I mean is that the tension which he now accepts has defined his vocation. He has touched people, made a mark in the world, left a "human stain" in Roth's sense. Even his trial and conviction testify to the significance of his life in contrast to that of Tolstoy's Ivan Ilych, who cannot let go of life because, having wasted it in the pursuit of trivialities, he has no life to lose. Only someone who knows how to live knows what it means to die.[30]

There is a fourth possible reading of the final scene and of the *Phaedo*, though it has a different status, given its general claim about Socratic dialogues and further assimilation of the *Phaedo* to the *Apology*. It argues that the *Phaedo* is aporetic. This means that its misdirections, reversals, impasses, incongruities, and warnings that what we hear is being reconstructed long after the fact create a complex irony that invites the reader to do more than absorb or simply disagree with whatever conclusion seems to be reached at any point in the dialogue, including the final one.[31] In these terms, Socrates' aim is to make the world seem strange and shocking, not to claim special authority or possession of the truth. He is inviting us to recognize that neither he nor anyone else has answers to questions that need to be reposed and rethought by widely disparate audiences, including the one reading *White Noise*. Though each of the four readings of the *Phaedo* finds thematic space in the novel, it is this last one that seems to frame it.

IV

While Socrates seems tranquil in the face of death, Jack Gladney is not. His fear of death is the text and subtext of his life (as it is of *White Noise* as a whole). His dread is so encompassing that it dominates his life, which is a frantic, if largely futile, effort to create institutions, practices, and cultural forms that might distract him from or conceal death: everyday routine and domesticity, supermarkets and shopping malls, TV and commodities, universities and popular culture, Hitler and Elvis, expertise and professionalism, class and status differences, drugs and families, technology and nostalgia, and, far from least, the cult of youth.

Why is Jack so vulnerable to the fear of death? One reason is his uncertainty of where death comes from, how to read the signs that might tell him, and where it fits in life.

With Hobbes we know who the enemy is, why he is one, and what steps can be taken to lessen hostilities. No such securities exist in *White Noise*. It is not simply that we continue to suffer the consequences of natural disasters such as earthquakes and floods, but that our inventive-

ness multiplies the sources of death as in plane and car crashes and chemical spills, which are felt to be real only to the degree they catch the flick-
ering glance of TV. Worse, death lurks where one least expects to find it:
in schools (lined with asbestos), around a cozy fire (burning artificial
logs), in labyrinthine malls (an elderly couple is traumatized in a deserted
one), in the acts of eating and watching TV (while being subject to waves
emanating from kitchen appliances and the set itself).

Jack is unable to decipher the codes or find patterns in the events that
shape his life and his world. Those moments when he thinks he has, turn
out absurdly. For instance, he is told that his exposure to the Airborne
Toxic Event means he will die in ten, twenty, or thirty years, a "fact" that
communicates nothing to a middle-aged man. Nonetheless, it increases
his dread. The second, his confrontation with Mink/Gray (which I will
examine in a moment) reads like a bad drug experience. In Plato, particulars are intimations of a Form that give the occasional and singular ontological dignity. But in *White Noise*, particulars are intimations of themselves or of a general formlessness.

But as my previous discussion suggests, this is not quite true of either
the dialogue or the novel. Let us leave aside the question of whether Plato
unequivocally endorses the theory of the Forms; the *Phaedo* leaves us
uncertain about whether Socrates believes that his story of the soul's odyssey is true or just useful, and perplexed by the dialogue's rapid shifts of
mood, preoccupation, and argument. As for *White Noise*, it tantalizes
Jack and us with possible intimations of transcendence in the ordinary
occurrences of watching sunsets, hearing a child's crying, reading tabloids, or listening to advertising jingles.

Jack's uncertainty is mirrored by the frequent but unpredictable non
sequiturs that disrupt the narrative's coherence. We do not know where
they come from, or what they mean and signify. Perhaps they are erup-
tions of a reality beyond the virtual, voices of the repressed or the oppressed, or the preconscious articulations of media-besotted, commodity-
driven souls.

What this adds up to is that death, including the physical fact of it, has
become increasingly mysterious as we have become more knowing and
possess more information. Achilles knows that avenging the death of Pa-
troclus will result in his own. But his ability to coauthor the script of his
life and death is an extension of his prowess (and his being the son of an
immortal mother), as well as his mortality (being the son of a human
father). Something similar could be said of Socrates. He brought the accusations on himself, purposely provoked the jury, refused exile, and died
with equanimity, his death being a final act in the script of his life he
"wrote" and performed so memorably. But there is no place for the hero-

ism of an Achilles or Socrates in *White Noise*, and Jack's mock-heroic battle with Gray/Mink is more mock than heroic.

Jack's motives in confronting Mink are mixed. What matters is that he thinks this is the moment when he can figure everything out, penetrate the veil, hear the messages, decipher the codes. Now he can become coauthor of his life because he will understand the novel of which he is a part. He feels himself decisive, finally taking control of his life, escaping history.

Jack is convinced that committing an act of violence can give his perceptions an epistemological authority they otherwise lack. The fact of killing someone simplifies the world and his place in it, brings clarity to his ruminations and purpose to his intellectual meanderings, which are now finally leading to some decisive action. Violence pushes past representations and the representation of representations to reality itself. Now he sees things as they truly are, grasps their form and essence. He has never felt so fully alive, so in tune with the universe, so much part of a magnificent drama. "I sensed I was part of a network of structures and channels," Jack says as he enters his white-walled, TV-dominated, nondescript motel room in which the technocrat composite Mink/Gray barely exists. "I knew the precise nature of events," he goes on. "I was moving closer to things in their actual state as I approached a violence, a smashing intensity. Water fell in drops, surfaces gleamed" (305). Later: "I continued to advance in consciousness. Things glowed, a secret life rising out of them. . . . I knew for the first time what rain really was." His son, the sophist who "proved" the senses lied and that we could never know it was really raining, is wrong. Plato, as he is conventionally interpreted, is right.

In this scene, the world appears to Jack as one of infinite possibilities. Like the *Phaedo*'s philosophers (and Oedipus before his identity is revealed), he feels liberated from boundaries, free of particular attachments and conventional moral inhibitions, as he revels in the "beauty" of Mink's fear and pain. As a man of action Jack grows larger and more substantial, safer, inured, even immune to death. He sees himself as "looming, dominant, gaining life-power, storing up life-credit" (312).

But the whole thing is a fiasco, more a scene from the Three Stooges than one from Homer. First, after Jack shoots Mink, Mink shoots Jack in the wrist. The two go to a hospital in Germantown run by German nuns who are aggressively atheistic and contemptuous of those, like Jack, who need to believe they believe. Leaving the hospital, he is more fearful than ever. Second, it is clear that Mink once thought himself larger than life, indeed capable of altering people's view of life, since he was the project manager for Dylar, a pharmaceutical that can purportedly inhibit our fear of death. But the project failed, and he is a mental and physical wreck, in part because of popping the pills that seem only to increase the fear of death, if they do anything at all. This means that Mink is yet another reminder of death's hold. Worse still, even if the pill had succeeded, it would not have worked. "There will eventually be an effective medication, you're saying," Jack asks Mink, to which Mink replies, "Followed by a greater death."

Finally, as I suggested, the surreal quality of the scene gives it the feel of a drug experience or madness. Jack plans the deed meticulously and recites his plan three or four times. Yet each time he repeats it, the plan has changed dramatically, though he does not recognize this, and none of the plans has much bearing on what actually transpires. Here is the reductio ad absurdum of Weber's disjunction between intentions and consequences.

For Socrates, philosophy as a preparation for death purifies the soul, allowing it access to meaning and truth. For Jack Gladney, the search for meaning and truth is linked to violence. These seem so different that we might just want to note the fact and leave it at that. But one could, with Nietzsche, press the point to find the ways Jack's theory of violence owes something to philosophy, to see that philosophy is less innocent of violence than it supposes and wants itself to be. Incoherence and randomness have their price, which is part of the story *White Noise* tells. But so do consistency and order, which is the other part. I have suggested that the *Phaedo* makes an analogous point.

A second reason why Jack is so "consumed" by death is the porousness of those narratives of American culture and history that might distract him from it. One such narrative is that of the most photographed barn in America. Jack and his colleague Murray, a professor of cultural studies, see "signs" telling them that they are approaching it. When they get there, they find the place full of buses with tourists taking pictures not only of the barn but of each other taking pictures of the barn. A man in a kiosk is selling postcards of the barn. (Murray and Jack are the only ones not taking pictures.) The notoriety of this barn is entirely arbitrary. There is nothing to differentiate it from thousands of others except for accidental celebrity. It is no longer a "real" barn but a simulacrum mediated by signs, consumed by a self-satisfied presentism that happily absorbs the past in an omniscient here and now. There is no sense of its possible history. No one speaks of the family that owned it and worked the land, of yeoman farmers, or of the livestock, hay, and food that were stored there, or of "our" pioneering past. Everything is absorbed into what Murray with his New Age psychobabble calls its "aura." It is as if we had no debt to the dead, as if "our" culture and lives did not come from them, as if we are not continuing what was already underway before we got here. We pretend to have invented the world yesterday and so arrogate to ourselves the authorship of those who authored us, even if that means making us our own progenitors in a parody of Oedipean incest.[32]

In the essay on death from which I quoted earlier, Robert Harrison argues that uncertainty about the provenance of one's food and the destination of one's corpse are part of a single-minded effort undertaken in "the West" in the last few centuries to emancipate ourselves from bondage to the land and the dead. What he calls "a staggering proportion of American children" respond to the question of where milk comes from with the assertion that it comes from a can, and believe that the supermarkets—Murray's favorite place—are the origin of our food. The world we live in, he concludes, "draws a veil over the process of generation" and obscures our relationship to the earth, which is ultimately the terms of our relation to death as well. Death, like the barn, is dissociated from the lives we think we lead, an abstraction that enables emergency crews to treat actual deaths as experiments so that simulated disasters can be enacted more efficiently. Recall chapter 2 and Nietzsche's contempt for those who become tourists of their own history, those irresolute, feeble, and despairing idlers prowling around the past as if it were a series of pictures (now photographs) in a gallery rather than a repository of monumental words and deeds for contemporary imitation.

Murray is thrilled with the scene, but Jack says nothing. Perhaps there is nothing to say, or he is stunned into silence. Or perhaps his silence signals DeLillo's desire to resist nostalgia as well as presentism. It may be that the past is something given, rather than a piece of artifice, and that robbing us of our memory means destroying something as crucial to our identity as our physical person.[33] In this sense, the past remains a submerged aspect of white noise, and all our efforts at deliberate or involuntary censoring are at best unstable strategies of forgetting. But it is also true that the days when one could invoke a seamless web of memory uniting the entirety of a national community in a common narrative of the past are gone (if they ever existed), and such narratives were anyway written over the enslaved and oppressed. Here again, white signifies whiteness. Thus DeLillo is equally suspicious of Murray's celebration of the contemporary aura and the romanticizing of a past which presumes that at some time culture stood in an unmediated relationship to reality.

Of course the idea of self-invention, that the present must be freed from the burden of the past, is a dominant theme in American history, which suggests that the distancing of the barn from its past is a cultural trope. It's Tocqueville who connects this trope to the melancholy Americans exhibit in the midst of abundance. The pursuit of wealth is haunted by the fear of old age and death (which helps explain why Jack buys things to build himself up and gives things away when informed he will die). Those men who attain a certain equality of condition can never attain as much as they desire. "They are near enough to see its charms but too far off to enjoy them; and before they have fully tested its delights, they die."[34]

In chapter 4, I offered an argument that television helps sustain, if it did not create, a presentism in which memoryless citizens became politically passive. All standards of critique were dissolved in successive moments of the here and now. DeLillo seems to agree. Again, it is Murray who makes the point, when he insists, in what might almost be a parody of Nietzsche's demand that we live in more than one time, that humans inhabit two places at once: those shown on TV and wherever they are, which is often where they watch TV. It is not merely that what we know beyond the circumference of our lives we know from watching television, but that what we know about our own life comes from it. The disasters we live through are real only if they are certified by being on television. Worse still, TV hungers for death, providing increasing dosages of it to hold our attention, like some drug we need more of as we adapt to it. (Recall in this regard Ignatieff's discussion in chapter 4 of TV's presentation of the Ethiopian famine). As Jack's reaction to the Airborne Toxic Event (itself a euphemism) indicates, the media alienates individuals from their own death by transforming death into yet another commodity for mass consumption.

A second narrative, that of technological mastery, has also become porous. Equally true, technology has promised abundance and has in many respects delivered it, however selectively. The supermarket in Blacksmith has products from twenty different countries, each product carrying a suppressed history, labeled and priced. One can choose what to eat and choose a lifestyle, replenish the soul as well as the body, and with such abundant choice sacralize one's freedom and power through consumer choice. Along with shopping malls and supermarkets (the word alone carries a certain weight), technology provides material and spiritual sustenance enabling us to bulk up against death. Buying is Jack's attempt to recapture his aura of power. For him abundance is neither the satiation of desire, the filling of "basic" needs, the necessary condition for generosity, nor a sign of being among the elect. It is, or rather he hoped it would be, protection against mortality. After all, if food, shelter, and clothes were necessary for primitive man to survive, it stands to reason that the more of these you have, the longer you live. This is why Babette, reflecting on the parental wealth of Jack's students, finds it hard to imagine death at that income level. But the consolation of commodities fails after everything has been commodified. When Jack realizes this, he begins to give things away in a gesture that is both defiant and defeatist.

Technology and science have produced cures for diseases, artificial limbs, transplants, plastic surgery, genetic engineering, and promises, as we saw earlier, of even more spectacular ways of extending life. But in holding out the prospect of immortality, they release what Nietzsche, retelling the story of Pandora, regarded as the ultimate curse: hope.

Jack asks a chemist colleague name Winnie to analyze Dylar. She warns
Jack against the drug and against losing one's fear of death. "Isn't death,"
she asks, in what seems to be DeLillo's voice, "the boundary we need?
Doesn't it give precious texture to life, a sense of definition?" You have
to ask yourself (as well as anyone who believes philosophy is a preparation for death) whether anything in this life would have beauty and meaning without the knowledge you carry of a final line, a border, a limit.
Jack's "answer" is a non sequitur that he speaks but does not hear: "Clor-
ets, Velamints, Freedent" (228–29).

To the question that defines his life, Jack responds not with his conscious mind but with brand names that momentarily surface from the
preconscious recesses of his soul.

If Winnie is right, Jack's life has been a quest for fool's gold, his desperate efforts to deflect death's presence a way of denying life. His "response," a non sequitur, suggests she is right. So does one of the primary
meanings of white noise: the communicative mush created by the absence
of distinction's borders and boundaries. The place where such borders
most fully disappear is in Gray's motel room, with its blaring TV, surreal
whiteness, desperate popping of Dylar, comic violence, and random connection of statement and referent, intention and consequence.

In the face of these no longer impregnable narratives of progress and
liberation, Jack attempts to fashion a narrative of his own. He invents the
field of Hitler Studies as a way to advance his academic career, whose
success he hopes can provide sufficient stature, power, and safety to calm
his fear of death. But he also wants to hide inside the enormity of Hitler's
crimes, as if death could not find him there or was already sated by the
millions killed in the death camps.[35] He names his son Heinrich to give
him authority and shield him from the fear of death, and seeks to learn
German to use it as a charm and protective device. Besides, Hitler's evil
offers the one remaining moral trump card against sophistry and relativ-
ism. But the whole enterprise is as much a fiasco as the confrontation with
Mink/Gray. Jack has a thoroughly superficial relationship to his subject.
His attempt to learn German fails, leaving him afraid that someone will
discover this deficiency, and he reads an English translation of *Mein
Kampf* in Dunkin Donuts. In addition, as his manic attempts to overcome
the fear of death attest, he does not feel himself part of something so large
and powerful that he can hide his dread inside it. Moreover, making Hitler
into an academic department like any other routinizes his evil and undermines the moral certainty Nazi evil represented. As for Jack's son Heinrich, he turns out to be the sophist who completes the disestablishment
of Nazi atrocities as a moral compass. He is also the one who has to
remind his father of the simple fact, which apparently eludes Jack, that
the Germans lost the war.

Yet for all his failures and mock-heroism, there is a nobility to Jack's struggle. In chapter 2, Nietzsche talked about the deathlike state of anonymity and indifference, and argued that seeing oneself as the culmination of history is not a form of self-congratulation but a paralyzing acceptance of weakness that diminishes rather than augments our activity. Despite everything, Jack refuses to accept either anonymity or indifference, and his failures represent the incapacities of those Greekless men and women who stand or think of themselves as the final product of history.

V

Politics is the subtext rather than the text of *White Noise*,[36] which is a point the novel makes about the status of politics in the America it portrays. At most, it exists at the margins of consciousness (as it does in the *Phaedo*), not as an object of it. We never see Jack doing anything political in the conventional sense (which is largely true of Socrates as well). He never votes or participates in a meeting or rally or talks with anyone about *a* political issue. We know nothing about the structure of power in Blacksmith or America. His exposure to public life seems confined to the disasters he watches on television. The novel's explicit focus is on his private life, his friendship with Murray, his family, and his career as a professor of Hitler Studies. Certainly there is no evidence that Jack (or any other character) participates in the sort of rich associational life Tocqueville found in America and Robert Putnam doesn't.

Politics may not be the text of *White Noise*, but it is the subtext just as it is in the *Phaedo*. Mostly it is part of the hum that exists just out of earshot and consciousness, a kind of non sequitur that disrupts the narrative. Of course the question is, how does politics work as an absent presence in the novel and in America?

Politics is present in the casual remarks about wealth as insurance against death and the community of privilege symbolized by the lines of new station wagons (read SUVs) signaling the return of students. It is there in Jack's disbelief that an environmental disaster should affect the chairman of an academic department instead of the poor people who live at the edge of town in mobile homes, and in the officiousness of experts and bureaucrats whose language codes make death an abstraction in a way that ratchets up the fear of it. Politics is there in the novel's portrait of popular culture, environmental disasters, commodity capitalism, and the way various soporifics function as drugs of the rich and powerful. But most of all, it is there in the confrontation between Mink and Jack, which makes many of these preoccupations more explicit.

Generally, the novel presents whiteness as blandness, lack of color, generic. But in this scene, whiteness becomes race rather than the absence of race. Here, white noise becomes WHITE noise, WHITE violence, WHITE America, the WHITE man's burden, anything but neutral and nondescript. We do not know what ethnicity Mink is—probably an amalgam—but there is much talk of it, just as there is a sudden emphasis on Jack's whiteness. At one point, in an echo of TV "Indian" talk, Mink asks Jack, "Why are you here, white man?"—a question that extends well beyond the room or the moment. In this scene, the normal and generic become murderous, the neutral packaging a cover for violence, and the hum of white noise a distraction from the politics of race and imperialism. Here, too, the erasure of boundaries becomes the erasure of distinctions and differences by those multinationals sponsoring research into Dylar and supporting media-speak, the preferred language of oblivion.

Recall Wolin's argument (from chapter 4) that the political animal has become the domesticated creature of such media-speak, subject to successive images whose arbitrary arrests of sound, motion, and fashion dissociate definitions of reality from the past. American citizens, he suggests, have developed a political amnesia that reifies the present. The politically lethal cocktail of bureaucratic rule, a common sense unable to grasp the interlocking operations of public and private power, an ersatz freedom defined as consumer sovereignty, and boundless amounts of formless data threatens to make democratic citizenship as anachronistic as the barn celebrated for being celebrated. All this at the moment when democracy is universally acclaimed.

No wonder Jack wanders and reacts rather than acts. The irrationality he experiences is far more vertiginous than the one Weber envisages in the concluding pages of "Politics as a Vocation." What Weber saw as the ethical irrationality of the world has expanded exponentially in the America of *White Noise*. For all its commercial civilization, America has become a political wilderness similar to the one Machiavelli envisaged in the opening lines of his discussion of fortune in *The Prince* (which I considered in chapter 5), where he acknowledges that even *his* will to act is sapped by the dizzying pace of change that characterizes the politics of his time. Because there seemed no way to map the frenzied violence that impelled the course of events, men succumbed to the temptations of trivial excitation, nostalgia, or a passive acceptance of fate.

It is not that Americans lack shared sentiments, a sense of belonging, or common worship, but that they lack a sense of engagement in common enterprises. At least, that seems to be a conclusion of the mirror images that frame *White Noise*.

The novel opens with students returning to school in a long line of shiny station wagons—evidence of wealth, success, technological achievement, and "massive insurance coverages." The parents are "a collection of the like-minded and spiritually akin, a people, a nation," engaged in ritual of common worship. The novel ends with a different sort of community and a very different tone, though the whisper of death is present in the opening tableau with its "massive insurance coverages."

They gather at the overpass, this other community of the helpless, crippled, and diseased. Mostly middle-aged and elderly, they whisper as if in church. No one plays a radio or TV; there are no non sequiturs. They come to view the sunsets, "unbearably beautiful" since the Airborne Toxic Event, with a combination of dread and wonder that parallels the sentiments expressed in the choral ode from *Antigone*. Though awestruck, they do not know what it all means. Early in the book, Jack worried about whether Heinrich's premature baldness was due to the terrible pollutants that gave the sunsets their unique beauty. Later, attempting to flee the ATE, Jack expresses a fear accompanied by religious awe in the face of what seems implacable, elemental, and willful cosmic forces. But he cannot be sure whether what he sees is permanent and significant, or "just some atmospheric weirdness soon to pass" (325). The questions are unending and in the end perhaps paralyzing. Is this the apocalypse, the day of reckoning and judgment exacted by God for man's hubris, chutzpah, and pride, or something utterly mundane? Are we to take as mysterious and beautiful his daughter's sleep-filled utterances, like "Toyota Celica," and Wilder's seven hours of crying Platonic-like recollections of hidden wonders and places? Is the name of a car an intimation of an ancient power or the nonsense uttered by a child? Has Wilder visited places where "things are said, sights are seen, distances reached which we in our ordinary toil can only regard with the mingled reverence and wonder we hold in reserve for feats of the most sublime and difficult dimensions" (79)? Do his cries signify the ironic view Nietzsche tells us is close behind the pride of modern man, aware that he lives in a historicizing twilight in which youthful hopes and energy will survive into the future? Is he unable to talk because he is like the "wild child" Murray describes, whose TV-deprived life leaves him ignorant of the "deeper codes and messages that mark his species as unique" (50)? Or is he the child who shall lead them, which would explain both why Jack and Babette cling to him so desperately and his miraculous bicycle ride across a busy freeway? Has he seen untold horrors, such as those visited on Shirley Wilder, a young black girl for whom no foster home could be found, and who, having been banished to reform school, was gang-raped and died of AIDS three weeks before a lawsuit filed on her behalf was successful?[37] Or is he just a child crying for one of a hundred reasons? What is "there," and how much of it have humans invented? Remember that the toxins that give the sunsets their shimmer are our creations. We have made nature more beautiful than is natural, and then stand in awe and dread of our own handiwork. Here is the metaphysical dimension of Marx's notion of alienation, of the way men and women make history before the revolution, of the function he assigns to religion, of the fetishism of commodities. Perhaps the recognition of this can provide a spark of recognition or an impetus for renewal, if not redemption.

It can only if crisis means opportunity as well as danger. The particular crisis with which the book concludes occurs, appropriately enough, in the supermarket, the place of power and freedom, abundance and life, order as well as being. It is also a place of white noise.

The crisis occurs because "the" supermarket decides to rearrange the shelves, which results not in frustration but panic. People are agitated and dismayed, unable to figure out the pattern, the underlying logic, the form, the reason for the change. And so their carts run into each other, and otherwise decent people go over the edge. Like Jack, they wander aimlessly, haunted, betrayed, powerless to read the labels. America, history, has changed, and in this "new and improved" world they, the middle-aged and the elderly, are lost.

Perhaps their discomfiture will be as temporary as the glorious sunsets. For one thing, the supermarkets have installed holographic scanners that infallibly decode the price of each commodity, like theories that conjure up a rational, predictable world to provide metaphysical solace and auras of invincibility and invulnerability. For another, as the slow-moving checkout line gets to the counter, everyone on it will have time to be reassured by the tabloid stories of the supernatural and extraterrestrial, the miracle vitamins, the cures for cancer, the remedies for obesity, the cults of the famous and the dead (326).

VI

Some years ago, Walter Benjamin argued that the triumph of the bourgeoisie meant that death was pushed from a perceptual world to a conceptual one.[38] The *Phaedo* and *White Noise* dramatize what such a movement might entail philosophically, culturally, and politically, though in obviously different ways. But Benjamin had something more specific in mind: the removal of death as an everyday sight and experience. Before the shift from the perceptual to the conceptual, "in every house there was hardly a room in which someone had not died." After it, all indications of mortality were fastidiously removed and isolated in special places. But DeLillo suggests that something more complicated is now occurring—that television and popular culture generally are mesmerized by death but commodify it; that images of death are ubiquitous *and* distant. "We" have never been so engaged by death or so ignorant about it. In these terms, the frantic desire to prolong life or erase the dread of mortality is a product of this peculiarly modern or postmodern condition.

Part of that condition has been the knowingness Nietzsche warned about and Žižek described in a passage I quoted earlier. Part of that knowingness is the porousness of the various narratives that helped distract us from death. It would be foolish to proclaim that these narratives have totally lost their power and hold. Clearly, they remain potent images of history in America, their ascendancy depending in part on the fate of the U.S. economy and the self-image of godlike power. Yet both the disappointment with and sometimes frantic iteration of these narratives of progress and self-fashioning suggest that they no longer monopolize public discourse (if they ever did). I hesitate to call what "we" confront a crisis, given how banal the word and idea have become. But I cannot think of a better word.

Writing about the nature of crisis, Arendt insists that the disappearance of "prejudices" means "that we have lost the answers on which we ordinarily rely without even realizing they were originally answers to questions." A crisis "forces us back to the questions themselves and requires from us either new or old answers, but in any case direct judgments." A crisis only becomes a disaster when "we respond to it with preformed judgments." Such a response not only sharpens the crisis but makes us forfeit the opportunity for reflection.[39] I have argued that the reading of *White Noise* and the *Phaedo* in terms of each other helps us reflect on politics, political theory, and mortality.

But what, in this instance, are the questions themselves? First, given the debate over abortion, cloning, stem cell research, reproductive technology, and the many efforts to prolong life, what sort of life is worth living? Second, how does the transposition of the Socratic question about the good life to Jack's about how to escape the dread, if not fact, of death change our notion of agency and politics? Third, how is it possible to be alive to death, to live with its presence without resentment at the uncertainty and finitude death signifies? How are we to avoid a rage that insists on the finality of Truth and Violence as the ultimate arbiters of life?

Socrates insisted that the unexamined life is not worth living. But it is all too easy to turn against thinking when it denies a final resting place. Socrates' demand is traumatic. The sting that keeps his compatriots awake can all too easily become the sleeplessness Nietzsche talked about. Moreover, Socrates' question "How shall we live?" created an unbridgeable gap between the demand to take one's whole life into account in everything one does and the need to decide, to act, and to forget.[40] Yet it is precisely this gap that provides the space for non sequiturs and the need for thought. Non sequiturs appear out of nowhere. They disturb the surface meanings (without necessarily pointing to some stable meaning above or below). They jar events and pry experience loose from the categories that cradle them and interrupt the logic of an argument, reminding us how arguments about death domesticate the subject just as Hitler Studies does. Whether reminders of what we didn't know we had forgotten, the return of the repressed, some mystical dimension of the ordinary, or the momentary surfacing of thoughts beyond thoughts, they push us out of our comfort zone.

The gap in the collective version of the Socratic question—how shall we live, and what shall we do?—provides the space for political theory. Here non sequiturs afford the opportunity and inspiration for rethinking aspects of public life. But when these spaces are filled with such a profusion of data that the non sequiturs are undifferentiated noise, the Socratic question is stillborn, and human action vacillates between routinization and violence, passivity and frantic movement, as it does in *White Noise*.

A fourth question: is Winnie right that Jack's frenetic search for a drug to erase his fear of death—like Marcuse's attempt to reduce death to a biological fact or Marx's to give individuals life through species being— transgresses a boundary that gives a precious texture to life? Would life lose its beauty and meaning(s) without our knowledge of a final line, a border, a limit, a horizon?

If she is right, then death is a condition of meaning because it makes our choices consequential. If we lived forever, there would be no choice that was irreversible, no need for forgiveness, no tragedy. But death is always a tragedy because it represents the loss of someone who is irreplaceable. The someone need not be Socrates. It includes Michael Eugene Mullen and Jack Gladney. If so, then knowledge of death gives our lives shape, and eternal life entails a loss of dignity.

As this implies, "we" cannot do without narratives of meaning. The very ideas of life and death demand it. But such narratives need to be more like stories, whether they be of Socrates and Athens or Jack and America. Stories help reconcile us to the bitter gauntlet thrown down by Silenus: the first day of our life is the first day of our death.

So does politics, or so Arendt claims Theseus, Sophocles, and the Athenians believed. This is not the view of Socrates or DeLillo, though my interpretation of Socrates' final words and the subtext of *White Noise* do give politics more of a place in the living of a human life than may at first appear in these texts. But in the case of Plato that is more grudging admission than a redemptive or celebratory moment, a necessary sacrifice but a sacrifice nonetheless. And though politics plays a more significant role in DeLillo, I wonder if he is not too enthralled by the world's white noise, too smitten by connections that go everywhere but point to nothing beyond themselves, too in love with the world he half-critiques to offer a vision of political possibilities.[41] Perhaps that is unfair, beside the point, an imposed project. He is not, as he says, a political theorist. But the question is whether a constructivist vision of politics can be built upon the ironic "foundations" *White Noise* provides, whether, to recall Critchly, we are ready and able to generate a chastened utopianism.

Notes

CHAPTER ONE
INTRODUCTION

1. Boston: Houghton Mifflin, 2000. Page references appear in the text.

2. I would dissociate myself from some of what Roth says about Greek tragedy, but that is not really the point.

3. The novel's view of race is consistently provocative, even or especially when it remains ambivalent. Far less can be said for its view of gender, which is clearer and more problematic.

4. The mirror image is Toni Morrison's claim in the *New Yorker* that Clinton was coded black by the Christian right:

> African-American men seemed to understand it right away. Years ago, in the middle of the Whitewater investigation, one heard the first murmurs: white skin notwithstanding, this is our first black President. Blacker than any actual black person who could ever be elected in our children's lifetime. After all, Clinton displays almost every trope of blackness: single-parent household, born poor, working class, saxophone-playing, McDonald's-and-junk-food-loving boy from Arkansas. And when . . . the President's body, his privacy, his unpoliced sexuality became the focus of the persecution, when he was metaphorically seized and body-searched, who could gainsay these black men who knew whereof they spoke? The message was clear: No matter how smart you are, hard you work . . . we will put you in your place or put you out of the place you have somehow, albeit with our permission, achieved. . . . Unless you do as we say (i.e., assimilate at once) your expletives belong to us.

5. The first part of the definition of the human stain comes from Faunia, Coleman's lover, who has been molested and brutalized for much of her life. The second and third aspects are presented by the narrator.

6. Again, the narrator is somewhat distant from what is said, and given the crudity of the conversation we, though not Roth, may be further from it still.

7. Richard Posner, *An Affair of State: The Investigation, Impeachment, and Trial of President Clinton* (Cambridge: Harvard University Press, 2000).

8. In Jean-Pierre Vernant and Pierre Vidal-Naquet, *Tragedy and Myth in Ancient Greece*, quoted in Bernard Williams, *Shame and Necessity* (Berkeley and Los Angeles: University of California Press, 1993), 19.

9. In *The Greek City from Homer to Alexander*, ed. Oswyn Murray and Simon Price (Oxford: Clarendon Press, 1990), 1–24.

10. Ibid., 3.

11. Pratap Bhanu Mehta, "Cosmopolitanism and the Circle of Reason," *Political Theory* 28, no. 5 (October 2000): 631.

12. Murray and Price, *The Greek City*, 4–5.

13. Ibid.

14. See Donna Haraway, *Primate Visions: Gender, Race and Nature in the World of Modern Science* (London: Verso, 1989).

15. Quoted by Gabriel Josipovici, "The Second Adams," *Times Literary Supplement*, April 13, 2001, 27.

16. "Rorty on Gadamer," *London Review of Books*, March 16, 2000, 25.

17. Jonathan Lear, *Open Minded: Working Out the Logic of the Soul* (Cambridge: Harvard University Press), 50–51.

18. I take some of the language from Josiah Ober, *Political Dissent in Democratic Athens* (Princeton, NJ: Princeton University Press, 1998).

19. Assertions about "origins" and "The West" can no longer be made unproblematically.

20. I take this story from Mel Gordon, "Noise Sound Creation in the Nineteenth Century," in *Wireless Imagination: Sound, Radio and Avant Garde*, ed. Douglas Kaplan and Gregory Whitehead (Cambridge: MIT Press, 1992).

21. The December 21, 1997, front page of the *San Francisco Chronicle*, in a story opposite one about organ transplants, quoted the complaint by astronomers that a sky full of noise was jamming their radio telescopes. The booming use of cellular phones, radios, pagers, communication satellites, and wireless links to the World Wide Web was flooding the atmosphere, making it more and more difficult to study "galaxy-gobbling black holes, hellfire-spewing stars and perhaps intelligent beings."

22. Michael Valdez Moses, "Lust Removed from Nature," in *New Essays on White Noise*, ed. Frank Lentricchia (New York: Cambridge University Press, 1991), 64.

CHAPTER TWO
ON THE USES AND DISADVANTAGES OF HELLENIC STUDIES
FOR POLITICAL AND THEORETICAL LIFE

1. I have used the Hollingdale translation by Daniel Breazeale in *Untimely Meditations* (New York: Cambridge University Press, 1997); page references appear in the text. In those few instances when I have not, I have used the Walter de Gruyter edition of *Vom Nutzen und Machtheil der Historie fur das Leben* (Berlin, 1972).

2. I am *not* using Nietzsche's work as a whole to do this, which means that I am avoiding the challenging question of Nietzsche's view of "The Greeks" as a whole and the way he comes to differentiate among them, e.g., in his critique of

NOTES TO CHAPTER TWO

Socratism, his admiration for the Sophists and Thucydides, his assessment of Homer and Hesiod, his analysis of pre-Socratic philosophy, and his judgments about Greek drama, Athenian democracy, and the role of the Dionysian. Who the Greeks were for him and the role they come to play (or not play) in his thought changes substantially from this essay, *The Birth of Tragedy*, and *The Genealogy of Morals* through *Twilight of the Idols* to *Zarathustra*. In part it is the "un-Nietzschean" things he says in this essay that attracted me to it. One could say that in terms of many contemporary uses of Nietzsche, my reading is untimely. Cf. Foucault's "use" of Nietzsche in "Nietzsche, Genealogy, History," in *Language, Counter-Memory, Practice: Selected Essays and Interviews*, ed. Donald Bouchard (Ithaca, NY: Cornell University Press, 1977), 139–64, esp. 95–97.

3. Joel Whitebrook argues that "utopia has been exhausted as a project and discredited as a body of thought." *Perversion and Utopia* (Cambridge: MIT Press, 1995), 76.

4. On the meaning of *betrachtungen* as well as *unzeitgemasse*, see Breazeale, *Untimely Meditations,* xliv.

5. Something like this is going on when Martin Luther King, Jr. (in "Letter from a Birmingham Jail") "uses" subordinate aspects of the Western philosophical religious traditions and the American political tradition to recast the dominant interpretations of them, and when Adam Michnik interprets the Warsaw Ghetto uprising as a form of Polish resistance to foreign invasion. When Machiavelli attempts to insert Florence and Italy into a Roman past he is partly inventing, he is acting out Nietzsche's advice about the need to choose a past when our own offers no examples of great action.

6. Thus I will have little to say about the way "On the Uses and Disadvantages of History for Life" is related to contemporary events, intellectual currents, or figures (such as Grillparzer, Hartmann, Wagner, Strauss, and Hegel).

7. It has the same explosive potential Machiavelli's opposition between success and morality had for those enamored of the Mirror of Princes literature.

8. As I will argue in chapter 4, Machiavelli laments the fact that his contemporaries are in thrall to a literary, aesthetic, and philosophical past but ignore its political uses. Indeed, their veneration of its culture becomes the excuse for ignoring its political potential. Of course he, unlike Nietzsche, is referring to Rome, or rather Livy's Rome.

9. Here is Marx's famous characterization of capitalism in *The Communist Manifesto*: "Constant revolutionizing of production, uninterrupted disturbance of all social conditions, everlasting uncertainty, and agitation distinguish the bourgeois epoch from all earlier ones. All fixed, fast-frozen relations . . . are swept away, all new-formed ones become antiquated before they can ossify. All that is solid melts into air, all that is holy is profaned, and man is at last compelled to face with sober senses, his real conditions of life, and his relations with his kind."

10. Milan Kundera, *The Book of Laughter and Forgetting* (New York: Knopf, 1980), 91.

11. See Joan Wallach Scott, "After History?" *Common Knowledge* 5, no. 3 (Winter 1996): 9–26.

12. In *Wir Philologen*, Nietzsche complains that classical education almost always reflects a "bloodless recollection of the past" and represents a "nauseating erudition" that fosters a "sluggish timid indifference to life." (I quote from William Arrowsmith's translation in *Arion* 2, nos. 1 and 2 [1963].)

13. The significance of historical contextualization, the way it generates shifting perspectives and precludes moralistic condemnations, is suggested by Dan Fowler in a review of a recent book on classical scholarship. "It is an irony," he writes, that "one of the reasons that Classical philology made this attempt at objectivity was to free itself from Victorian and Edwardian moralizing, so as to be able to examine 'coolly' and 'historically' phenomena such as same-sex relationships in Sappho without Christian prejudice." He adds that the professionalization of classics now under attack was driven by younger scholars who were tired of raptures about "The Greek Spirit." See "Expertise and Experience," *Times Literary Supplement*, October 24, 1997, 33.

14. See the discussion in Scott, "After History?"

15. Peter Dews, *The Limits of Disenchantment* (London: Verso, 1995), chap. 1.

16. Wolin develops the idea in *Hobbes and the Epic Tradition of Political Theory* (William Andrews Clark Memorial Library, University of California, Los Angeles, 1970).

17. I do not mean to single out any particular school, since what Weber called (in a different context) the routinization of charisma is a frequent occurrence when theoretical provocations become methods of analysis.

18. "Politics as a Vocation," in *From Max Weber: Essays in Sociology*, ed. H. H. Gerth and C. Wright Mills (New York: Oxford University Press, 1958). Page references appear in the text.

19. Where the structure of society produces a war, people with a "manly and controlled attitude" would tell the enemy, "We lost the war. You have won it. That is now all over. Now let us discuss what conclusions must be drawn according to the *objective* interests that come into play and what is the main thing in view of the responsibility towards *the future* which above all burdens the victor. Anything else is undignified and will become a boomerang." Weber contrasts this "manly" attitude with that of an "old woman" who searches for the guilty one (118).

20. Weber distinguishes this from measuring up to the world as it is. But it is not entirely clear how he can do this without an unacknowledged idealizing moment: a "real" world exists distinct from the one we actually live in.

21. This project, though hardly the nature of the specific conditions, is analogous to that of Hannah Arendt (see *The Human Condition* [Chicago: University of Chicago Press, 1958]) and Sheldon Wolin. Here is Wolin (in "Fugitive Democracy," in *Democracy and Difference: Contesting the Boundaries of the Political*, ed. Seyla Benhabib [Princeton: Princeton University Press, 1996]):

I shall take the *political* to be an expression of the idea that a free society composed of diversities can nonetheless enjoy moments of commonality when, through public deliberations, collective power is used to promote or protect the well-being of the collectivity. *Politics* refers to the legitimized and public contestation, primarily by organized and unequal social power, overaccess to the resources available to the public authorities of the collectivity. Politics is continuous and ceaseless and endless. In contrast, the political is episodic and rare (171).

In many respects Arendt and Wolin developed their idea of the political as a critique of Weber.

22. Hannah Arendt, "The Crisis in Education," in *Between Past and Future: Eight Exercises in Political Thought* (New York: Viking, 1983), 196.

CHAPTER THREE
HANNAH ARENDT AT COLONUS

1. William Connolly asks the right questions and provides a generally persuasive answer. Why, he asks, "do so many contemporary intellectuals draw selective sustenance from this untimely aristocrat in rethinking democracy? . . . How does this protean thinker contribute distinctive elements to the nobility of democracy while he himself, after *Human All Too Human*, disparages it?" The paradox is that the distinctive sensibility through which Nietzsche opens the door "to an ennobling of democracy is also one that inhibits him from walking through it." See his "The Nobility of Democracy" in *Vocations of Political Theory*, ed. Jason A. Frank and John Tambornino (Minneapolis: University of Minnesota Press, 2000), 305–25. (The quotations are on 305–6.)

2. Hanna Pitkin, "Justice: On Relating Public and Private," *Political Theory* 9, no. 3 (August 1981): 327–52.

3. See Shoshana Felman, *Jacques Lacan and the Adventure of Insight: Psychoanalysis in Contemporary Culture* (Cambridge: Harvard University Press, 1987).

4. The essay is in *Between Past and Future: Eight Exercises in Political Thought* (New York: Penguin, 1968), 165.

5. Hannah Arendt, *The Human Condition* (Chicago: University of Chicago Press, 1958), 187 (*HC*). On this and on Arendt as a tragic thinker, see Robert C. Pirro, *Hannah Arendt and the Politics of Tragedy* (DeKalb, IL: Northern Illinois University Press, 2001).

6. Simon Goldhill, "Refracting Classical Vision: Changing Cultures of Viewing," in *Visions in Context: Historical and Contemporary Perspectives on Sight*, ed. Teresa Brennan and Martin Jay (New York: Routledge, 1996), 19.

7. Hannah Arendt, *Men in Dark Times* (New York: Harcourt Brace and World, 1968), 104 (*MDT*). There are some striking similarities between this play about exile and Arendt's own life.

8. Hannah Arendt, *The Life of the Mind*, vol. 1, *One Thinking* (London: Secker and Warburg, 1978), 164 (*LOM*).

9. With a few exceptions I rely on the David Grene translation (with a few minor emendations): *The Complete Greek Tragedies*, vol. 1, *Sophocles*, ed. David Grene and Richard Latimore, 2d ed. (Chicago: University of Chicago Press, 1991). Here I am using the translation by Dudley Fitts and Robert Fitzgerald, *The Oedipus Cycle: An English Version* (New York: Harcourt, Brace & World, 1949).

10. See, for instance, Sheldon Wolin, "Hannah Arendt: Democracy and the Political," *Salmagundi* 60 (1983): 3–19.

11. See *The Jew as Pariah*, edited and with an introduction by Ron H. Feldman (New York: Grove Press, 1978).

12. Hannah Arendt, *On Revolution* (New York: Viking), 1963, 285 (*OR*). Nietzsche's version of Silenus's wisdom and his remarks about Olympian gods can be found in "The Birth of Tragedy," in *The Birth of Tragedy and the Case of Wagner*, trans. Walter Kaufmann (New York: Vintage, 1967), 42 and 41, respectively.

13. There is the further bond of their both being exiles. Perhaps this explains why, as P. E. Easterling suggests, they "talk the same language." Only "brief exchanges are needed between them so secure is their understanding of one another." The quotations are from her "Plain Words in Sophocles," in *Sophocles Revisited: Essays Presented to Sir Hugh Lloyd-Jones*, ed. Jasper Griffin (New York: Oxford University Press, 1999), 105.

14. See Easterling's reading of line 618 (ibid., 103).

15. See Jacques Taminiaux, *The Thracian Maid and the Professional Thinker: Arendt and Heidegger*, trans. and ed. Michael Gendre (Albany: State University of New York Press, 1997), 155.

16. *The Heroic Temper: Studies in Sophoclean Tragedy* (Berkeley and Los Angeles: University of California Press, 1964), 155.

17. See the discussion of Sophie Mills, *Theseus, Tragedy and the Athenian Empire* (Oxford: Oxford University Press, 1996), 168.

18. R. P. Winnington-Ingram has a good discussion of this scene. But in an effort to correct the argument that Oedipus is the definitive spokesman of the play, he goes too far by underestimating the degree to which Polyneices is being manipulative and the fact that the son never answers, let alone refutes, the charges Oedipus levels at him. (See *Sophocles: An Interpretation* [Cambridge: Cambridge University Press, 1980], chap. 2.)

19. Ibid., 263.

20. We might read this scene in terms of Arendt. For one thing, Oedipus's explosive reactions against his powerlessness echo Arendt's fears (in her analysis of the French Revolution) of the "masses" taking revenge for their poverty. For another, Oedipus's new power and confidence are connected with his newly acquired citizenship and so illustrate Arendt's ideas of collective power. Of course the problem with any such analogy is that Arendt is relentlessly secular in her reading of Greek literature. One could say that for her the role Nietzsche assigned the Olympian gods is played by a myth of politics.

21. Arendt also speaks about the dangers of the old dictating to the young and the past to the future. See "The Crisis in Education," in *Between Past and Future: Eight Exercises in Political Thought* (New York: Penguin), 1968, 173–96.

22. C. M. Bowra, *Sophoclean Tragedy* (Oxford: Clarendon Press, 1945), 349.

23. See Peter Burian, "Suppliant and Saviour: Oedipus at Colonus," *Phoenix* 28, no. 4 (Winter 1974): 408–29.

24. The quotation and argument are from Deborah Roberts, "The Frustrated Mourner: Strategies of Closure in Greek Tragedy," in *Nomodeiktes*, ed. Ralph M. Rosen and Joseph Farrell (Ann Arbor: University of Michigan Press, 1993), 573–89.

25. Felman, *Jacques Lacan*, 142.

26. Bernard Williams, *Shame and Necessity* (Berkeley and Los Angeles: University of California Press, 1993), 158–59.

27. Jasper Griffin's impatience with political readings of tragedy (the polis "makes its way into the discussion because of an a priori conviction that tragedy must be political in something like our sense") is a useful warning. But "politics" in "our" sense has, for better or worse, expanded to include issues of culture, religion, sexuality, etc. He is also right to warn about the great difficulty of determining just what the political content of a play or passage should be taken to be, but apparently thinks it easy to say what the political content is not. And his question "[W]ere the audience on the lookout for subtly disguised or obliquely presented political meanings or were they absorbed in the primary meaning of the words and events?" may rest on a false dichotomy and begs the question. See his "Sophocles and the Democratic City" in *Sophocles Revisited*, 189–90.

28. Dudley Fitts and Robert Fitzgerald, *The Oedipus Cycle* (New York: Harcourt Brace, 1958), 174.

29. On the degree to which the valorization of Theseus's Athens is a critique of Periclean Athens, see Mary Whitlock Blundell. "The Ideal of Athens in Oedipus at Colonus," in *Tragedy, Comedy and the Polis*, ed. Alan Sommerstein et al. (Bari: Levante Editori, 1990), 287–306. On 290 ff. she has a fine discussion of the significance of the Chorus's honoring both Poseidon Hippios (the horse god patron of the elite class of knights) and the sea god associated with the demos.

30. See her "Thebes: Theater of Self and Society in Athenian Drama," in *Greek Tragedy and Political Theory*, ed. J. Peter Euben (Berkeley and Los Angeles: University of California Press, 1986), 121–22, 126. But in this play Thebes is as plural as Athens. Thus Theseus distinguishes Creon from Theban citizenry as a whole, as the play does between the mythical and the contemporary. Thus there are four, not two, terms involved in the contrasts in the play.

31. On exclusivist Athenians' self-understanding, see Carol Dougherty, "Democratic Contradictions and the Synoptic Illusion of Euripedes' Ion," in *Demokratia: A Conversation on Democracies, Ancient and Modern*, ed. Josiah Ober and Charles Hedrick (Princeton, NJ: Princeton University Press, 1996). Cf. Barry Strauss, "The Melting Pot, the Mosaic and the Agora," in *Athenian Political*

Thought and the Reconstruction of American Democracy, ed. J. Peter Euben et al. (Ithaca, NY: Cornell University Press, 1994), and Laura Slatkin, "Oedipus at Colonus: Exile and Integration," in Euben, *Greek Tragedy and Political Theory*, 210–21. I do not want to exaggerate about the "openness" of even mythical Athens or the sense in which it can serve as an ideal for "us." We are talking about relative exclusiveness, since it, like perhaps all structures of power, establishes exclusions merely by defining even the most capacious notion of inside. Indeed, one could argue that the more a society captures honorific terms such as "democratic," "open," and "inclusive," the more its exclusions are erased.

32. For a discussion of what these are and how they function, see Dana R. Villa, *Arendt and Heidegger: The Fate of the Political* (Princeton, NJ: Princeton University Press, 1996).

33. Arendt's translation takes considerable liberties with the Greek. For instance, it is not clear that when Theseus talks about endowing life with splendor, he is talking about the city or polis in general rather than his life, or what he shares with Oedipus (to whom the lines are directed). Nor is it clear that Theseus is the spokesman for the city as a whole or how exactly the line about endowing life with splendor relates to the Wisdom of Silenus, which comes some eighty lines later. In sum, Arendt's claim that the play proclaims the redemptive nature of politics is a stretch at best.

34. Blundell, "The Ideal of Athens," 298.

35. "Democratic Contradictions," 262.

36. Jean-Pierre Vernant and Pierre Vidal-Naquet, *Tragedy and Myth in Ancient Greece* (New York: Zone Books, 1988).

37. The phrases are from Jonathan Lear's *Open Minded: Working Out the Logic of the Soul* (Cambridge: Harvard University Press, 1998), 50.

38. This is a paraphrase of Hanna Fenichel Pitkin's characterization of Arendt's project in *The Attack of the Blob: Hannah Arendt's Concept of the Social* (Chicago: University of Chicago Press, 1998), 1 and passim.

39. Ibid., 88

40. George Kateb, *Hannah Arendt, Politics, Conscience, Evil* (Totowa, NJ: Rowman & Allanheld, 1984), 149.

41. Easterling, "Plain Words in Sophocles," 98–99, 101–2.

CHAPTER FOUR

ARISTOPHANES IN AMERICA

1. I chose TV comedy because, as David Marc has put it, "Television is America's jester. It has assumed the guise of an idiot while actually accruing the advantages of power and authority behind the smoke screen of its self-degradation." See his *Demographic Vistas: Television in American Culture*, rev. ed. (Philadelphia: University of Pennsylvania Press, 1996), 7.

2. As anyone who has heard Jerry Lewis expound on the subject can attest. White's argument is in the preface to the Modern Library edition of *A Subtreasury of American Humor* (New York: Random House, 1948), xvii.

3. Rush Rehm, *Greek Tragic Theater* (London: Routledge, 1992), vii, 3–5. See Oddone Longo, "The Theater of the Polis," and John J. Winkler, "The Ephebes Song: Tragoida and Polis," in *Nothing To Do with Dionysos? Athenian Drama in Its Social Context*, ed. John J. Winkler and Froma I. Zeitlin (Princeton, NJ: Princeton University Press, 1990), 12–19 and 20–61, respectively.

4. See the introduction to *Three Plays by Aristophanes: Staging Women*, trans. and ed. Jeffrey Henderson (New York: Routledge, 1996), 5–7.

5. See his "Drama and Community: Aristophanes and Some of His Rivals," in Winkler and Zeitlin, *Nothing to Do with Dionysos?*, 237–70.

6. Thucydides 1.142, and Josiah Ober, *Political Dissent in Democratic Athens: Intellectual Critics of Popular Culture* (Princeton, NJ: Princeton, University Press, 1998), 135–40.

7. David Konstan, *Greek Comedy and Ideology* (New York: Oxford University Press, 1995), 8, 165–67.

8. As Anthony Grafton has argued, humor is "the most delicate of subjects in scholarship and everyday life." The phrase "we are not amused" is one of the most fearful we can hear, and the disapproving comment "I don't think that's funny" makes most intellectuals neurotic. No social task is harder "than explaining a joke to someone who does not get it and no intellectual task is harder than trying to understand what makes jokes funny in another society or in the earlier history of one's own." See his "Beyond the Joke," *Times Literary Supplement*, April 10, 1998, 4–5.

9. Malcolm Heath (in *Political Comedy in Aristophanes*, [Göttingen: Vandenhoeck and Reprecht, 1987]) argues that Plato is not blaming Aristophanes here but ridiculing Meletus for constructing a travesty of Socrates no different from the purposeful caricatures of comedy.

10. See Stephen Halliwell, "Comic Satire and Freedom of Speech in Classical Athens," *Journal of Hellenic Studies* 111 (1991): 48–70.

11. Jeffrey Henderson, "The Demos and the Comic Competition," in Winkler and Zeitlin, *Nothing To Do with Dionysos?* 293–97.

12. See Daphne Elizabeth O'Regan, *Rhetoric, Comedy, and the Violence of Language in Aristophanes' Clouds* (New York: Oxford University Press, 1992), 132.

13. There is a certain affinity between comedy and Socrates' project as he describes and exemplifies it in Plato's *Apology*, insofar as both are engaged in political education without normative blueprints and practical solutions. Elsewhere (*Corrupting Youth: Political Education, Democratic Culture, and Political Theory* [Princeton, NJ: Princeton University Press, 1997], chap. 5) I have argued that comedy helped constitute a tradition of democratic self-critique upon which Socrates built even as he criticized democracy's shortcomings. Without denying the obvious ways in which comedy and philosophy are very different things, or that

philosophers have frequently rejected with disgust the idea that irreverence, ridicule, parody, scatology, and vulgarity could ever be a ground for "serious" ethical and political critique, there are, nonetheless, continuities between Socratic political theory and comedic political education as I describe it here. (My discussion of ancient comedy draws on that chapter.)

14. My *Corrupting Youth* offers an extended analysis of the question, using *The Clouds* as an example.

15. I take the idea of a "democratic ethos" and *some* of its substance from William Connolly, "Democracy and Territoriality," in *The Rhetorical Republic: Governing Representations in American Politics*, ed. Thomas Dumm and Frederick Dolan (Amherst: University of Massachusetts Press, 1993), 249–74.

16. Henderson, *Three Plays*, introduction, 13. Christopher Carey argues that comedy required radical democracy. Given the "scale, rigor and tone of comic attacks on powerful figures," there must have been a "patron" more powerful than any of the targets. That patron "was the demos." See "Comic Ridicule and Democracy," in *Democratic Accounts* (Oxford: Clarendon Press, 1994), 69.

17. Henderson, *Three Plays*, introduction, 12.

18. Halliwell, "Comic Satire," 66. Simon Goldhill, "Comic Inversion and Inverted Commas: Aristophanes and Parody," in *The Poet's Voice: Essays on Poetics and Greek Literature*, ed. Simon Goldhill (New York: Cambridge University Press, 1991), 167–222.

19. Henderson, "The Demos and Dramatic Competition," 307.

20. Anthony T. Edwards, "Aristophanes' Comic Poetics: TRUX, Scatology, Skomma," *Transactions of the American Philological Association* 121 (1991): 179.

21. Robert Wallace, "Poet, Public, and Theatrocracy: Audience Performance in Classical Athens," in *Poets, Public and Performance in Ancient Greece*, ed. Lowell Edmunds and Robert W. Wallace (Baltimore: Johns Hopkins University Press, 1997). Cf. Ober, *Political Dissent*.

22. See George Lipsitz, *Time Passages: Collective Memory and American Popular Culture* (Minneapolis: University of Minnesota Press, 1990).

23. Ibid., chap. 1.

24. Ibid., 7–11.

25. Ibid., 19. But see the provocative argument by Robert Meister in "Beyond Satisfaction: Desire, Consumption and the Future of Socialism," *Topoi* 15 (1996): 189–210.

26. Neil Postman, *Amusing Ourselves to Death: Public Discourse in the Age of Show Business* (New York: Penguin, 1986), 92.

27. Jean-Pierre Vernant, *The Origins of Greek Thought* (Ithaca, NY: Cornell University Press, 1982).

28. See Robert Putnam, "Bowling Alone: America's Declining Social Capital," *Current*, June 1995, 3–14.

29. Eric Barnouw, *Tube of Plenty: The Making of American Television*, rev. ed. (New York: Oxford University Press, 1982), 300. Caren Kaplan argues that

television "contributed to the rise of a consumer culture by flattening or homogenizing U.S. national identity; increasingly by eliminating or subduing the vaudeville-inspired ethnic comics and through the representation of middle-class, white, WASP suburban families in situation comedies" ("The Good Neighbor Policy Meets the 'Feminine Mystique': The Geopolitics of the Domestic Sitcom" [lecture delivered at the University of Southern California, April 1993]). Robert Bork criticizes the same phenomenon for very different reasons when he laments how American popular culture has become a threat to democracy because it "trashes our values." See his comments in the *New York Times*, June 14, 1992, sec. 1, 24. On the "balkanization" of TV audiences, see chap. 6 of Marc, *Democratic Vistas*.

30. See the discussion in Anne Norton's *Republic of Signs: Liberal Theory and American Popular Culture* (Chicago: University of Chicago Press, 1993), chap. 2.

31. See Lipsitz, *Time Passages*, 4–5, 18.

32. Ibid. Without ignoring the omnivorous appetite of commodification, Melissa Orlie has suggested that "the practices of commodity consumption reveal a persistent desire for freedom and a capacity for the deliberate exercise of power in conditions that otherwise would appear to extinguish them." What she is doing with commodification I am trying to do with television: opening up possibilities for thought and action by disaggregating a monolithic pessimism which (in her case) insists that commodity consumption "is at best distracting, and therefore politically and ethically bankrupt." See her "Political Capitalism and the Consumption of Democracy," in *Democracy and Vision: Sheldon Wolin and the Vicissitudes of the Political*, ed. Aryeh Botwinick and William E. Connolly (Princeton, NJ: Princeton University Press, 2001). The quotations are on 139.

33. Norton, *Republic of Signs*, 116, and Mark Danner, "The Shame of the Political TV," *New York Review of Books*, September 21, 2000, 101.

34. On television's role in levitating John F. Kennedy and his presidency into "an historiographic mythosphere," see Marc, *Demographic Vistas*, 133–34.

35. Jim Cullen, *The Art of Democracy: A Concise History of Popular Culture in the United States* (New York: Monthly Review Press, 1996), 278–79.

36. Pierre Bourdieu, "Sport and Social Class," in *Rethinking Popular Culture: Contemporary Perspectives in Cultural Studies*, ed. Chandra Mukerji and Michael Schudson (Berkeley and Los Angeles: University of California Press, 1991), 357–73.

37. Why look at anything for longer than the duration of its allure, when dozens more *imagi mundi*—all of them bouncing and shifting through endless permutations—seductively tickle the fingertips? David Marc, *Comic Visions: Television Comedy and American Culture* (New York: Routledge, 1992), 204.

38. In *Seducing America: How Television Charms the Modern Voter* (New York: Oxford University Press, 1994), Roderick P. Hart warns of the peril to democracy "when its people do not know what they think they know and when they do not care about what they do not know. Television miseducates the citizenry, but worse, it makes that miseducation attractive" (13). Postman makes a similar

argument about how television changes the structure of discourse "by encouraging certain uses of the intellect, by favoring certain definitions of intelligence and wisdom, and by demanding a certain kind of content—in a phrase by creating new forms of truth telling," (*Amusing Ourselves to Death*, 27).

39. Michael Ignatieff, "Is Nothing Sacred? The Ethics of Television," *Daedalus* 4 (1985): 70–71.

40. Ibid.

41. Sheldon W. Wolin, "Democracy without the Citizen," in *The Presence of the Past* (Baltimore: Johns Hopkins University Press, 1989), 180–91.

42. Robert Putnam, *Bowling Alone* (New York: Simon and Schuster, 2000).

43. Lipsitz, *Time Passages*, 18.

44. See Dana R. Villa, "Theatricality in the Public Realm of Hannah Arendt," in *Public Space and Democracy*, ed. Marcel Henaff and Tracy B. Strong (Minneapolis: University of Minnesota Press, 2001), 144–71.

45. See Todd Gitlin's discussion in the introduction to his edited book, *Watching Television* (New York: Pantheon, 1986), and Andrew Ross, *No Respect: Intellectuals and Popular Culture* (New York: Routledge, 1989).

46. See the discussion in John Corner, *Television Form and Public Address* (London: Edward Arnold, 1995).

47. See Stuart Hall, "Notes on Deconstructing 'the Popular,' " in *People's History and Socialist Theory*, ed. Raphael Samuel (London: Routledge, 1981), and "Encoding and Decoding," in *Culture, Media, Language*, ed. Stuart Hall et al. (London: Hutchinson, 1980).

48. As Gitlin argues, while television may not have invented the superficiality or triviality of American political or public expression and there may be precedent for a "shriveled politics" of slogans, deceit, and pageantry, "precedent is nothing to be complacent about when ignorance is the product." See his "Blips, Bites and Savvy Talk: Television's Impact on American Politics," *Dissent* 37, no. 1 (Winter 1990): 26.

49. For an example, see Roger Sanjek, *The Future of Us All: Race and Neighborhood Politics in New York City* (Ithaca, NY: Cornell University Press, 1998); Dolores Hayden, *The Power of Place: Urban Landscapes as Public History* (Cambridge: MIT Press, 1995); and, for the importance of hip-hop culture and music in these negotiations, George Lipsitz, *Dangerous Crossroads: Popular Music, Postmodernism and the Poetics of Place* (New York: Verso, 1994). For Arendt's discussion of the polis, see *The Human Condition* (Chicago: University of Chicago Press, 1958), esp. 192–99.

50. Goldhill, "Comic Inversions and Inverted Commas," and Nicole Loraux, *The Invention of Athens: The Funeral Oration in the Classical City*, trans. Alan Sheridan (Cambridge: Harvard University Press, 1986), 302–11.

51. Marc, *Demographic Vistas*, chap. 6, "What Was Broadcasting?" 65–66.

52. Karen Hudes, "It's the Sitcom Cartoons That Have Character," *New York Times*, March 8, 1998, sec. 4, 36–37. The quotation is on 37.

53. Konstan, *Greek Comedy*, 5.

54. See Blaine Harden, "Ralph Had Dreams. Archie Had Opinions. Jerry Had Neuroses. But They All Told a Story about Life and Times in the Big Apple," *Washington Post*, May 14, 1998, sec. C, 1, 8.

55. Marc, *Demographic Vistas*, 112; Marc has an excellent discussion of *The Honeymooners*.

56. I take these points from Paul A. Cantor, "The Simpsons: Atomistic Politics and the Nuclear Family," *Political Theory* 27, no. 6 (December 1999): 734–49.

57. See Jeff MacGregor, "More Than Sight Gags and Subversive Satire," *New York Times*, June 20, 1999, sec. 2, 97.

58. See Paul A. Cantor, "In Praise of Television: The Greatest TV Show Ever ('The Simpsons')," *American Enterprise* 8, no. 5 (September–October 1997): 34–37.

59. Cantor (in "The Simpsons: Atomistic Politics and the Nuclear Family") makes much of the fact and of what he sees as the Simpsons' postmodern traditionalism.

60. See "The New Political Theater," *Mother Jones*, November–December 2000, 30–33.

61. Ober, *Political Dissent*, chap. 2.

62. See Charles McGrath, "No Kidding: Does Irony Illuminate or Corrupt?" *New York Times*, August 5, 2000, A15.

63. C.L.R. James, *American Civilization*, ed. and introduced by Anna Grimshaw and Keith Hart, with an afterword by Robert A. Hill (Cambridge: Blackwell, 1993), 123.

64. Stanley Cavell, "The Fact of Television," in *Themes Out of School* (Chicago: University of Chicago Press, 1988).

65. Alexander Nehamas, "Plato and the Mass Media," in *The Virtues of Authenticity: Essays on Plato and Aristotle* (Princeton, NJ: Princeton University Press, 1999). For Nehamas, Plato accuses poetry of perverting its audience because it is essentially suited to the representation of inferior characters and vulgar subjects, both of which are easy to imitate and are what the already corrupt crowd wants to see and hear. In these terms, reactions to poetry are transferred directly to the rest of life because we regard it as being as real as the world "outside" it. Only when we come to recognize it as an art form requiring interpretation does this duplicating function come to be seen as naive.

CHAPTER FIVE

THE POLITICS OF NOSTALGIA AND THEORIES OF LOSS

1. C.D.B. Bryan, *Friendly Fire* (New York: Putnam, 1976), 139–40.

2. This does not mean that all theories can be read as (or as part of) a narrative of loss, or that any theorist can be wholly read that way. Nor would I deny that

the very act of writing about loss is often an act of compensation and redemption, no matter what the explicit argument.

3. Nicole Loraux, *Mothers in Mourning*, translated from the French by Corinne Pache (Ithaca, NY: Cornell University Press, 1998), 83–84.

4. See Jackson Lears, "Looking Backward: In Defense of Nostalgia," *Lingua Franca*, December–January 1998, 59–66.

5. Peter Laslett, *The World We Have Lost: England before the Industrial Age* (New York: Scribner, 1965), 5. Robert Wiebe, *The Search for Order: 1877–1920* (New York: Hill & Wang, 1967), 12.

6. Judith Butler, *The Psychic Life of Power: Theories in Subjection* (Stanford, CA: Stanford University Press, 1997), 139.

7. In Homer, *hērōs* is related to *hōrē*, meaning season, especially the season of spring, so that a hero is seasonal "in that he comes into his prime, like flowers in the spring, only to be cut down once and for all." See Seth Schein, *The Mortal Hero: An Introduction to Homer's Iliad* (Berkeley and Los Angeles: University of California Press, 1984), 69. In my view Schein's book is far and away the best introduction to the *Iliad* available in English.

8. Hesiod is, wrongly I believe, sometimes considered an exception to this statement.

9. Simon Goldhill, "Intimations of Immortality: Fame and Tradition from Homer to Pindar," in *The Poet's Voice* (New York: Cambridge University Press, 1991), 76.

10. Schein, *The Mortal Hero*, 72. The wrath of Achilles is also the wrath of his mother, Thetis, who is forced to marry a mortal man who is about to die. In Loraux's words: "Homer has displaced the wrath from a mother to her son and because the maternal me-nis 'becomes absorbed in the actual wrath of her son' we credit the hero with a Great Mother's wrath without seeing that mourning and wrath are undivided between the mother and son," 49. (She is quoting Laura Slatkin's "The Wrath of Thetis," *Transactions of the American Philological Association* 116 [1986]: 22.)

11. Goldhill, "Intimations of Immortality," 86.

12. See Margaret Anne Doody, "Finales, Apocalypses, Trailings-off," *Raritan* 15, no. 3 (Winter 1996): 24–46.

13. See the discussion of this in Goldhill, "Intimations of Immortality," 93–94.

14. Doody, "Finales," 28–29.

15. *The Complete Greek Tragedies*, vol. 1, *Sophocles*, ed. David Grene and Richard Latimore, trans. with an introduction by David Grene, 2d ed (Chicago: University of Chicago Press, 1991).

16. Blanco translation of Thucydides' *The Peloponnesian War*, ed. Walter Blanco and Jennifer Tolbert Roberts (New York: W. W. Norton, 1998).

17. Michael Janover, "Nostalgias," in *Critical Horizons* 1, no. 1 (February 2000): 113–33.

18. I have discussed this at length in *The Tragedy of Political Theory: The Road Not Taken* (Princeton, NJ: Princeton University Press, 1990), chaps. 1 and 2.

19. Sheldon Wolin, *Hobbes and the Epic Tradition of Political Theory* (William Andrews Clark Memorial Library, University of California, Los Angeles, 1970), 4–5.

20. Though there are serious questions about the authenticity of *The Seventh Letter*, I think the same conclusions about *The Republic* and Syracuse can be made more circuitously on the basis of other sources.

21. 325 b–c. I have relied on the Morrow translation (New York: Library of Liberal Arts, 1962).

22. 325 d–e. Cf. *The Republic*, 473d, 487e, 499b, 501e.

23. The phrase is Sheldon Wolin's from *Politics and Vision: Continuity and Innovation in Western Political Thought* (Boston: Little, Brown, 1960), chap. 2.

24. At the end of Book 1 (354b–c), Socrates berates himself and warns his readers/interlocutors about their impatience in arriving at conclusions. By itself this is simply advice to be more cautious in discussing issues of such complexity. But when the beginning of Book 5 (449–451b) dramatically as well as substantively recapitulates the opening of the entire dialogue—as if we need to begin the entire discussion again—the caution becomes a general wariness about beginnings and endings. That warning becomes even more significant if we read the Myth of Er as violating the conditions of the dialogue as they were stipulated at the beginning of Book 2 (357a–367e, esp. 366e), where Socrates accepts the challenge to defend justice without recourse to rewards and punishments. Here, at "the end," he does exactly what he has promised not to do.

25. Doody, "Finales," 42–43.

26. J. H. Plumb, *Renaissance Italy* (New York: American Heritage, 1961).

27. *The Portable Machiavelli*, trans. and ed. Peter Bondanella and Mark Musa (New York: Penguin, 1980), 159. Hereafter, page references appear in the text.

28. See the perceptive analysis of Machiavelli's realism in Robert Hariman, *Political Style: The Artistry of Power* (Chicago: University of Chicago Press, 1995).

29. If I am right in following Hariman on this point, Machiavelli changes from a successful realist into an unsuccessful republican in the sense that his means (*The Prince*) to an end (*The Discourses*) become the end. While we take Machiavelli's realism as his final word and reject politics because it relies on deceit, power, and appearances, he saw this as a spur to political engagement. Thus he has contributed to a political cynicism he was trying to combat. Since it is *The Prince*, not *The Discourses*, that is honored as a "great book," few people aside from political theorists know anything about Machiavelli's views of civic virtue, the dignity of citizenship, public spiritedness (which he defends), confrontational politics, the people as the appropriate repository of liberty, or civic religion.

30. The most powerful modern restatement of Machiavelli's views on this subject remains the concluding section of Max Weber's *Politics as a Vocation*.

31. See *The Discourses*, esp. 297–99.

32. See Claude Lefort, "Machiavelli: History, Politics, Discourse," in *The States of "Theory": History, Art, and Critical Discourse*, ed. with an introduction by David Carroll (New York: Columbia University Press, 1990), 113–24.

33. Lefort, "Machiavelli," 138.

34. Machiavelli's critique of religion parallels Marx's argument about God. We project our powers onto an alien being and need to recover them for ourselves. Capitalism's corrosive effect on religious belief and affiliation is "progressive" in this respect.

35. In a discussion of "high minded nostalgia" Mary Beard argues that ever "since the Romans it has been an underlying tenet of most classical scholarship that the present generation is strikingly less capable than its predecessors at the job of preserving and passing on the great traditions, that 'we' unlike our illustrious forebears are simply not up to it" ("Not You," *London Review of Books*, January 23, 1997, 10–11). If Beard is right, then Machiavelli learned about the problem of nostalgia from the Romans.

36. Sigmund Freud, "Mourning and Melancholia," in *The Freud Reader*, ed. Peter Gay (New York: W. W. Norton, 1989), 584–89. Freud has a quite different analysis in *The Ego and the Id*. On the significance of the differences, see Butler, *The Psychic Life of Power*, 132–41.

37. Machiavelli implies that the dual perspective essential for political knowledge and power was institutionalized in the Roman mixed constitution. Because that constitution was composed of (at least) two classes, each of which stood for different principles (the Senate for tradition, authority, order, property, and continuity; the people for innovation and liberty) and interpreted events in those terms, Rome was able to change with the times. In other words, a healthy society like Rome has no need of the theorist's special qualifications as they are presented in the image of the landscape painter.

38. Hannah Arendt, "What Is Authority?" in *Between Past and Future: Eight Exercises in Political Thought* (New York: Penguin, 1977), 120–21.

39. Ibid., 120–21. No doubt Machiavelli also chose fratricide to contest Augustine's version, which he would have seen as a further instance of Christianity's political naïveté.

40. See *The Discourses* 1:xi.

41. Of course if I am right that Machiavelli finds prudential reasons why the prince must modify his immoral impulses, then this is far less of a blanket endorsement than it seems.

42. Lefort, "Machiavelli," 124.

43. Marx, "Manifesto of the Communist Party," in *The Marx-Engels Reader*, ed. Richard Tucker, 2d ed. (New York: W. W. Norton, 1978), 475–76.

44. Ibid., 595–96. With this description Marx "transformed, by a sort of reverse rhetorical alchemy, the golden *exempla* of humanist favor into the leaden burdens of a dead past" (Kirstie McClure, "Affect in Action: Figurae, the 'Com-

munity Sense,' and Political Prose" [paper delivered at the American Political Science Association Meetings, September 1998]). For Machiavelli this *was* often a result of invoking Rome, but it need not be one.

45. See Jonathan Dollimore, *Death, Desire and Loss in Western Culture* (New York: Routledge, 1998).

46. I do not mean to exaggerate. Religion for Marx was delusional only in the sense that the objective conditions that brought it into being and made it an opiate would be transformed. Moreover, many criticisms of Marx come from Marx himself, which is why he denied that he was a Marxist.

47. Victor Nee, "A Theory of Market Transition: From Redistribution to Markets in State Socialism," *American Sociological Review* 54 (October 1989): 663–81.

48. See the introduction to *Global Dreams: Imperial Corporations and the New World Order*, by Richard J. Barnet and John Cavanagh (New York: Simon and Schuster, 1997).

49. "Newsreel History," *London Review of Books*, November 12, 1998, 8.

50. See Elaine Showalter, "Foucault in America," *Times Literary Supplement*, November 28, 1997, 28.

51. See the discussions in Simon Critchley, *Very Little—Almost Nothing: Death, Philosophy, Literature* (New York: Routledge, 1997), 2–3, 24.

CHAPTER SIX
THE POLIS, GLOBALIZATION, AND THE CITIZENSHIP OF PLACE

1. Peter Green, *Alexander to Actium: The Historical Evolution of the Hellenistic Age* (Berkeley and Los Angeles: University of California Press, 1990), xxi. Green is ambivalent or perhaps coy about fulfilling the promise present in the quotation, for he goes on: "I have . . . steadfastly tried to avoid drawing such factitious parallels in my text, or coloring ancient phenomena with modern associations. . . . What this parallelism signifies I do not pretend to know, and think it wiser not to speculate; but it does suggest, forcibly, that there may indeed be something more in the Hellenistic age for concerned modern readers than mere antiquarian interest."

2. Ralf Dahrendorf, *Betrachtunger über die Revolution in Europa* (Stuttgart: Deutsche Verlag-Anstalt, 1990). Quoted by Pietr Sztompka, "Mistrusting Civility: Predicament of a Post-Communist Society," in *Real Civil Societies: Dilemmas of Institutionalization*, ed. Jeffrey C. Alexander (Thousand Oaks, CA: Sage, 1998), 191.

3. William Connolly, "Democracy and Territoriality," in *The Rhetorical Republic: Governing Representations in American Politics*, ed. Thomas Dumm and Frederick Dolan (Amherst: University of Massachusetts Press, 1993); and Richard Falk, "The Making of Global Citizenship," in *Global Visions: Beyond the New*

World Order, ed. Jeremy Brecher, John Brown Childs, and Jill Cutler (Boston: South End Press, 1993).

4. See the introduction to *Global Dreams: Imperial Corporations and the New World Order*, ed. Richard J. Barnet and John Cavanagh (New York: Simon and Schuster, 1994); and see Mike Featherstone, "Global Culture: An Introduction," in his edited volume, *Global Culture: Nationalism, Globalization and Modernity* (Newbury Park, CA: Sage, 1990).

5. John B. Thompson, *The Media and Modernity: A Social History of the Media* (Stanford, CA: Stanford University Press, 1995), 236.

6. Mary Beard, "An Open Forum? New Emphasis on the Place of the Citizen in the Roman Polity," *Times Literary Supplement*, May 29, 1999, 3–4. Beard is making her arguments against those who denigrate Rome by romanticizing Athens. Kenneth Minogue calls "the legend" of Athenian participatory democracy a "will-o-the-wisp," since "the reality of governing must always be a top-down activity, in which the rulers, despite their democratic parades of humility, must be remote from the people" ("Creed for Democrats," *Times Literary Supplement*, June 18, 1999, 8).

7. W. G. Runciman, "Doomed to Extinction: The Polis as an Evolutionary Dead-End," in *The Greek State: From Homer to Alexander*, ed. Oswyn Murray and Simon Price (Oxford: Clarendon Press, 1990), 364.

8. Hannah Arendt, *The Human Condition* (Chicago: University of Chicago Press, 1998), 2d ed., 198.

9. Here and in general I owe a great deal to Ronnie Lipschutz's "Members Only? Citizenship and Civic Virtue in a Time of Globalization," *International Politics* 36 (June 1999): 203–33.

10. I take the idea and much of the content of this ethos from Connolly's "Democracy and Territoriality."

11. The previous paragraphs paraphrase Jean-Pierre Vernant's *The Origins of Greek Thought* (Ithaca, NY: Cornell University Press, 1962), 47–48, 51–52.

12. I have argued this in detail in "The Battle of Salamis and the Origins of Political Theory," in my *Corrupting Youth: Political Education, Democratic Culture and Political Theory* (Princeton, NJ: Princeton University Press, 1997), 64–90, as has Josiah Ober in many of his essays. For a very different view, see Nicole Loraux, *The Invention of Athens: The Funeral Oration in the Classical City* (Cambridge: Harvard University Press, 1982).

13. Josiah Ober, *The Athenian Revolution: Essays on Ancient Greek Democracy and Political Thought* (Princeton, NJ: Princeton University Press, 1996), 35.

14. See Ober, *Political Dissent in Democratic Athens: Intellectual Critics of Popular Rule* (Princeton, NJ: Princeton University Press, 1998), 6–7, 40–41, 368–69; and J. Peter Euben, "Political Equality and the Greek Polis," in *Liberalism and the Modern Polity: Essays in Contemporary Political Theory*, ed. Michael J. Gargas McGrath (New York: Bael Marcel Dekker, 1978).

15. On how citizenship functioned to limit forms of economic exploitation, see Ellen Wood, *Peasant-Citizen and Slave: The Foundations of Athenian Democracy* (London: Verso, 1988).

16. Ober, *Athenian Revolution*, 63.

17. Ibid., 150.

18. Ibid., 4.

19. On the ancient economy and Aristotle's views of it, see M. I. Finley, "Aristotle and Economic Analysis," *Past and Present* 47 (1970): 3–25, and *The Ancient Economy* (Berkeley and Los Angeles: University of California Press, 1973); Karl Polanyi, "Aristotle Discovers the Economy," in *Primitive, Archaic, and Modern Economics*, ed. G. Dalton (Garden City, NY: Doubleday, 1968); M. M. Austin and P. Vidal-Naquet, *Economic and Social History of Ancient Greece* (Berkeley and Los Angeles: University of California Press, 1977); Paul A. Rahe, "The Primacy of Politics in Classical Greece," *American Historical Review* 89, no. 2 (1989): 265–93; Thomas J. Lewis, "Acquisition and Anxiety: Aristotle's Case against the Market," *Canadian Journal of Economics* 2 (1978): 70; and *Trade and Market in Early Empires: Economies in History and Theory*, ed. Karl Polanyi, C. Arensberg, and H. W. Pearson (Chicago: Free Press, 1957), 255; as well as Book 2 of the *Politics* and Books 5 and 6 of the *Ethics*.

20. Ober, *Political Dissent*, 303–4. None of this is to suggest that Aristotle was a democrat, though he is much less antidemocratic than is usually supposed.

21. For example, when we place an ad to sell a car, we are likely to ask the maximum price and exaggerate the quality of the car's condition while remaining silent about unobvious malfunctions. But if a friend becomes interested, everything changes; we may well lower the car's price and tell our friend exactly what is wrong with it, while he or she may insist on paying the original price so we do not lose money. What intervenes is a concern about the other with whom we have had a history and with whom we expect to have a future. We think now not only of our profit but of their needs and the importance of maintaining the friendship. I take the example from Lewis, "Acquisition and Anxiety," 72–73.

22. Ober, *Athenian Revolution*, 11.

23. See Erich S. Gruen, "The Polis in the Hellenistic World," in *Nomodeiktes: Studies in Honor of Martin Ostwald*, ed. Ralph M. Rosen and Joseph Farrell (Ann Arbor: University of Michigan Press, 1993). The quotation in the next paragraph is on 340. In general, Gruen argues against the position taken here. He insists that the very existence of treaties between city-states, with the pledges of their citizenry and external witnesses, is proof of "the continued vitality of the *polis*, its political and territorial integrity, and its autonomous nature" (342–43). Similarly, Mogens Herman Hansen argues that since a polis did not lose its identity as a polis by being subjected to another political entity, such as the king of Persia or Macedon or Hellenistic monarchies, one should not talk about the loss of autonomy. (See his "The Polis as a Citizen State," in his edited book *The Ancient Greek City-State* [Copenhagen: Royal Danish Academy of Sciences and Letters, 1993], 19–

22.) For him the culprit is Aristotle. But Hansen makes unintelligible the reasons why poleis would fight at such risk for the autonomy he says is not that important and the terms in which Athenians (in Thucydides) celebrate their victory over Persia.

24. See Sheldon Wolin, *Politics and Vision: Continuity and Innovation in Western Political Thought* (Boston: Little, Brown, 1960), chap. 3, "The Age of Empire: Space and Community"; and T. A. Sinclair, *A History of Greek Political Thought* (London: Routledge & Kegan Paul, 1967), chap. 12.

25. Wolin, *Politics and Vision*, 83.

26. Ober, *Political Dissent*, 343, makes a very different claim. He thinks Aristotle not only took account of the conditions of his time but thought they presented an opportunity to create new political constitutions.

27. Wolin, *Politics and Vision*, 70.

28. See the introduction by André Laks and Malcolm Schofield to their edited book, *Justice and Generosity: Studies in Hellenistic Social and Political Philosophy* (New York: Cambridge University Press, 1995), 1–17; and J. L. Moles, "The Cynics and Politics," in the same volume, 129–60.

29. See Fragment 17M and the gloss on it by Sinclair, *History of Greek Political Thought*, 246 ff.

30. Moles, "The Cynics and Politics," 143–44.

31. Malcolm Schofield, *The Stoic Idea of the City* (Chicago: University of Chicago Press, 1999), 24.

32. The transition from man as citizen of a polis to man as a moral being meant removing all contingencies, such as physical proximity or mutual acquaintance, from the idea of citizenship. Thus citizens were simply those who were in obedience to the law of nature. No political dimension of citizenship is necessary or indeed desirable in this formulation. See ibid., chap. 4, esp. 102–3.

33. Marcus Aurelius, *Meditations* 4.

34. See Schofield's discussion of instrumental and substantive reason, *The Stoic Idea*, 93.

35. In *de otio* 4 (Schofield translation).

36. *Epistulae Morales* 1.

37. *Of the Nature of Things* 2.

38. A. A. Long, "Hellenistic Ethics and Political Power," in *Hellenistic History and Culture*, ed. Peter Green (Berkeley and Los Angeles: University of California Press, 1993), 143.

39. Schofield, *The Stoic Idea*, epilogue.

40. Wolin, *Politics and Vision*, 78–80.

41. In addition to chap. 2 of *Cultivating Humanity* (Cambridge: Harvard University Press, 1997), see chaps. 9 and 10 in Nussbaum's *The Therapy of Desire* (Princeton, NJ: Princeton University Press, 1994) and *For Love of Country: Debating the Limits of Patriotism*, ed. Joshua Cohen (Boston: Beacon Press, 1996), 2–20.

42. *For Love of Country*, 13.

43. Nussbaum, *Cultivating Humanity*, 60.

44. Ibid., 58.

45. Ibid., 57–58.

46. Ibid., 61.

47. Ibid., 58–61, and *The Therapy of Desire*, 343.

48. *Cultivating Humanity*, 59, 60, 62, and *For Love of Country*, 7–9.

49. Cosmopolitanism has a fascinating political history. For Spengler cosmopolitanism was a code for Jews whose lack of belonging made them dangerous outsiders to European society. Stalin traded on the same association when he condemned Jews as "intellectuals" and cosmopolitans. But cosmopolitanism also played a conservative role in this country when used as a basis for anti-Stalinism. On this, see Bruce Robbins's "Introduction, Part I," in *Cosmopolitics: Thinking and Feeling beyond the Nation*, ed. Pheng Cheah and Bruce Robbins (Minneapolis: University of Minnesota Press), 1998.

50. *Cultivating Humanity*, 59. Nussbaum italicizes "no" while I have italicized "mere."

51. Michael Walzer, "Spheres of Affection," in *For Love of Country*, 125.

52. Wolin, *Politics and Vision*, 82.

53. Cheah and Robbins, *Cosmopolitics*, 6.

54. *For Love of Country*, 11.

55. See Pratap Bhanu Mehta, "Cosmopolitanism and the Circle of Reason" *Political Theory* 28, no. 5 (October 2000): 631.

56. Nussbaum argues that if we believe we owe more respect to a nation because it is democratic, then we do so because we regard democracy as a universal value. (See her argument in *For Love of Country*.) But this seems misleading because arguments for democracy need not be universalistic, or, if they are, it is in a way different from those Nussbaum defends. For instance, Connolly and I see democracy as interrogating its own claims to superiority. For the distinction between cosmopolitanism and universalism, see Amanda Anderson, "Cosmopolitanism, Universalism and the Divided Legacies of Modernity," in Cheah and Robbins, *Cosmopolitics*, 265–89.

57. See Featherstone, "Global Culture," 12. Thus an "Indian scientist or intellectual in New Delhi who wishes to develop contacts or exchange information with his Japanese opposite numbers, must do so in English."

58. See Kwame Anthony Appiah's discussion of "rooted cosmopolitanism" in "Cosmopolitan Roots," in Cheah and Robbins, *Cosmopolitics*, 91–114; Christopher Lasch's argument as to how traditional cultures within and outside imperialist states have managed to resist industrial capitalism despite all predictions to the contrary, *The World of Nations: Reflections on American History, Politics, and Culture* (New York: Knopf, 1973); and Veit Bader on how commitments to cosmopolitanism are rooted in bonds of language, culture, and history, in "For Love of Country," a review essay in *Political Theory* 27, no. 3 (Fall 1999): 379–97.

59. *Cultivating Humanity*, 59.

60. Jürgen Habermas, "Remarks on Legitimation," *Philosophy and Social Criticism* 24, nos. 2–3 (1998): 162, quoted in Mehta, "Cosmopolitanism," 8.

61. Mehta, "Cosmopolitanism," 9–11. Roxanne L. Euben, *Enemy in the Mirror: Islamic Fundamentalism and the Limits of Modern Rationalism* (Princeton, NJ: Princeton University Press, 1999), and the essays in pt. 3 of Cheah and Robbins, *Cosmopolitics*.

62. Cheah and Robbins, *Cosmopolitics*, 1.

63. See, for instance, her "Aristotelian Social Democracy," in *Liberalism and the Good*, ed. R. Bruce Douglass, Gerald M. Mara, and Henry S. Richardson (New York: Routledge, 1990), 203–52; "Human Functioning and Social Justice: In Defense of Aristotelian Essentialism," *Political Theory* 20, no. 2 (May 1992): 202–46; "Nature, Function and Capability: Aristotle on Political Distribution," *Oxford Studies in Ancient Philosophy*, supplemental volume (1988): 145–84.

64. See Anderson, "Cosmopolitanism," 268.

65. Falk, "The Making of Global Citizenship," 40. Hereafter page references to Falk are in the text.

66. "Democracy and Territoriality." Page references are in the text.

67. See Saskia Sassen, *Globalization and Its Discontents* (New York: The New Press, 1998), xxxii. Hereafter page references will be in the text.

68. See Roger Sanjek, *The Future of Us All: Race and Neighborhood Politics in New York City* (Ithaca, NY: Cornell University Press, 1998).

69. On the "parallel polis," see Václav Benda et al., "Parallel Polis or an Independent Society in Central and Eastern Europe: An Inquiry," *Social Research* 1–2 (1988): 211–46; Jeffrey C. Isaac, "The Meaning of 1989," *Social Research* 63, no. 2 (1996); H. Gordon Skilling, *Charter 77 and Human Rights in Czechoslovakia* (Boston: Allen and Unwin, 1981); Václav Havel, *The Power of the Powerless* (Armonk, NY: M. E. Sharpe, 1985); and Jonathan Schell's introduction to Adam Michnik's *Letters from Prison* (Berkeley and Los Angeles: University of California Press, 1985), xvii–xliii, and Michnik's essay in that volume "Maggots and Angels," 169–98.

70. Sheldon S. Wolin, "Democracy without the Citizen," in *The Presence of the Past* (Baltimore: Johns Hopkins University Press, 1989), 180–91.

71. Ibid.

CHAPTER SEVEN
PLATONIC NOISE

1. See John E. Seery, *Political Theory for Mortals: Shades of Justice, Mirages of Death* (Ithaca, NY: Cornell University Press). Though I disagree with some of Seery's interpretations and formulations, I have learned much from his book.

2. Quoted by Hannah Arendt, *Men in Dark Times* (New York: Harcourt Brace and World, 1968), 105.

3. Ibid., 8.

4. Ibid., 105–6.

5. *The Human Condition*, 2d. ed. (Chicago: University of Chicago Press, 1998).

6. Walter Benjamin, "The Storyteller: Reflections on the Works of Nikolai Leskov," in *Illuminations: Essays and Reflections*, ed. Hannah Arendt (New York: Harcourt Brace and World, 1968), 95.

7. Here is the full quotation: "I don't have a political theory or doctrine that I'm espousing. I follow characters where they take me and I don't know what I can say beyond that." Quoted by Louis Menand, "Market Report: Review of Mao II," *New Yorker*, June 24, 1991, 81.

8. John Leonard, "The Hunger Artist," *New York Review of Books*, February 22, 2001, 4. Don DeLillo, *White Noise* (New York: Penguin, 1984). All page references will be given in the text.

9. Ibid. and A. O. Scott, "The Page Floats," *New York Times*, June 16, 2000, E1–4.

10. Leonard, "The Hunger Artist."

11. Nietzsche, "The Gay Science," sec. 9, and William E. Connolly, *Why I Am Not a Secularist* (Minneapolis: University of Minnesota Press, 1999), 25–29.

12. The phrase is Terry Eagleton's in "For the Hell of It," *London Review of Books*, February 22, 2001, 30.

13. Hannah Arendt, *Eichmann in Jerusalem* (New York: Viking, 1964), 287.

14. *The Life of the Mind*, vol. 1, *Thinking* (London: Socker and Warburg, 1978), 5.

15. Pratap Bhanu Mehta, "Cosmopolitanism and the Circle of Reason," *Political Theory* 28, no. 5 (October 2000): 626. As Mehta points out, appropriation of Eastern religions seldom includes the broader premise and practices that give those religions meaning.

16. Given the Orphic and Pythagorean influences on the dialogue, this is hardly surprising.

17. I take this discussion from Ian Donaldson, "The Importance of Dying Well," *Times Literary Supplement*, February 13, 1998, 13–14.

18. Robert A. Harrison, "Food and Graves" (manuscript). Portions of that paper appear in "Hic Jacet," *Critical Inquiry* 27 (Spring 2001): 393–407.

19. Thomas Lynch, "Why Buy More Time?" *New York Times*, March 14, 1999, sec. 4, p. 15.

20. Herbert Marcuse, "The Ideology of Death," in *The Meaning of Death*, ed. H. Feifel (New York: McGraw Hill, 1959), 64–76; and the discussion in Jonathan Dollimore, *Death, Desire and Loss in Western Culture* (New York: Routledge, 1998), 220–27. It was Dollimore's book that brought the Marcuse essay to my attention.

21. Slavoj Žižek, *London Review of Books*, March 18, 1999, 3.

22. *The Essence of Christianity*, trans. George Eliot, introduction by Karl Barth and foreword by H. Richard Niebuhr (New York: Harper, 1953), 152–53.

23. See George Shulman, "Hope and American Politics" manuscript.

24. Jonathan Lear, *Happiness, Death, and the Remainder of Life* (Cambridge: Harvard University Press, 2000), 102.

25. See Glenn W. Most, "A Cock for Aesclepius," *Classical Quarterly* 43, no. 1 (January–June 1993):1–16.

26. Ibid., 15.

27. "The Problem of Socrates," in *Twilight of the Idols*, in Walter Kaufmann, *The Portable Nietzsche* (New York: Viking, 1968), 473–79.

28. *The Gay Science*, 340. Foucault found something quite different in the dialogue and its final words. Treating the *Apology*, *Crito*, and the *Phaedo* as a cycle, he finds them an ethic of care for the self confirmed by the other two dialogues. See Thomas Flynn, "Foucault as Paresiast: His Last Course at the College de France," in *The Final Foucault*, ed. James Bernauer and David Rasmussen (Cambridge: MIT Press, 1994). A more direct source is the lecture Foucault gave at UCSC. Alexander Nehamas thinks Foucault is wrong to link the *Phaedo* with these much earlier works and insists that Plato's animosity toward the body is "so intense, so passionate" that one cannot look past it. Yet he agrees with Foucault that Plato was developing a discourse that is primarily concerned with the care of the self. See his *The Art of Living: Socratic Reflections from Plato to Foucault* (Berkeley and Los Angeles: University of California Press, 1998), chap. 6.

29. Arlene Saxonhouse makes a parallel argument about Xanthippe. She suggests that "Xanthippe's presence [in *The Phaedo*] emphasizes the aporetic quality of the Platonic dialogue by questioning the adequacy of Socrates' apparent, but often ineffective, efforts to pursue dichotomies, in particular the dichotomy between body and soul, between life and death, between waking and sleeping." See her "Xanthippe and Philosophy: Who Really Wins?" *Proceedings of the Boston Colloquium on Ancient Philosophy* 14 (1998):111–29.

30. Leo Tolstoy, *The Death of Ivan Ilych*, trans. Lynn Solotaroff (New York: Bantam, 1981), and Tobin Siebers, *Morals and Stories* (New York: Columbia University Press, 1992), 161–63.

31. See Mary Margaret McCabe, "Listening to Plato's Niece," *Times Literary Supplement*, July 7, 2000, 10.

32. Harrison, "Food and Graves," 4.

33. James Booth, "Communities of Memory: On Identity, Memory and Debt," *American Political Science Review* 93 (June 1999):249–62.

34. Alexis de Tocqueville, *Democracy in America*, ed. J. P. Mayer and Max Lerner, trans. George Lawrence (New York: Harper & Row, 1966).

35. See Anthony DeCurtis, " 'An Outside in the Society': An Interview with Don DeLillo," *South Atlantic Quarterly* 89, no. 2 (1990): 301, and Paul A. Cantor, "Adolph, We Hardly Knew You," in *New Essays on While Noise*, ed. Frank Lentricchia (New York: Cambridge University Press, 1991), 39–62.

36. Frank Lentricchia, "Tales of the Electronic Tribe," in Lentricchia, *New Essays*, 87–113.

37. See Nina Bernstein, *The Lost Children of Wilder: The Epic Struggle to Change Foster Care* (New York: Pantheon, 2001).

38. "The Storyteller," 34–5.

39. Hannah Arendt, "The Crisis in Education," in *Between Past and Future: Eight Exercises in Political Thought* (New York: Penguin, 1977), 174–75.

40. Jonathan Lear, *Happiness, Death, and the Remainder of Life* (Cambridge: Harvard University Press, 2000), 101–2.

41. See Michael Gorra, "Voices Off," *Times Literary Supplement*, February 16, 2001, 21.

Index

Absolutely Fabulous (TV show), 79
Achilles (*Iliad*), 89, 90, 91, 98, 149, 161, 188n.10
"Action" (Arendt), 55
actions. *See* public life/actions
Aeschylus (*Agamemnon*), 14
The Akharnians, 67
Alger, Horatio, 145
Ally McBeal (TV show), 79
America: "distended society" of late-nineteenth-century, 88; examining role of TV comedy in democracy of, 64–65; impact of television on citizenship/politics in, 73–77, 84, 165; as political wilderness, 168; three political concerns for citizens of, 128–29
American Political Science Association, 142
Antigone: characters assert reasonableness in, 131; "choral ode to man" of, 10, 32, 91–93, 109, 169; in context of Platonic philosophy, 94; sense of loss at heart of triumph in, 10, 32; synchronicity found in, 91–93; tension between agonistic/deliberative in, 43
Antigone (*Antigone*): excluded from the burial, 51–52; likened to bird that others seek to yoke, 92; on Oedipus's refusal to hear Polyneices, 50
antimethodological method: four related elements of, 18–19; Nietzsche's expression of his, 16
antiquarian history, 21, 22–23
Apology of Socrates (Plato), 31, 147, 152–57
aporetic dialogue (*The Republic*), 97
arche (power, initiative, sovereignty, rule), 116
Arendt, Hannah: admiration of Athenian democracy by, 40–41; on Adolph Eich-

mann, 147; on dangers of old dictating to young, 181n.21; on death as bestowing completedness to life, 50, 143–44; dramatization of modernity by, 42–43, 61; on education as taking responsibility, 39; exploring Hellenism of, 9–10, 61–63; fears of revenge by "masses" by, 180n.20; idea of judgment by, 59–60; on meaning revealed by storytelling, 143; misused terminology when speaking of the Greeks, 58–59; on morality as political problem, 141; on polis as giving meaning to life, 54–58, 77–78, 92; on political greatness of different historic occasions, 60; and political thought revealed through use of tragedy, 58–61; on role of forgiveness in action, 52; story of Oedipus as reflecting ideas of, 43; totalitarianism as described by, 62
Ariès, Philippe, 148
Aristophanes: caricature of Socrates by, 69; Cleon's lawsuit against, 69; on ethical import of ridicule and parody, 65; as nostalgic for simpler times, 69; as political educator of Athenian democracy, 68; two audiences addressed by, 77; as writer for *The Honeymooners*, 66, 81; as writer for *The Simpsons*, 66, 81
Aristophanic comedy: comparing American TV comedies to, 10, 79–84; comparing *The Honeymooners* to, 79–81; comparing *The Simpsons* to, 79, 81–84; cultural climate producing, 65–66; modern stand-up comics as fitting into, 78–79; as providing stage for self-critique, 71–72; public ridicule expressed by, 67–68. *See also* comedy; Old Comedy
Aristotle: on benefits of political participation, 119; citizenship as conceptualized by, 125; comparison of Stoicism thought

illusions of, 20–21; dangers of excessive cultivation/overvaluation of, 19–20; forgetting element of serving life, 25–28; Machiavelli on political reading of, 102–4; Marx's rejection of Machiavelli's political use of, 109; monumental, 21–22; Nietzsche on history serving life, 21–25; Nietzsche's antimethodological method approach to, 16, 18–19; Nietzsche's criticism of historicizing, 21; passion for objectivity of, 25–26; recasting dominant interpretations of, 177n.5; television as being ahistorical and ignoring, 75; three kinds of, 21. *See also* nostalgia
Hobbes, Thomas, 129, 160
Hofstadter, Richard, 88
Hogan's Heroes (TV show), 79
Homer, 60, 88
The Honeymooners (TV show): Aristophanes as writer for, 66, 81; cultural ladder position of, 65; Gleason (Kramden) character of, 79–81, 82; social divisions dramatized in, 79–80; unspoken ironies of, 80–81
The Human Condition (Arendt), 55, 59, 60, 62
human stain, 3–4, 175n.5
The Human Stain (Roth), 1, 2, 5, 142
humor, 183n.8
Huntington, Samuel, 110

idealism/moralism critique, 101–3
Ignatieff, Michael, 75, 165
Iliad (Homer), 89–90, 93, 98
In Living Color (TV show), 65
irony, 19, 83–84
Ismene (*Oedipus at Colonus*), 47, 48

James, C.L.R., 84
Janover, Michael, 93
Jocasta (*Oedipus at Colonus*), 46
justice: comparing Aristotle's/Stoicism definitions of, 124; Nietzsche on man of, 35; Nietzsche on strength of speaking for, 29

Kateb, George, 63
King Lear (Shakespeare), 85
kleos (fame, glory, renown), 89, 90
The Knights, 68
"Know Thyself" (Delphic Apollo), 17, 31, 33
Knox, Bernard, 48, 60

Konstan, David, 79
kosmopolites (citizenship of the world), 122
Kramden, Alice (*The Honeymooners*), 80–81
Kramden, Ralph (*The Honeymooners*), 79–81, 82
Kundera, Milan, 25

Lacan, Jacques, (*Oedipus at Colonus*), 52
Laertes (*Odyssey*), 91
Laius (*Oedipus at Colonus*), 46
Laks, André, 122
Laslett, Peter, 88, 109, 136
Lear, Jonathan, 8
Lefort, Claude, 103, 108
Leonard, John, 145
Lessing, Gotthold, 143
Lewinsky, Monica, 2
life: capacity to prolong, 149–50; as completed by death, 50, 143–44; death as final hurdle of, 150; Socrates on unexamined, 171, 172; uncertainty of, 160, 161, 164. *See also* death; mortality
The Life of the Mind (Arendt), 55
Lipsitz, George, 72
Loraux, Nicole, 78
loss: aspects of political, 98; diachronic narrative of, 88, 108–9; four types of narratives of, 88; Freud on melancholic's sense of, 103–4; as issue in tragedy, 94; *nostos* (homecoming) [nostalgia] and, 90, 110; Peg Mullen's story on, 85–87, 94, 96, 108; perspectival narrative of, 88, 98–108; as pervading our public discourse, 110–11; philosophic narrative of, 88, 96–98; Plato's response to Socrates' death and, 96–98, 108; political theory and dealing with, 111; political theory as emerging from personal, 87–88, 96; profound disorientation attending, 108; synchronic narrative of, 88, 89–94
Luce, Henry, 110
Lucretius, 124
Lysistrata, 67

Machiavelli, Niccolò: compares himself to landscape painter, 105; discussion of fortune by, 28; dramas/stories used by, 104; on Fortuna, 99–100, 108, 168; moralism/idealism critique by, 101–3; perspectival narrative of loss by, 88, 98–108; on political knowledge/power,

political knowledge: Athenian democracy
connecting action with, 116–17; democratic ethos as presuming, 115; Machiavelli on requirements of, 104–7, 190n.37
political loss, 98
political power. *See* power
political theory: Arendt's connection of theater, democracy, and, 42–43; as beginning
with loss, 87–88, 96; using classical studies in debates on aims of, 14–15; dealing
with sense of loss, 111; deflationary tendency of, 33–34; making case for "usefulness" of, 11; reading Peg Mullen's
story as emergence of, 87; reflections on
mortality, politics, and, 10, 142, 147–48,
171; story on the social ontology of, 10;
White Noise foundation for, 173
political thought: Arendt's connection of
theater, democracy, and theory in, 42–
43; impact of changing categories of traditional, 113; loss of capacity for, 62; origins of Western, 11; tragedy used to reveal Arendt's, 58–61
politics: Arendt on life gaining meaning
through, 54–58; comparing views of
Arendt, Nietzsche, and Sophocles on,
62; disaffection with, 38; impact of globalization on, 114; late-night comics' satire of, 82–83; Machiavelli's view of,
100–101, 105–7; Nietzsche and Weber
on vocation for, 35–37, 168; Plato's rejection of, 95–96, 108; political community as opposed to, 56; "post-totalitarian," 138–39; reflections on political
theory, mortality, and, 10, 142, 147–48,
171; relationship between Athenian theater and, 66–72; as requiring public
realm or community, 55–57; *The Seventh Letter* (Plato) on, 95–96; Socrates
as healing rift between philosophy and,
159–60; Stoicism on, 121, 122–26; TV
comedies lampooning of cultural icons/
rituals of, 78–79; as *White Noise* subtext, 167–70; Wisdom of Silenus expressing redemptive power of, 43, 44–47, 54–
55
Politics (Aristotle), 120
"Politics as a Vocation" (Weber), 35,
168
Polyneices (*Oedipus at Colonus*), 49, 50–
51
Posner, Richard, 4–5

postmodernism deflationary tendency, 33
power: global city citizens' claims to, 137–
38; Machiavelli on political, 105–7; *The
Simpsons* (TV show) distrust of, 81; television distortion of workings of, 74–75;
television substitution of imaginary participation in, 75; television worship of,
74; three dimensions of, 116
presentism, 7–8
Priam (*Iliad*), 89, 91
The Prince (Machiavelli): compared to *The
Republic*, 105; comparison of self to
landscape painter in, 105; "Dedication"
to, 101; on Fortuna, 99–100, 108, 168;
imaginary republics scorned in, 104;
moralism/idealism critique in, 101–3; as
perspectival narrative of loss, 88, 98–
108; on political knowledge/power, 104–
7, 190n.37; realism strategy examined
in, 100–101, 107–8, 189n.29
Prizzi's Honor (film), 141
Pryor, Richard, 78
public life/actions: Arendt on role of forgiveness in, 52; Athenian democracy connecting knowledge to, 116–17; benefits
and power of, 55–57; challenges during
Hellenistic period on, 120–21; using classical studies in debates on quality of, 14–
15; by Creon (*Oedipus at Colonus*) ignoring laws/justice, 48; emergence of
Greek, 116; human plurality as basic
condition of speech in, 56; Machiavelli's
realism strategy for, 100–101, 107–8,
189n.29; Plato on reasons for staying
out of, 95–96, 108; polis as assuring recognition of, 56–57; *The Simpsons* as
playing interrogatory role in, 84; television as part of privatization of, 75–76.
See also political community
public realm, 55–57
public responsibilities, 74
public spaces: endowing life with meaning
through polis and, 54–55, 77–78, 92; as
function of theater, 59; public realm as
(space of appearance), 55–57; television
as closing in/down of, 74
Purdy, Jedidiah, 83
purity protest, 2–3
Putnam, Robert, 75, 83, 138

Rawls, John, 33
realism strategy, 100–101, 107–8, 189n.29

redemption: Arendt on politics and, 43;
Machiavelli's ideal of renewal in place
of, 106–7; philosophy as generating antipolitical vision of, 58; Wisdom of Silenus expressing power of political, 43,
44–47, 54–55
Redfield, James, 67
relevance, 8
renewal, 106–7
The Republic (Plato): antipolitical community represented by, 62; Arendt's reading
of, 40; criticisms of comedy in, 65; critique of democracy in, 69; on demos's
tendency toward self-deception, 69; epic
theory elements of, 94–95; everyday language used in Book 1 of, 87; as philosophic narrative of loss, 88; *The Prince*
compared to, 105; rarity of imaginary republics as in, 103; rejection of politics
by, 108; response to loss of Socrates'
death in, 96–98, 152; significance of
aporetic dialogue of, 97
"The Revolutionary Tradition and Its Lost
Treasure" (Arendt), 44–45
rhetorical speech, 28
Roberts, Deborah, 51
Rock, Chris, 78
Roots (TV series), 84
The Roseanne Barr Show (TV show), 65,
79
Rosenblum, Nancy, 139
Roth, Philip, 1, 2, 4, 7, 8, 160
Rousseau, Jean-Jacques, 113
Runciman, W. G., 114

sallekhana practice (fast unto death), 148
Sanjek, Roger, 115, 132, 138, 139
Sassen, Saskia, 115, 132, 137, 138, 139
Schlesinger, Arthur, 88
The Search for Order (Wiebe), 136
Seinfeld (TV show), 65, 83
Sen, Amartya, 132
Seneca, 123–24
September 11th, 78
The Seventh Letter (Plato), 95–96, 152
Silk, Coleman (*The Human Stain*), 1–3, 4
Simpson, Bart (*The Simpsons*), 82
Simpson, Homer (*The Simpsons*), 81–82
The Simpsons (TV show): Aristophanes as
writer for, 66, 81; contributions to politi-
cal education by, 82–84; cultural ladder
position of, 65; irony of, 83–84; popular

culture satirized by, 82; public life interrogatory role by, 84
Sisyphus, 145
Skinner, Quentin, 33
social capital: irony as eroding, 83; television and loss of citizen trust and, 75–76
social thought deflationary tendency, 33–34
Socrates: as choosing condition of his
death, 149; Cynics' claims of following,
122; death as presence throughout Platonic corpus, 152–57; as healing rift between philosophy and politics, 159–60;
intellectual tradition constituted by, 147;
last words of, 146, 157–60, 172; Old
Comedy ridicule of, 69; *Phaedo* as fram-
ing narratives on, 144, 146; Plato's response to Athenian treatment of, 95;
Plato's sense of loss from death of, 96–
98, 108; turn to writing of poetry by,
158; twofold loss signified by death of,
96; on unexamined life, 171, 172
Solon, 148
Sophocles, 53, 62
"the space of appearance" (public realm),
55–57
Sphinx's riddle, 149–50
Stoicism: citizenship/politics as viewed by,
121, 122–26; comparing Greek and
Roman, 128; Nussbaum's rearticulation
of, 126–32
stories/storyteller: authority borrowed from
death, 144; distinguished from information, 145–46; great men, 22; of Peg Mullen, 85, 86, 87, 94, 96, 108; as revealing
meaning without definition, 143–44; told
in *White Noise*, 148, 151, 162–63, 166–
70. *See also* narratives of loss
Strepsiades (Aristophanes character), 81, 82
synchronic narrative of loss: example of,
88; *Iliad* as, 89–90, 93; *Odyssey* as, 90–
91; Plato's rejection of, 94

technological mastery, 165
technophiles, 150–51
television: ability to dramatize modern life
through, 84; as contributing to political
passivity of citizens, 84, 165; criticized
as being antipolitical education, 73–74;
eleven elements of antipolitical education of, 73–76; as form of democratic political education, 73, 185n.38; late-night
comics of, 82–83; as "operating hypo-

television (*cont.*)
dermically," 77; as part of cultural dialectic, 76–77; studied as vehicle of corporate capitalism, 76; transforming citizens
into consumers, 74, 184n.29, 185n.32
television comedies: comparing Aristophanic comedy to, 10, 79–84; comparing Aristophanic comedy to *The Honeymooners*, 79–81; comparing Aristophanic
comedy to *The Simpsons*, 79, 81–84; examining role played in American democracy by, 64–65; lampooning of cultural
icons/political rituals by, 78–79
television news sound bites, 75
theater: Arendt's connection of political theory, democracy, and, 42–43; contemporary issues examined through, 61; parallels
between ancient and modern, 72–73; public space function of, 59; relationship between Athenian politics and, 66–72. *See
also* drama; Greek tragedy; Old Comedy
Themistocles, 139
Theseus (*Oedipus at Colonus*): as legendary unifier of Athens, 53; on mutability
of fortune, 46–47, 48, 52; Oedipus made
a citizen by, 44; as representing Athenian
democracy, 53–54; speaks against Oedipus's refusal to hear Polyneices, 50
"thin theory of the good" (Rawls), 33
Third Rock from the Sun (TV show), 79
Thompson, E. P., 88
Thucydides, 60, 117, 139
Tocqueville, Alexis de, 75, 138, 164
"to know" (*eidenia*), 42
"to see" (*idein*), 42
totalitarianism, 62
tragedy. *See* Greek tragedy
truth-speak, 28

uncertainty, 160, 161, 164
Underworld (DeLillo), 145
untimeliness, notion of, 15–18

Václav, Benda, 77
Vernant, Jean-Pierre, 5, 59, 73

Walzer, Michael, 129, 137
The Wasps, 67

Weber, Max: on manly attitude toward
war, 178n.19; on politics as vocation,
35–38, 168; on world as ethically irrational, 52
*Western Political Theory in the Face of the
Future* (Dunn), 113
"What Is Freedom?" (Arendt), 41
White, E. B., 65
white noise: DeLillo's novel on, 12–13,
172–73; meanings of, 12
White Noise (DeLillo): book's title as play
on, 12; comparison of to *Phaedo*, 142,
146–48; on facing fear of death, 160–63;
and parallels with choral ode from *Antigone*, 169; political theory built on foundation of, 173; politics as subtext in,
167–70; as quintessential postmodern
novel, 144; reflections on politics, political theory, and mortality in, 142, 147–
48, 171; story told in, 148, 151, 162–63,
166–70; as theodicy, 145
Wiebe, Robert, 88, 109, 136
Williams, Bernard, 52, 142
Winnie (*White Noise*), 166, 172
Wir Philologen (Nietzsche), 15
Wisdom of Silenus (*Oedipus at Colonus*):
Arendt on redemption of politics and,
43, 44–47, 54–55; Nietzsche's version
of, 44–45
Wolin, Sheldon, 34, 94–95, 120, 139, 168
world citizenship, 128–29
The World We Have Lost (Laslett), 136

Xanthippe (*Phaedo*), 198
Xenophon, 69

the young/youth: age as mimicking, 51;
Arendt on the old dictating to, 181n.21;
lament for lost youth in *Oedipus at Colonus*, 48–49; *Oedipus at Colonus* on revenge by old on, 51; as possessing plastic
power, 30; saving world from ruin by uncynical, 39. *See also* the old

Zeitlin, Froma, 54
Zeno, 125, 126
Zeno of Citium, 122
Žižek, Slavoj, 150, 171